Scalae Latinae:

Tiered Selections from
Book II of Livy's Ab Urbe Condita

Tiered by

Robert Amstutz

For Jennifer and Seneca

Table of Contents

Preface:

Preface to teachers:

Here's what you will find in the book:

- Tiered reading for the Livy Core choice.
- A segmented reading approach for every prose section
- A series of comprehension questions that model themselves on previous IB questions, or that elicit more discussion from students.
- Paper 1 practice sets for Ovid's *Heroides* and Aulus Gellius' *Atticae Noctes* selections.
- A glossary containing nearly every word used throughout each work.

Here is how the tiered readings in this book work:

- Carmen Ipsum, or Liber ipse- is always the unaltered text itself.
- The next tier down from the segmented reader or carmen ipsum, tier 2, alters the word order so that it is more approachable for students. Sometimes this does not follow proper Latin idiom. After years of working with students using tiers that adhered more closely to standard Latin idiom, I decided that focusing on the discussion of Latin idiom in the work itself was more important than maintaining Latin idiom throughout.
- The next tier down from that, tier 1, swaps in words more commonly found in textbook Latin.
- Students start at the lowest tier, then read through to the work itself. They can of course skip over any tiers that are not required to establish understanding. In my class for the prose texts, we often do tier 1, then the segmented reader, then the final version, skipping tier 2 unless the students are having a challenge.

You can always further reduce the complexity of the text to try to make it even more approachable for any of the students in your class. By creating the tiers, I have pretty much destroyed the artistry inherent in the Latin. This was purposefully done to make the text more approachable for the task of going from textbook Latin to large selections of unadapted classical Latin. Where the artistry has been destroyed, however, is a great place to begin a class discussion on why the writer wrote in such a way.

This book also contains questions for reading comprehension and deeper analysis for each of the selections included herein. Although this book is in no way related to

International Baccalaureate, I have created this for my students to have a workbook of sorts to go along with the IB syllabus first testing in 2024.

Preface to students:

Hi. Thank you for reading this. My hope is that you will find the way I have adapted the works collected herein more readable than if you were reading them with glossed notes typically found in student readers. As you move through the tiers from easier to more complex, I hope you pay attention to the words that the classical writers have chosen to use and the order in which they have written them. I have purposefully ruined their hard work to make your life a little easier when it comes to understanding Latin in Latin. Please make sure you put the effort into understanding Latin as it was meant to be understood.

Disclaimer: This book is in no way affiliated with or endorsed by International Baccalaureate.

Livy Selections

Livy AUC 2.9.1-4 Summary

Livy puts forward the demands that the Tarquins made of Porsenna and how Porsenna arrived at the decision to invade Rome.

Livy AUC 2.9.1-4 Tier 1

deinde P. Valerius et T. Lucretius consules facti sunt.

Tarquinii perfugerant ad Lartem Porsennam, regem Clusinum.

Tarquinii Porsennae consilium et preces suas dedit.

Tarquinii rogabant ne Tarquinios, qui Etrusci erant, et qui erant eiusdem sanguinis, essent exsules qui nihil habent.

nunc monebant ne Porsenna permitteret populum reges expellere sine poena.

monebant libertatem ipsam esse satis dulcem.

monebat finem regnis adesse nisi reges defendant regna tanta vi quanta civitates libertatem cupiant,

monebant futurum esse nullos nobiles qui supra alios civitates sint;

monebant adesse finem regnis, finem rei pulcherrimae inter deos et homines.

cogitatus non solum regem securum esse Romae, sed etiam regem ex Etruscis bonum esse, Porsenna venit Romam cum exercitu.

Livy AUC 2.9.1-4 Tier 2

inde P. valerius iterum (et) T. Lucretius consules facti (sunt).

Tarquinii ad Lartem Porsennam, regem Clusinum, iam perfugerant.

ibi nunc orabant miscendo consilium precesque ne se, oriundos ex Etruscis, eiusdem sanguinis nominisque, pateretur egentes exsulare,

nunc monebant etiam ne sineret inultum orientem morem pellendi reges.

(monebant) libertatem ipsam habere satis dulcedinis.

(monebant) adesse finem regnis nisi reges regna defendant tanta vi quanta civitates eam expetant,

(monebant) futurum esse nihil excelsum, nihil quod supra cetera emineat in civitatibus;

(monebant) adesse finem regnis, rei pulcherrimae inter deos hominesque.

ratus cum regem Romae esse tutum, tum regem gentis Etruscae, amplum Tuscis, Porsenna infesto exercitu Romam venit.

Livy AUC 2.9.1-4 Segmented Reader
Inde P. Valerius iterum T. Lucretius consules facti.
Iam Tarquinii ad Lartem Porsennam,
Clusinum regem,
perfugerant.
Ibi miscendo consilium precesque
nunc orabant, ne se,
oriundos ex Etruscis,
eiusdem sanguinis nominisque,
egentes exsulare pateretur,
nunc monebant etiam
ne
orientem morem pellendi reges
inultum sineret.
Satis libertatem ipsam habere dulcedinis.
Nisi quanta vi civitates eam expetant
tanta regna reges defendant,
aequari summa infimis;
nihil excelsum,
nihil quod supra cetera emineat,
in civitatibus fore;
adesse finem regnis,
rei inter deos hominesque pulcherrimae.
Porsenna
cum regem esse Romae tutum,
tum Etruscae gentis regem,
amplum Tuscis ratus,
Romam infesto exercitu venit.

Livy AUC 2.9.1-4 Liber Ipse

Inde P. Valerius iterum T. Lucretius consules facti. Iam Tarquinii ad Lartem Porsennam, Clusinum regem, perfugerant. Ibi miscendo consilium precesque nunc orabant, ne se, oriundos ex Etruscis, eiusdem sanguinis nominisque, egentes exsulare pateretur, nunc monebant etiam ne orientem morem pellendi reges inultum sineret. Satis libertatem ipsam habere dulcedinis. Nisi quanta vi civitates eam expetant tanta regna reges defendant, aequari summa infimis; nihil excelsum, nihil quod supra cetera emineat, in

9

civitatibus fore; adesse finem regnis, rei inter deos hominesque pulcherrimae. Porsenna cum regem esse Romae tutum, tum Etruscae gentis regem, amplum Tuscis ratus, Romam infesto exercitu venit.

Livy AUC 2.9.1-4 Questions

1. Identify *P. Valerius* and *T. Lucretius*.

2. Identify *Tarquinii*.

3. Identify *Lartem Porsennam*.

4. Identify and locate *Clusinum*.

5. Identify *Etruscis*.

6. *Ibi miscendo…inultum sineret*, outline how the Tarquins were appealing to Porsenna. Quote the Latin that supports your answer.

7. *Nisi quanta…pulcherrimae*, describe what might happen if Porsenna doesn't help the Tarquins retake Rome? Quote the Latin that supports your answer.

8. *Porsenna…venit,* why did Porsenna seem to ultimately decide to bring troops against Rome?

9. Translate *ibi miscendo…inultum siineret.*

Livy AUC 2.9.5-8 Summary

Livy described the actions that the Roman Senate took to appease the masses so that the people wouldn't turn on the newly formed republic.

Livy AUC 2.9.5-8 Tier 1

numquam tam perterritus fuit senatus;

tum Clusium erat fortis et nomen Porsenna magnum erat.

nec modo senatores ipsi timebant hostes sed etiam cives suos, ne Romana plebs, acta metu, acciperet reges in urbem vel acciperet pacem cum servitute.

igitur senatus multa blandimenta plebi dedit.

primo curavit ut copiam frumenti obtineret, et senatus alios in Volscos alios Cumas ad comparandum frumentum misit.

quoniam sal nimis pretiosa erat, senatus pretium a privatis in publicum transtulit;

et senatus plebes a stipendio liberavit, ut vri pecuniosi stipendium deberent:

senatus cogitavit pauperes pendere (pay) satis stipendi si liberos educent.

itaque senatus his indulgentiis tenuit concordem civitatem postquam res aspera erat in civitate cum urbs oppugnata est et famem habuit,

senatus tam bene tenuit concordem civitatem ut non modo pecuniosi populi horrerent nomen regium sed etiam pauperes nomen regium horrerent, nec quisquam postea demagogus malis artibus tam popularis esset quam senatus fuit bene imperando.

Livy AUC 2.9.5-8 Tier 2

non umquam ante alias invasit tantus terror senatum;

tum res Clusina adeo valida erat nomenque Porsennae magnum.

nec modo ipsi timebant hostes sed suosmet cives, ne Romana plebs, perculsa metu, regibus receptis in urbem vel acciperet pacem cum servitute.

igitur per id tempus multa blandimenta data plebi ab senatu.

in primis cura habita annonae, et alii missi in Volscos, alii Cumas ad comparandum frumentum.

arbitrium vendendi salis quoque, quia venibat impenso pretio, ademptum privatis sumptum in publicum omne;

plebesque liberata portoriis et tributo, ut conferrent divites qui essent oneri ferendo:

pauperes pendere satis stipendi, si liberos educent.

itaque haec indulgentia patrum adeo tenuit concordem civitatem postmodum asperis rebus in obsidione ac fame,

ut horrerent nomen regium non mags summi quam infimi, nec quisquam unus postea tam popularis esset malis artibus quam universus senatus tum fuit bene imperando.

Livy AUC 2.9.5-8 Segmented Reader
Non unquam alias ante
tantus terror
senatum invasit;
adeo valida res tum Clusina erat
magnumque Porsennae nomen.
Nec hostes modo timebant
sed suosmet ipsi cives,
ne Romana plebs,

metu perculsa,

receptis in urbem regibus

vel cum servitute pacem acciperet.

Multa igitur blandimenta plebi

per id tempus

ab senatu data.

Annonae in primis habita cura,

et ad frumentum comparandum

missi alii in Volscos, alii Cumas.

Salis quoque vendendi arbitrium,

quia impenso pretio venibat,

in publicum omne sumptum,

ademptum privatis;

portoriisque et tributo plebes liberata,

ut divites conferrent

qui oneri ferendo essent:

pauperes satis stipendii pendere,

si liberos educent.

Itaque haec indulgentia patrum

asperis postmodum rebus in obsidione

ac fame

adeo concordem civitatem tenuit,

ut regium nomen

non summi magis quam infimi horrerent,

nec quisquam unus malis artibus

postea tam popularis esset

quam tum bene imperando universus senatus fuit.

Livy AUC 2.9.5-8 Liber Ipse

Non unquam alias ante tantus terror senatum invasit; adeo valida res tum Clusina erat magnumque Porsennae nomen. Nec hostes modo timebant sed suosmet ipsi cives, ne Romana plebs, metu perculsa, receptis in urbem regibus vel cum servitute pacem acciperet. Multa igitur blandimenta plebi per id tempus ab senatu data. Annonae in primis habita cura, et ad frumentum comparandum missi alii in Volscos, alii Cumas. Salis quoque vendendi arbitrium, quia impenso pretio venibat, in publicum omne sumptum, ademptum privatis; portoriisque et tributo plebes liberata, ut divites conferrent qui oneri ferendo essent: pauperes satis stipendii pendere, si liberos educent. Itaque haec indulgentia patrum asperis postmodum rebus in obsidione ac fame adeo concordem civitatem tenuit, ut regium nomen non summi magis quam infimi horrerent, nec quisquam unus malis artibus postea tam popularis esset quam tum bene imperando universus senatus fuit.

Livy AUC 2.9.5-8 Questions

1. non unmquam…acciperet, Describe the fears of the Senate. Quote the Latin that supports your answer.

2. Identify *Volscos*.

3. Locate *Cumas*.

4. *ad frumentum…ferendo essent*, outline the steps the Senate took to calm the common people. Quote the Latin that supports your answer.

5. What were the poor expected to do if not pay taxes?

6. Translate *itaque haec indulgentia…infimi horrerent.*

7. Identify the hyperbole in *nec quisquam…senatus fuit.*

8. What did the Senate ultimately accomplish in this section?

Livy AUC 2.10.1-6 Summary

Livy describes the beginning of the Etruscan attack on Rome, and how there only seemed one way into the Palatine, a bridge, which a single man saw right to defend while his colleagues work to destroy it. The beginning of the story of Horatius Cocles.

Livy AUC 2.10.1-6 Tier 1

cum hostes adessent, omnes ex agris in urbem eunt; protegunt urbem custodibus.

alia videbantur tuta muris, alia videbantur tuta quia Tiberis erat inter se et hostes:

Pons Sublicius paene dedit viam hostibus, sed unus vir, Horatius Cocles, aderat;

illo die fortuna Romae habuit eum qui urbem defendit.

Horatius Cocles, qui fore in statione pontis erat cum vidisset Ianiculum captum impetu atque vidisset hostes ad urbem currere,

et vidisset turbam perterritam suorum relinquere arma et ordines, Horatius Cocles quemque virum timidum admonebat

Horatius Cocles quemque virum obstabat et dicebat eos in urbem sine custodibus frustra fugere,

Horatius dicebat si pontem ut viam hostibus reliquissent, plus hostium in urbem quam in Ianiculo futurum esse.

itaque monebat ut pontem rumpant ferro, ignit, quacumque possint:

dicebat se defensurum contra impetum hostium, quantum posset uno viro.

adit in primam partem pontis, Horatius Cocles erat notus quia is hostes expectabat inter omnes viros qui terga sua ad pugnam vertebant,

hostes videbat Horatium Coclitem ineundum ad proelium armis, preparatum pugnare manu contra manum, et audacia eius hostes obstupefecit.

Livy AUC 2.10.1-6 Tier 2

cum hostes adessent, quisque pro se demigrant in urbem ex agris; urbem ipsam praesidiis saepiunt.

alia videbantur tuta muris, alia (videbantur tuta) Tiberio obiecto:

Pons Sublicius paene dedit iter hostibus, ni unus vir fuisset, Horatius Cocles;

illo die fortuna urbis Romanae habuit id munimentum .

qui forte positus in statione pontis cum Ianiculum captum repentino impetu atque inde citatos hostes decurrere vidisset

trepidamque turbam suorum relinquere arma ordinesque, reprehensans singulos,

obsistens obtestansque testabatur fidem deum et hominum nequiquam eos fugere praesidio deserto;

si reliquissent transitum ponte a tergo, plus hostium in Palatio Capitolioque quam in Ianiculo iam fore.

itaque monere, praedicere ut pontem interrumpant ferro, igni, quacumque vi possint:

se excepturum impetum hostium, quantum posset obsisti corpore uno.

inde vadit in primum aditum pontis, insignisque obversis inter terga conspecta cedentium pugna,

(insignis) comminus ineundum ad proelium armis, obstupefecit hostes ipso miraculo audaciae.

Livy AUC 2.10.1-6 Segmented Reader
Cum hostes adessent,
pro se quisque
in urbem ex agris

demigrant;
urbem ipsam saepiunt praesidiis.
Alia muris,
alia Tiberi obiecto
videbantur tuta:
Pons Sublicius iter paene hostibus dedit,
ni unus vir fuisset,
Horatius Cocles;
id munimentum illo die
fortuna urbis Romanae habuit.
Qui positus forte in statione pontis
cum captum repentino impetu Ianiculum
atque inde citatos decurrere hostes
vidisset
trepidamque turbam suorum
arma ordinesque relinquere,
reprehensans singulos,
obsistens obtestansque
deum et hominum fidem testabatur
nequiquam deserto praesidio eos fugere;
si transitum ponte a tergo reliquissent,
iam plus hostium in Palatio Capitolioque
quam in Ianiculo fore.
Itaque monere,
praedicere ut pontem ferro,
igni, quacumque vi possint,
interrumpant:
se impetum hostium,
quantum corpore uno posset obsisti,
excepturum.
Vadit inde in primum aditum pontis,
insignisque
inter conspecta cedentium pugna terga obversis
comminus ad ineundum proelium armis,
ipso miraculo audaciae obstupefecit hostes.

Livy AUC 2.10.1-6 Liber ipse

Cum hostes adessent, pro se quisque in urbem ex agris demigrant; urbem ipsam saepiunt praesidiis. Alia muris, alia Tiberi obiecto videbantur tuta: Pons Sublicius iter paene hostibus dedit, ni unus vir fuisset, Horatius Cocles; id munimentum illo die fortuna urbis Romanae habuit. Qui positus forte in statione pontis cum captum repentino impetu Ianiculum atque inde citatos decurrere hostes vidisset trepidamque turbam suorum arma ordinesque relinquere, reprehensans singulos, obsistens obtestansque deum et hominum fidem testabatur nequiquam deserto praesidio eos fugere; si transitum ponte a tergo reliquissent, iam plus hostium in Palatio Capitolioque quam in Ianiculo fore. Itaque monere, praedicere ut pontem ferro, igni, quacumque vi possint, interrumpant: se impetum hostium, quantum corpore uno posset obsisti, excepturum. Vadit inde in primum aditum pontis, insignisque inter conspecta cedentium pugna terga obversis comminus ad ineundum proelium armis, ipso miraculo audaciae obstupefecit hostes.

Livy AUC 2.10.1-6 Questions

1. *Cum hostes…videbantur tuta*, what defense measures did the Romans take? Quote the Latin that supports your answer.

2. Identify and locate the *Pons Sublicius.*

3. Identify *Horatius Cocles.*

4. Locate *Ianiculum.*

5. *Iter paene…habuit,* what was the good fortune that Rome had that day?

6. Translate *Qui positus…relinquere.*

7. *reprehensans…in Ianiculo fore*, describe Cocles' actions. Quote the Latin that supports your response.

8. *Itaque monere…excepturum* How does Cocles plan to stop the enemy from using this route? Quote the Latin that supports your answer.

9. *vadit…hostes*, how does Livy portray Cocles heroically here?

10. Identify a rhetorical technique at use in this passage and explain its use. Quote the Latin that supports your response.

Livy AUC 2.10.7-10 Summary

Cocles was joined by two men to hold off the attack while the bridge is destroyed. When the bridge is almost destroyed, he sends the other two men back and challenges the enemies to one on one combat.

Livy AUC 2.10.7-10 Tier 1

pudor duos viros cum Horatio tenuit, ambos famosos familia et factis suis.

Horatius cum his duobus sustinuit primam tempestatem et partem pugnae quae pessima erat;

deinde Larcinus et Herminius revocati a quibus pontem frangebant, in tutum iverunt nam tantum parva pars pontis relicta est;

deinde Horatius saevis oculis minaciter spectabat Etruscos et provocabat singulos et omnes clamabat:

"servi estis regum arrogantium, immemores tuae libertatis, venitis oppugnatum libertatem alienam."

Etrusci haesitaverunt dum alius alium circumspectant ut proelium incipiant;

deinde pudor lineam Etruscorum movit, et clamore omnes Etrusci in unum hostem tela iaciunt.

Horatius omnia tela scuto capit, neque minus obstinatus, pontem tenet.

Etrusci temptabant Horatium expellere impetu, cum et fragor rupti pontis et clamor Romanorum sustinuit impetum subito metu.

Livy AUC 2.10.7-10 Tier 2

tamen pudor duos cum eo tenuit, Sp. Larcium ac T. Herminium, ambos claros genere factisque.

cum his parumper sustinuit primam procellam periculi et quod tumultuosissimum pugnae erat;

deinde exigua parte pontis relicta revocantibus qui rescindebant, eos quoque ipsos cedere in tutum coegit.

inde minaciter circumferens truces oculos ad proceres Etruscorum nunc provocare singulos, nunc increpare omnes:

servitia regum superborum, immemores suae libertatis, venire oppugnatum alienam.

cunctati sunt aliquamdiu, dum alius alium circumspectant ut proelium incipiant;

deinde pudor commovit aciem, et clamore sublato, undique tela coniciunt in unum hostem.

quae cum cuncta haesissent in obiecto scuto, neque ille minus obstinatus obtineret pontem ingenti gradu,

iam conabantur detrudere virum impetu, cum simul fragor rupti pontis, simul clamor Romanorum, sublatus alacritate perfecti operis, sustinuit impetum subito pavore.

Livy AUC 2.10.7-10 Segmented Reader

Duos tamen cum eo pudor tenuit,
Sp. Larcium ac T. Herminium,
ambos claros genere factisque.
Cum his
primam periculi procellam
et quod tumultuosissimum pugnae erat
parumper sustinuit;
deinde eos quoque ipsos
exigua parte pontis relicta
revocantibus
qui rescindebant cedere in tutum coegit.
Circumferens inde truces minaciter oculos
ad proceres Etruscorum
nunc singulos provocare,
nunc increpare omnes:
servitia regum superborum,
suae libertatis immemores
alienam oppugnatum venire.
Cunctati aliquamdiu sunt,
dum alius alium,
ut proelium incipiant,
circumspectant;
pudor deinde commovit aciem,
et clamore sublato
undique in unum hostem
tela coniciunt.
Quae cum in obiecto cuncta scuto haesissent,
neque ille minus obstinatus
ingenti pontem obtineret gradu,
iam impetu conabantur detrudere virum,

cum simul fragor rupti pontis,
simul clamor Romanorum,
alacritate perfecti operis sublatus,
pavore subito impetum sustinuit.

Livy AUC 2.10.7-10 Liber ipse

Duos tamen cum eo pudor tenuit, Sp. Larcium ac T. Herminium, ambos claros genere factisque. Cum his primam periculi procellam et quod tumultuosissimum pugnae erat parumper sustinuit; deinde eos quoque ipsos exigua parte pontis relicta revocantibus qui rescindebant cedere in tutum coegit. Circumferens inde truces minaciter oculos ad proceres Etruscorum nunc singulos provocare, nunc increpare omnes: servitia regum superborum, suae libertatis immemores alienam oppugnatum venire. Cunctati aliquamdiu sunt, dum alius alium, ut proelium incipiant, circumspectant; pudor deinde commovit aciem, et clamore sublato undique in unum hostem tela coniciunt. Quae cum in obiecto cuncta scuto haesissent, neque ille minus obstinatus ingenti pontem obtineret gradu, iam impetu conabantur detrudere virum, cum simul fragor rupti pontis, simul clamor Romanorum, alacritate perfecti operis sublatus, pavore subito impetum sustinuit.

Livy AUC 2.10.7-10 Questions

1. What made the two men stay back with Cocles?

2. *cum his…tutum coegit,* describe the actions of the Romans in this section. Quote the Latin that supports your answer.

3. *circumferens…venire,* outline how Cocles provokes the enemies. Quote the Latin that supports your response.

4. *quae …detrudere virum,* describe how the enemy attack on Cocles is carried out. Quote the Latin to support your response.

5. *cum simul…impetum sustinuit,* why do the Romans rejoice here?

6. How does the style of writing in this passage help convey the heroics of the Romans? Quote the Latin that supports your answer.

7. Translate: *cunctati…coniciunt.*

Livy AUC 2.10.11-13 Summary

LIvy describes the end of Cocles' great feat and how Rome honored him.

Livy AUC 2.10.11-13 Tier 1

tum Cocles "O sancte Tiberine pater" inquit," te precor accipias me armatum benigno flumine."

sic armatus Cocles in Tiberim desiluit. Etrusci multa tela iacuerunt neque eum transfixit. Cocles sine vulneri ad suos trans flumen navit. ausus est rem quae habemus plus fama quam fide.

Roma fuit grata ad tantam virtutem; Roma statuam Coclitis in foro posuit; Roma ei dedit quantum agri uno die circumaravit.

privati cives quoque ei dona dare voluerunt inter publicos honores;

etiam in re incerta, omnes ei aliud dedit, etiam non multum habuerunt.

Livy AUC 2.10.11-13 Tier 2

tum Cocles "sancte Tiberine pater" inquit, "te precor, accipias haec arma et hunc militem propitio flumine."

sic armatus in Tiberim ita desiluit, multisque telis superincidentibus, incolumis ad suos tranavit, rem ausus habituram ad posteros plus famae quam fidei.

civitas fuit grata erga tantam virtutem; statua posita in comitio; quantum agri uno die circumaravit, datum.

privata studia quoque inter publicos honores eminebant;

nam in magna inopia pro domesticis copiis unusquisque ei aliud contulit, fraudans se ipse victu suo.

Livy AUC 2.10.11-13 Segmented Reader
Tum Cocles
"Tiberine pater"
inquit,
"te sancte precor,
haec arma et hunc militem
propitio flumine accipias."
Ita sic armatus in Tiberim desiluit
multisque superincidentibus telis
incolumis ad suos tranavit,

rem ausus

plus famae habituram

ad posteros

quam fidei.

Grata erga tantam virtutem civitas fuit;

statua in comitio posita;

agri quantum uno die circumaravit,

datum.

Privata quoque inter publicos honores

studia eminebant;

nam

in magna inopia pro domesticis copiis

unusquisque ei aliquid,

fraudans se ipse victu suo,

contulit.

Livy AUC 2.10.11-13 Liber ipse

Tum Cocles "Tiberine pater" inquit, "te sancte precor, haec arma et hunc militem propitio flumine accipias." Ita sic armatus in Tiberim desiluit multisque superincidentibus telis incolumis ad suos tranavit, rem ausus plus famae habituram ad posteros quam fidei. Grata erga tantam virtutem civitas fuit; statua in comitio posita; agri quantum uno die circumaravit, datum. Privata quoque inter publicos honores studia eminebant; nam in magna inopia pro domesticis copiis unusquisque ei aliquid, fraudans se ipse victu suo, contulit.

Livy AUC 2.10.11-13 Questions

1. *Tum Cocles…tranavit*, outline Cocles' actions in terms of their praiseworthiness. Quote the Latin that supports your response.

2. *grata…contulit*, describe how the Romans celebrated Cocles' deeds. Quote the Latin that supports your response.

3. Translate: *rem ausus…fidei.*

4. Why does Livy separate out the honors bestowed upon Cocles into state and private?

5. Identify a rhetorical technique at use in this passage. Quote the Latin that supports your response.

Livy AUC 2.11.1-5 Summary

Since Porsenna isn't able to defeat the Romans in the first attack, he tries to lay siege and starve them out. Valerius, a Roman Consul, plans counter attacks.

Livy AUC 2.11.1-5 Tier 1

cum Porsenna Romanos in prima pugna non vicerit, is consilium suum vertit ab oppugnando urbe ad capiendam urbem per longum tempus.

Porsenna milites in colle Ianiculo posuit, et posuit castra in plano ad Tiberim, navibus importatis ab omni loco et ad custodiam ut nullum cibum ad Romam vehi sineret, et ut milites trans flumen mitteret ad res capiendas cum occasio esset;

et brevi tempore Porsenna omnem campum Romanum tam periculosum fecit ut Romani non solum cetera ex campis sed omnes oves et boves quoque in urbem ferrent,

neque quisquam auderet oves bovesque movere extra portas.

hoc concessum solum licebat Etruscis, (id est Romani campis consilio discedebant) non quod Romani timebant sed quod Romani consilium habebant.

namque consul Valerius fuit cupidus impetus magni contra numerum magnum Etruscorum. Valerius Etruscos impetum non expectantem oppugnare voluit, itaque Valerius non curavit punire impetus parvos Etruscorum.

itaque Valerius iussit populum suum agere multas oves bovesque ex porta Esquilina, quia porta Esquilina procul ab hoste fuit, et quia Valerius voluit praedatores trahere.

Valerius putavit hostes scituros id quod servi ad Etruscos transfugerunt.

Livy AUC 2.11.1-5 Tier 2

Porsenna, repulsus primo conatu, consiliis versis ab oppugnanda urbe ad obsidendam, praesidio locato in Ianiculo, (Porsenna) ipse castra posuit in plano ripisque Tiberis,

navibus undique accitis et ad custodiam ne quid frumenti Romam subvehi sineret, et ut milites trans flumen traiceret praedatum per occasiones aliis atque aliis locis;

brevique omnem agrum Romanum adeo infestum reddidit ut non solum cetera ex agris sed omne pecus quoque in urbem compelleretur,

neque quisquam auderet propellere extra portas.

hoc tantum concessum licentiae Etruscis non metu magis quam consilio.

namque consul Valerius, intentus in occasionem adoriundi multos simul et improviso, se gravem vindicem ad maiora servabat, neglegens ultor in parvis rebus.

itaque edicit suis postero die expellerent frequentes pecus porta Esquilina quae aversissima ab hoste erat ut eliceret praedatores,

ratus hostes scituros id quod servitia infida in obsidione et fame transfugerent.

Livy AUC 2.11.1-5 Segmented Reader

Porsenna
primo conatu repulsus,
consiliis
ab oppugnanda urbe ad obsidendam
versis,
praesidio in Ianiculo locato,
ipse in plano ripisque Tiberis
castra posuit,
navibus undique accitis
et ad custodiam
ne quid Romam frumenti subvehi sineret,
et ut praedatum milites trans flumen
per occasiones
aliis atque aliis locis traiceret;
brevique
adeo infestum
omnem Romanum agrum reddidit
ut non cetera solum ex agris
sed pecus quoque omne
in urbem compelleretur,
neque quisquam extra portas propellere auderet.
Hoc tantum licentiae Etruscis
non metu magis quam consilio
concessum.
Namque Valerius consul
intentus in occasionem
multos simul
et effusos improviso adoriundi,
in parvis rebus neglegens ultor,
gravem se ad maiora vindicem servabat.
Itaque ut eliceret praedatores,

edicit suis
postero die
frequentes porta Esquilina,
quae aversissima ab hoste erat,
expellerent pecus,
scituros id hostes ratus,
quod in obsidione et fame
servitia infida transfugerent.

Livy AUC 2.11.1-5 Liber Ipse

Porsenna primo conatu repulsus, consiliis ab oppugnanda urbe ad obsidendam versis, praesidio in Ianiculo locato, ipse in plano ripisque Tiberis castra posuit, navibus undique accitis et ad custodiam ne quid Romam frumenti subvehi sineret, et ut praedatum milites trans flumen per occasiones aliis atque aliis locis traiceret; brevique adeo infestum omnem Romanum agrum reddidit ut non cetera solum ex agris sed pecus quoque omne in urbem compelleretur, neque quisquam extra portas propellere auderet. Hoc tantum licentiae Etruscis non metu magis quam consilio concessum. Namque Valerius consul intentus in occasionem multos simul et effusos improviso adoriundi, in parvis rebus neglegens ultor, gravem se ad maiora vindicem servabat. Itaque ut eliceret praedatores, edicit suis postero die frequentes porta Esquilina, quae aversissima ab hoste erat, expellerent pecus, scituros id hostes ratus, quod in obsidione et fame servitia infida transfugerent.

Livy AUC 2.11.1-5 Questions

1. Locate *Ianiculo.*

2. *consiliis…traiceret,* what actions did Porsenna take after the intial assault on the city failed? Quote the Latin that supports your answer.

3. *brevique…auderet,* what was the immediate result of the siege for the Romans?

4. *hoc tantum…servabat,* what do we learn about Rome's leader in this section? Quote the Latin that supports your answer.

5. *itaque…transfugerent,* outline the different aspects of Valerius' plan. Quote the Latin that supports your response.

6. Translate *Porsenna primo…sineret.*

7. Identify a figure of speech used in this passage.

Livy AUC 2.11.6-10 Summary

Valerius' plan for an ambush is put into practice, and thoroughly defeats a force of plundering Etruscans.

Livy AUC 2.11.6-10 Tier 1

Et servi Etruscis id dixerunt; Etrusci miserunt plures milites multo trans flumen ut multas res capiant.

Publius Valerius inde iubet Titum Herminium considere occultum in via Gabina cum parvo numero militum,

Valerius iubet Spurium Larcium expectare ad portam Collinam cum manu iuvenum armis levibus dum hostis ante Spurium it, deinde se obicere ne ad flumen reditus sit.

alter consulum duorum, Titus Lucretius, exivit porta Naevia cum multis militibus;

Valerius ipse educit cohortes delectas monte Caelio, et hostes primum viderunt hos milites.

Ubi Herminius tumultum sensit, cucurrit ex loco secreto, et impetum fecit contra Etruscos qui ad Lucretium versi sunt;

clamor redditus ab dextra et ab sinistra hinc a porta Collina, illinc ab Naevia porta;

ita praedatores in medio victi sunt, neque praedatores aequi ad pugnam Romanis fortibus, neque praedatores viam ad fugam habuerunt.

et ille fuit finis Etruscis errandi tam late.

Livy AUC 2.11.6-10 Tier 2

Et sciverunt indicio perfugae; traiciuntque multo plures flumen, ut in spem universae praedae.

Publius Valerius inde iubet Titum Herminium via Gabina considere occultum cum modicis copiis ad secundum lapidem,

(Valerius iubet) Spurium Larcium stare ad portam Collinam cum expedita iuventute donec hostis praetereat; inde se obicere ne ad flumen reditus sit.

Consulum (duorum) alter, Titus Lucretius, egressus porta Naevia cum aliquot manipulis militum;

Valerius ipse educit cohortes delectas Caelio monte, hique primi apparuerunt hosti.

Ubi tumultum sensit, Herminius concurrit ex insidiis, et caedit terga Etruscis versis in Lucretium;

clamor redditus dextra laevaque, hinc a porta Collina, illinc ab Naevia;

ita caesi praedatores in medio, neque pares ad pugnam viribus et saeptis omnibus viis ad fugam.

et ille fuit finis Etruscis evagandi tam effuse.

Livy AUC 2.11.6-10 Segmented Reader

Et sciere perfugae indicio;
multoque plures,
ut in spem universae praedae,
flumen traiciunt.
P. Valerius inde
T. Herminium
cum modicis copiis ad secundum lapidem
Gabina via occultum considere iubet,
Sp. Larcium
cum expedita iuventute
ad portam Collinam stare
donec hostis praetereat;
 inde se obicere
ne sit ad flumen reditus.
Consulum
alter T. Lucretius porta Naevia
cum aliquot manipulis militum
egressus;
ipse Valerius Caelio monte cohortes delectas educit,
hique primi apparuere hosti.
Herminius
ubi tumultum sensit,
concurrit ex insidiis,
versisque in Lucretium Etruscis terga caedit;
dextra laevaque,
hinc a porta Collina,
illinc ab Naevia,
redditus clamor;
ita caesi in medio praedatores,
 neque ad pugnam viribus pares
et ad fugam saeptis omnibus viis.
Finisque ille tam effuse evagandi Etruscis fuit.

Livy AUC 2.11.6-10 Liber Ipse

Et sciere perfugae indicio; multoque plures, ut in spem universae praedae, flumen traiciunt. P. Valerius inde T. Herminium cum modicis copiis ad secundum lapidem Gabina via occultum considere iubet, Sp. Larcium cum expedita iuventute ad portam Collinam stare donec hostis praetereat; inde se obicere ne sit ad flumen reditus. Consulum alter T. Lucretius porta Naevia cum aliquot manipulis militum egressus; ipse Valerius Caelio monte cohortes delectas educit, hique primi apparuere hosti. Herminius ubi tumultum sensit, concurrit ex insidiis, versisque in Lucretium Etruscis terga caedit; dextra laevaque, hinc a porta Collina, illinc ab Naevia, redditus clamor; ita caesi in medio praedatores, neque ad pugnam viribus pares et ad fugam saeptis omnibus viis. Finisque ille tam effuse evagandi Etruscis fuit.

Livy AUC 2.11.6-10 Questions

1. *et sciere…traiciunt*, what part of Valerius' plan worked based on this selection?

2. P. Valerius inde…reditus, what are the different components of Valerius' plans for the Etruscans? Quote the Latin that supports your answer.

3. Who is Titus Lucretius again?

4. locate *Caelio monte*.

5. Which forces did the Etruscans first encounter?

6. *Herminius…reditus clamor*, describe the attack on the Etruscan raiders. Quote the Latin that supports your answer.

7. Translate *ita caesi…fuit*.

8. For your own notes, draw out a map of the plan described and carried out in this section.

Livy AUC 2.12.1- 6 Summary

Gaius Mucius, fed up with the blockade, decides to inform the Senate of his plans to do a daring deed.

Livy AUC 2.12.1-6 Tier 1

non minus erat obsidio et inopia frumenti fecit pretium nimis magnum, Porsenna habebat spem se expugnaturum urbem expectando,

cum Gaius Mucius, adulescens nobilis, consilium fecit.

Gaio Mucio, obsidio indigna esse videbatur quia populus Romanus sub regibus, nullo bello, obsione non habebatur

et iam, sine regibus, populus Romanus habetur obsidione ab Etruscis quorum exercitum Romani saepe vicerunt,

Gaius Mucius ei indignitati consilium audacem fecit,

primo constituit penetrare in castra hostium;

dein adit senatum, quia Mucius metuit ne custodes Romani eum caperet ut fugitivum, si iret sine imperio senatus.

"volo" inquit Mucius, "transire Tiberim, patres, et si possim, intrare castra hostium,

nolo esse praedo nec esse ultor; habeo in animo aliquid maius, si di iuvant."

patres adprobant; Mucius ad castra hostium it gladio occulto sub veste.

Livy AUC 2.12.1-6 Tier 2

obsidio erat minus nihilo et inopia frumenti cum summa caritate, et Porsenna habebat spem se expugnaturum urbem sedendo,

cum Gaius Mucius, adulescens nobilis, cui videbantur indignum populum Romanum servientem

cum esset sub regibus obsessum esse nullo bello nec ab hostibus ullis,

eundum populum (Romanum) obsideri ab iisdem Etruscis quorum exercitus saepe fuderit,

-itaque (Gaius Mucius) ratus eam indignitatem vindicandam aliquo magno audacio facinore,

primo constituit sua sponte penetrare in castra hostium;

dein senatum adit, metuens ne forte deprehensus a custodibus Romanis retraheretur ut transfuga,

tum fortuna urbis adfirmante crimen,

si iret iniussu consulum et omnibus ignaris.

"volo" inquit, "transire Tiberim patres, et si possim, intrare castra hostium,

non praedo nec ultor in vicem populationum; facinus in animo est maius, si di iuvant."

patres adprobant; proficiscitur ferro abdito intra vestem.

Livy AUC 2.12.1-6 Segmented Reader

Obsidio erat nihilo minus
 et frumenti cum summa caritate inopia,
sedendoque
expugnaturum se urbem spem Porsenna habebat,
cum C. Mucius,
adulescens nobilis,
cui indignum videbatur populum Romanum servientem
cum sub regibus esset nullo bello
nec ab hostibus ullis obsessum esse,
liberum eundem populum
ab iisdem Etruscis obsideri
quorum saepe exercitus fuderit,
—itaque magno audacique aliquo facinore
eam indignitatem vindicandam ratus,
primo sua sponte penetrare in hostium castra constituit;
dein metuens ne
si consulum iniussu
et ignaris omnibus iret,
forte deprehensus a custodibus Romanis retraheretur
ut transfuga,
fortuna tum urbis crimen adfirmante,
senatum adit.
"Transire Tiberim" inquit, "patres,
et intrare,
si possim,
castra hostium volo,
non praedo
nec populationum in vicem ultor;
maius
si di iuvant
in animo est facinus."
Adprobant patres;
abdito intra vestem ferro proficiscitur.

Livy AUC 2.12.1-6 Liber Ipse

Obsidio erat nihilo minus et frumenti cum summa caritate inopia, sedendoque
expugnaturum se urbem spem Porsenna habebat, cum C. Mucius, adulescens nobilis,
cui indignum videbatur populum Romanum servientem cum sub regibus esset nullo

bello nec ab hostibus ullis obsessum esse, liberum eundem populum ab iisdem Etruscis obsideri quorum saepe exercitus fuderit, — itaque magno audacique aliquo facinore eam indignitatem vindicandam ratus, primo sua sponte penetrare in hostium castra constituit; dein metuens ne si consulum iniussu et ignaris omnibus iret, forte deprehensus a custodibus Romanis retraheretur ut transfuga, fortuna tum urbis crimen adfirmante, senatum adit. "Transire Tiberim" inquit, "patres, et intrare, si possim, castra hostium volo, non praedo nec populationum in vicem ultor; maius si di iuvant in animo est facinus." Adprobant patres; abdito intra vestem ferro proficiscitur.

Livy AUC 2.12.1-6 Questions

1. *Obsidio …Porsenna habebat*, explain why Porsenna felt he would win. Quote the Latin that supports your response.

2. Identify *C. Mucius.*

3. *cui indignum…ratus*, explain Mucius' thoughts about the siege. Quote the Latin that supports your response.

4. Why did Mucius ask permission of the Sente? Quote the Latin that supports your answer.

5. *Transire…facinus*, how does Mucius persuade the Senate?

6. Translate: *cum C. Mucius…fuderit.*

Livy AUC 2.12.7-12 Summary

Mucius assassinates the wrong man and threatens the king that he should fear a long line of such assassins.

Livy AUC 2.12.7-12 Tier 1

Cum Mucius castra intravit, se occultavit prope tribunal regium in turba plena.

eo tempore milites pecuniam accipiebant et scriba cum rege sedebat gerens vestimenta similia, multa agebat et milites ad scribam adibant,

itaque Mucius non volebat rogare uter Porsenna esset, quia Mucius volebat se occultum remanere,

fortuna traxit factum, Mucius scribam pro rege caedit.

deinde Mucius viam sibi fecerat cruento gladio per turbam timidam, quamquam viri regis Mucium ceperunt et ad tribunal retraxerunt, et quamquam Mucius sine amicis erat, Mucius not timidus erat.

etiam inter tantum periculum, Mucius non metuit, sed necesse fuit Etruscis Mucium metuere, "Romanus sum," inquit Mucius, "civis;

Romani me Gaium Mucium vocant. ego ut hostis volui hostem occidere, et tam paratus sum mori quam hostem occidere; et facere et obdurare fortia est Romanum.

nec ego solus habui hos animos in te; post me est linea longa virorum qui gloriam te occidentis volunt.

si tibi placet, para te in hanc difficultatem, ut pugnes omnes horas pro capite tuo. habeas gladium et hostem in domo tua.

iuventus Romana ferimus hoc bellum tibi. in futuro, timueris nullam lineam militum, nullum pugnam inter exercitus; unus post unum, singuli te unum petemus."

Livy AUC 2.12.7-12 Tier 2

ubi eo venit, constitit prope tribunal regium in confertissima turba.

ibi cum forte stipendium militibus daretur et scriba sedens cum rege, fere pari ornatu, multa ageret eumque milites volgo adirent,

(Mucius) timens sciscitari uter Porsenna esset, ne ignorando regem quis esset semet ipse aperiret,

quo temere fortuna facinus traxit, obtruncat scribam pro rege.

inde qua ipse fecerat viam sibi per vadentem trepidam turbam cruento mucrone,

cum concursu facto ad clamorem satellites regii (Mucium) comprehensum retraxissent,

ante tribunal regis (Mucius) destitutus tum quoque inter tantas minas fortunae, metuendus magis quam metuens, "Romanus sum" inquit, "civis;

C. Mucium vocant. hostis volui hostem occidere, nec animi est minus ad mortem. quam fuit ad caedam; et facere et pati fortia est Romanum.

nec ego unus gessi hos animos in te; post me est longus ordo petentium idem decus.

si iuvat, proinde accingere in hoc discrimen, ut dimices in singulas horas capite tuo, habeas ferrum hostemque in vestibulo regiae.

iuventus Romana indicimus hoc bellum tibi. timueris nullam aciem, nullum proelium; res erit tibi uni cum singulis."

Livy AUC 2.12.7-12 Segmented Reader

Ubi eo venit,
in confertissima turba
prope regium tribunal constitit.
Ibi cum stipendium militibus forte daretur
et scriba cum rege sedens
pari fere ornatu
multa ageret
eumque milites volgo adirent,
timens sciscitari uter Porsenna esset,
ne ignorando regem semet ipse aperiret quis esset,
quo temere traxit fortuna facinus,
scribam pro rege obtruncat.
Vadentem inde qua
per trepidam turbam
cruento mucrone sibi ipse fecerat viam,
cum concursu ad clamorem facto
comprehensum regii satellites retraxissent,
ante tribunal regis destitutus,
tum quoque inter tantas fortunae minas
metuendus magis quam metuens,
"Romanus sum" inquit, "civis;
C. Mucium vocant.
Hostis hostem occidere volui,
nec ad mortem minus animi est,
quam fuit ad caedem;
et facere et pati fortia Romanum est.
Nec unus in te ego hos animos gessi;
longus post me ordo est
idem petentium decus.
Proinde in hoc discrimen, si iuvat, accingere,
ut in singulas horas capite dimices tuo,
ferrum hostemque in vestibulo habeas regiae.
Hoc tibi iuventus Romana indicimus bellum.
Nullam aciem,
nullum proelium timueris;
uni tibi et cum singulis res erit."

Livy AUC 2.12.7-12 Liber Ipse

Ubi eo venit, in confertissima turba prope regium tribunal constitit. Ibi cum stipendium militibus forte daretur et scriba cum rege sedens pari fere ornatu multa ageret eumque milites volgo adirent, timens sciscitari uter Porsenna esset, ne ignorando regem semet ipse aperiret quis esset, quo temere traxit fortuna facinus, scribam pro rege obtruncat. Vadentem inde qua per trepidam turbam cruento mucrone sibi ipse fecerat viam, cum concursu ad clamorem facto comprehensum regii satellites retraxissent, ante tribunal regis destitutus, tum quoque inter tantas fortunae minas metuendus magis quam metuens, "Romanus sum" inquit, "civis; C. Mucium vocant. Hostis hostem occidere volui, nec ad mortem minus animi est, quam fuit ad caedem; et facere et pati fortia Romanum est. Nec unus in te ego hos animos gessi; longus post me ordo est idem petentium decus. Proinde in hoc discrimen, si iuvat, accingere, ut in singulas horas capite dimices tuo, ferrum hostemque in vestibulo habeas regiae. Hoc tibi iuventus Romana indicimus bellum. Nullam aciem, nullum proelium timueris; uni tibi et cum singulis res erit."

Livy AUC 2.12.7-12 Questions

1. *Ibi cum stipendium…obtrucat*, explain why Mucius killed the wrong man. Quote the Latin that supports your answer.

2. *vandentem…regis destitutus*, outline Mucius' capture. Quote the Latin that supports your response.

3. *tum quoque…metuens*, which rhetorical technique is Livy using here to highlight how monstrous Mucius would have seemed to the Etruscans?

4. *hostis hostem…Romanum est*, how does Mucius describe his being in the Etruscan camp? Quote the Latin that supports your answer.

5. *nec unus…regiae*, describe the threat Mucius makes against Porsenna. Quote the Latin to support your answer.

6. Translate *hoc tibi…res erit*.

Livy AUC 2.12.13-16 Summary

Porsenna threatens to kill Mucius unless he unveils the plot, and Mucius displays the commitment of the Romans.

Livy AUC 2.12.13-16 Tier 1

rex Porsenna, territus iratusque minis Mucii, Mucium in ignibus poni iussit,

nisi Mucius statim insidiam, quam Mucius ambigue iacuit, planam fecit,

"ecce," inquit Mucius, " ut sentias quam leve corpus sit iis qui magnam gloriam vident;"

et Mucius dextram ad sacrificium in igne posuit.

Mucius manum torruit velut Mucius sine sensu erat, et rex ab hoc miratus est.

dum Porsenna ab sede sua salivit et iussit Mucium moveri ab altaribus,

"tu abi," inquit Porsenna, "ausus nocere tibi magis quam me.

iuberem te laudari esse virtute, si ista virtus pro mea patria staret;

nunc te liberum dimitto iure belli, te integrum et inviolatum. "

tunc Mucius, quasi rediens meritum, "certe," inquit Mucius, "quando honos virtuti est apud te, ut tuleris a me benficio quod minis nequisti,

trecenti principes Romani consilium habuimus ut contra te hac via veniremus.

prima sors (lot, chance) fuit mea; ceteri aderunt tempore suo, ut fata ceciderint, dum fortuna opportunum dederit."

Livy AUC 2.12.13-16 Tier 2

rex, simul cum conterritus periculo infensusque ira, minitabundus circumdari ignes iuberet,

nisi (Mucius) propere expromeret minas insidiarum sibi quas per ambages iaceret,

"en tibi" inquit (Mucius), "ut sentias quam vile corpus sit iis qui magnam gloriam vident;"

dextramque inicit foculo accenso ad sacrificium.

quam cum torreret velut animo alienato ab sensu, rex, prope attonitus miraculo,

cum (Porsenna) ab sede sua prosiluisset iussissetque iuvenem amoveri ab altaribus,

"tu vero abi," inquit (Porsenna), ausus hostilia in te magis quam in me.

iuberem (te) macte esse virtute, si ista virtus pro mea patria staret;

nunc iure belli hinc dimmitto te liberum, intactum inviolatumque."

tunc Mucius, quasi renumerans meritum, "quidem," inquit (Mucius) "quando honos est apud te virtuti, ut tuleris beneficio a me quod nequisti minis,

trecenti principes iuventutis Romanae coniuravimus ut hac via grassaremur in te.

prima sors fuit mea; ceteri quisque aderunt tempore suo ut ceciderint cuiusque primi quoad fortuna opportunum te dederit."

Livy AUC 2.12.13-16 Segmented Reader

Cum rex simul
ira infensus periculoque conterritus
circumdari ignes minitabundus iuberet
nisi expromeret propere
quas insidiarum sibi minas
per ambages iaceret,
"en tibi" inquit, "ut sentias
quam vile corpus sit
iis qui magnam gloriam vident";
dextramque
accenso ad sacrificium
foculo inicit.
Quam cum
velut alienato ab sensu
torreret
animo,
prope attonitus miraculo
rex cum ab sede sua prosiluisset
amoverique ab altaribus iuvenem iussisset,
"tu vero abi" inquit,
"in te magis quam in me hostilia ausus.
Iuberem macte virtute esse,
si pro mea patria ista virtus staret;
nunc iure belli liberum te,
intactum inviolatumque
hinc dimitto."
Tunc Mucius,
quasi remunerans meritum,
"quando quidem" inquit, "est apud te virtuti honos,

ut beneficio tuleris a me
quod minis nequisti,
trecenti coniuravimus principes iuventutis Romanae
ut in te hac via grassaremur.
Mea prima sors fuit;
ceteri
ut cuiusque ceciderit primi
quoad te opportunum fortuna dederit,
suo quisque tempore aderunt."

Livy AUC 2.12.13-16 Liber Ipse

Cum rex simul ira infensus periculoque conterritus circumdari ignes minitabundus iuberet nisi expromeret propere quas insidiarum sibi minas per ambages iaceret, "en tibi" inquit, "ut sentias quam vile corpus sit iis qui magnam gloriam vident"; dextramque accenso ad sacrificium foculo inicit. Quam cum velut alienato ab sensu torreret animo, prope attonitus miraculo rex cum ab sede sua prosiluisset amoverique ab altaribus iuvenem iussisset, "tu vero abi" inquit, "in te magis quam in me hostilia ausus. Iuberem macte virtute esse, si pro mea patria ista virtus staret; nunc iure belli liberum te, intactum inviolatumque hinc dimitto." Tunc Mucius, quasi remunerans meritum, "quando quidem" inquit, "est apud te virtuti honos, ut beneficio tuleris a me quod minis nequisti, trecenti coniuravimus principes iuventutis Romanae ut in te hac via grassaremur. Mea prima sors fuit; ceteri ut cuiusque ceciderit primi quoad te opportunum fortuna dederit, suo quisque tempore aderunt."

Livy AUC 2.12.13-16 Questions

1. *cum rex…iaceret*, what two emotions has Mucius created within the king?

2. *en tibi…animo*, outline Mucius' actions that will go on to bewilder the king. Quote the Latin that supports your answer.

3. Translate: *prope attonitus…hostilia ausus.*

4. *Iuberem…dimitto*, outline how Porsenna's opinion of Mucius has changed. Quote the Latin that supports your response.

5. What is the importance of the word *quasi*, in *quasi remunerans meritum*?

6. *quando quidem…aderunt*, outline the 'threat' that hangs over Porsenna. Quote the Latin that supports your answer.

Livy AUC 2.13.1-5 Summary 1-5

Mucius goes back to Rome along with Porsenna's negotiations for peace. Mucius is honored for his bravery.

Livy AUC 2.13.1-5 Tier 1

Legati Mucium ad Romam secuti sunt. Postea cognomen 'Scaevola' Mucio datum erat quia Mucius non manum dextram iam habuit.

Et casus primi impeti, a quo nihil praeter errorem Mucii se protexisset

et certamen subeundum, tam moverat Porsennam ut Porsenna libenter mitteret condiciones pacis Romanis.

Frustra Porsenna addidit condicionem de Tarquiniis restituendis in regnum quia Porsenna non potuerat dicere Tarquiniis "minime." Porsenna scivit Romanos id negatum esse sibi.

Porsenna imperavit condicionem de restituendo agro Veientibus. Porsenna imperavit Romanos dare obsides ei si Romani vellent Porsennam deducere exercitum ab Ianiculo.

Patres Romani agrum trans Tiberim C. Mucio causa virtutis dederunt.

Livy AUC 2.13.1-5 Tier 2

legati a Porsenna Romam secuti sunt Mucium dimissum, cui postea cognomen inditum est Scaevolae a clade dextrae.

et casus primi periculi, a quo nihil praeter errorem insidiatoris se texisset,

et dimicatio subeunda, totiens quot coniurati superessent, adeo moverat eum ut ultor (libenter) Rex Porsenna ferret condiciones pacis Romanis.

iactatum in condicionibus nequiquam (frustra) de Tarquiniis restituendis in regnum,

magis quia ipse id negare Tarquiniis nequiverat (non potuerat) quam quod ignoraret id negatum iri sibi ab Romanis.

condicio de agro restituendo Veientibus impetratum est ab Porsenna, necessitas dandi obsides expressa est ex Romanis, si Romani vellent praesidium deduci Ianiculo.

pace composita his condicionibus, Porsenna deducit exercitum ab Ianiculo et agro Romano excessit.

patres dedere(dederunt) dono C. Mucio, causa virtutis, agrum trans Tiberim, quae postea Mucia prata apellata sunt.

Livy AUC 2.13.1-5 Segmented Reader

Mucium dimissum,
cui postea Scaevolae
a clade dextrae manus
cognomen inditum,
legati a Porsenna Romam secuti sunt;
adeo moverat eum
et primi periculi casus,
a quo nihil se praeter errorem insidiatoris texisset,
et subeunda dimicatio totiens quot coniurati superessent,
ut pacis condiciones ultro ferret Romanis.
Iactatum in condicionibus nequiquam
de Tarquiniis in regnum restituendis,
magis quia id negare ipse nequiverat Tarquiniis
quam quod negatum iri sibi ab Romanis ignoraret.
De agro Veientibus restituendo impetratum,
expressaque necessitas obsides dandi Romanis,
si Ianiculo praesidium deduci vellent.
His condicionibus composita pace,
exercitum ab Ianiculo deduxit Porsenna
et agro Romano excessit.
Patres C. Mucio
virtutis causa
trans Tiberim agrum dono dedere,
quae postea sunt Mucia prata appellata.

Livy AUC 2.13.1-5 Liber Ipse

Mucium dimissum, cui postea Scaevolae a clade dextrae manus cognomen inditum, legati a Porsenna Romam secuti sunt; adeo moverat eum et primi periculi casus, a quo nihil se praeter errorem insidiatoris texisset, et subeunda dimicatio totiens quot coniurati superessent, ut pacis condiciones ultro ferret Romanis. Iactatum in condicionibus nequiquam de Tarquiniis in regnum restituendis, magis quia id negare ipse nequiverat Tarquiniis quam quod negatum iri sibi ab Romanis ignoraret. De agro Veientibus restituendo impetratum, expressaque necessitas obsides dandi Romanis, si Ianiculo praesidium deduci vellent. His condicionibus composita pace, exercitum ab Ianiculo deduxit Porsenna et agro Romano excessit. Patres C. Mucio virtutis causa trans Tiberim agrum dono dedere, quae postea sunt Mucia prata appellata.

Livy AUC 2.13.1-5 Questions

1. *Mucium dimissum…inditum* why did Mucius receive the cognomen Scaevola?

2. *legati…Romanis,* explain why Porsenna sent legates to Rome with Scaevola. Quote the Latin that supports your response.

3. Translate *iactatum…ignoraret.*

4. Identify *Tarquiniis.*

5. Identify *Veientibus.*

6. *Iactatum in condicionibus…deduci vellent,* outline the terms of peace that Porsenna included. Which did he actually achieve? Quote the Latin that supports your answer.

7. Translate *his condicionibus…prata appellata.*

8. Identify one rhetorical technique at use in this passage and explain its effect. Quote the Latin that supports your answer.

Livy AUC 2.13.6-11 Summary

One of the female hostages, Cloelia, is moved to great action by the example of Mucius, and she leads some hostages back to Rome.

Livy AUC 2.13.6-11 Tier 1

Quoniam virtus Mucii ita honorata est, feminae quoque excitatae sunt ad publica decora.

Cloelia, una virgo ex obsidibus, dux virginum trans Tiberim ad Romam natavit, quia castra Etruscorum prope ripam Tiberis locata sunt.

Cloelia inter tela hostium natavit et omnes puellas ad familias suas restituit.

id quod cum rex Porsenna audivit, primum incensus ira rex oratores ad Romam misit ad deposcendam Cloeliam obsidem:

Oratores dixerunt regem alias puellas non velle.

Deinde rex versus in admirationem dixit factum Cloeliae superare facta Coclitis Muciique.

Rex quoque dixit foedus pro rupto se habiturum esse si Cloelia non dedatur obses,

sed Cloeliam sic deditam se (Porsenna) intactam inviolatamque ad familiam suam remissurum esse.

Utrimque fides constitit. Romani pignus pacis ex foedere restituerunt, et virtus Cloeliae non solum tuta sed etiam honorata fuit,

et rex dixit se donare Cloeliam parte obsidium; ipsa pueros quos vellet legeret.

Post omnes pueros producti erant, dicitur eam impubes elegisse, quod virginitatem convenit et obsidibus ipsis placuit quia pueri minimi erant itaque iis necesse est liberari ab hoste.

Pace redintegrata, Romani novam virtutem in femina novo genere honoris donaverunt, statua equestri;

virgo sedens in equo posita fuit in summa Sacra Via.

Livy AUC 2.13.6-11 Tier 2

Ergo ita honorata virtute Mucii feminae quoque excitatae ad publica decora, et, cum castra Etruscorum forte locata essent haud procul a ripa Tiberis,

una virgo ex obsidibus, Cloelia ,dux agminis virginum, frustrata custodes Tiberim Romam tranavit (trans Tiberim ad Romam natavit) inter tela hostium

 sospitesque omnes ad propinquos restituit.

Quod ubi nuntiatum est regi, primo (primum) rex incensus ira oratores ad Romam misit ad deposcendam Cloeliam obsidem:

Oratores dixerunt facere alias haud magni;

deinde rex versus in admirationem supra Coclites Muciosque dicere id esse facinus (factum),

prae se ferre (he made known) quemadmodum (how) pro rupto foedus se habiturum esse, si obses non dedatur;

sic deditam intactam inviolatamque eam ad suos remissurum esse.

Utrimque fides constitit: et Romani restituerunt pignus pacis ex foedere, et apud regem Etruscum (Porsenna) virtus fuit non solum tuta sed etiam honorata,

et rex dixit se donare laudatam virginem parte obsidium; Cloelia ipsa legeret quos vellet.

(Cloelia) dicitur elegisse impubes ex productis omnibus, quod et decorum virginitati et consensu obsidium ipsorum probabile (dignum) erat eam aetatem potissimum (praesertim) quae maxime opportuna iniuriae esset liberari ab hoste.

Pace redintegrata, Romani donavere (donaverunt) novam virtutem in femina novo genere honoris, statua equestri;

virgo insidens equo (sedens in equo) posita fuit in summa Sacra Via.

Livy AUC 2.13.6-11 Segmented Reader

Ergo ita honorata virtute,
feminae quoque ad publica decora excitatae,
et Cloelia virgo una ex obsidibus,
cum castra Etruscorum forte
haud procul ripa Tiberis locata essent,
frustrata custodes,
dux agminis virginum
inter tela hostium
Tiberim tranavit,
sospitesque omnes Romam ad propinquos restituit.
Quod ubi regi nuntiatum est,
primo incensus ira
oratores Romam misit ad Cloeliam obsidem deposcendam:
alias haud magni facere.
Deinde in admirationem versus,
supra Coclites Muciosque dicere id facinus esse,
et prae se ferre quemadmodum si non dedatur obses,
pro rupto foedus se habiturum,
sic deditam
intactam inviolatamque ad suos remissurum.
Utrimque constitit fides;
et Romani pignus pacis ex foedere restituerunt,
et apud regem Etruscum
non tuta solum sed honorata etiam virtus fuit,
laudatamque virginem parte obsidum se donare dixit;
ipsa quos vellet legeret.
Productis omnibus elegisse impubes dicitur;
quod et virginitati decorum
et consensu obsidum ipsorum
probabile erat eam aetatem potissimum liberari ab hoste
quae maxime opportuna iniuriae esset.
Pace redintegrata
Romani novam in femina virtutem novo genere honoris,
statua equestri, donavere;
in summa Sacra via fuit posita virgo insidens equo.

Livy AUC 2.13.6-11 Liber Ipse

Ergo ita honorata virtute, feminae quoque ad publica decora excitatae, et Cloelia virgo una ex obsidibus, cum castra Etruscorum forte haud procul ripa Tiberis locata essent, frustrata custodes, dux agminis virginum inter tela hostium Tiberim tranavit, sospitesque omnes Romam ad propinquos restituit. Quod ubi regi nuntiatum est, primo incensus ira oratores Romam misit ad Cloeliam obsidem deposcendam: alias haud magni facere. Deinde in admirationem versus, supra Coclites Muciosque dicere id facinus esse, et prae se ferre quemadmodum si non dedatur obses, pro rupto foedus se habiturum, sic deditam intactam inviolatamque ad suos remissurum. Utrimque constitit fides; et Romani pignus pacis ex foedere restituerunt, et apud regem Etruscum non tuta solum sed honorata etiam virtus fuit, laudatamque virginem parte obsidum se donare dixit; ipsa quos vellet legeret. Productis omnibus elegisse impubes dicitur; quod et virginitati decorum et consensu obsidum ipsorum probabile erat eam aetatem potissimum liberari ab hoste quae maxime opportuna iniuriae esset. Pace redintegrata Romani novam in femina virtutem novo genere honoris, statua equestri, donavere; in summa Sacra via fuit posita virgo insidens equo.

Livy AUC 2.13.6-11 Questions

1. Identify *Cloelia*.

2. Locate *Tiberis*.

3. What does Livy credit as the inspiration for Cloelia's brave deed?

4. *Cloelia…restituit*, describe Cloelia's escape from the Etruscan camp. Quote the Latin that supports your answer.

5. Translate *Quod ubi…facere*.

6. Why did Porsenna change his mind concerning Cloelia? Quote the Latin that supports your answer.

7. Identify *Coclites* and *Mucios*.

8. *et prae se ferre…remissurum*, outline Porsenna's offer. Quote the Latin thta supports your response.

9. *apud regem…legeret*, describe how Porsenna goes above and beyond what he said in his offer to praise Cloelia. Quote the Latin that supports your answer.

10. *productis omnibus…iniuriae esset*, why did Cloelia choose those she did?

11. *pace...equo*, outline how Cloelia was celbrated at Rome. Quote the Latin that supports your answer.

12. Locate *Sacra via*.

13. What is particularly unique about the way that Cloelia is celebrated?

Livy AUC 2.14 Summary

Porsenna sets off from Rome, but because he doesn't want his people to think they went to war for nothing, he gives his son command to beseige Aricia, and the Etruscans lose.

Livy AUC 2.14 Tier 1

dissimile tam pacatae finis belli inter Romanos et Etruscos, est mos, qui ab antiquis usque ad nunc traditus est, inter foedum Romanorum et Etruscorum Romani bona regis Porsennae vendidit.

necesse est originem cuius moris aut quia Romani bona Porsennae in bello et post pacem vendiderunt

aut mos est ex benigniore principio quam hoc nomen vendendi bona male dicatur,

hoc est quod credibile est: Porsenna discedens ab Ianiculo dedit castra plena Romanis dedit,

erat castra plena rerum quae ex agris fertilibus Etruriae importatae sunt,

porsenna castra dedit Romanis quia tum Romani nihil habuerunt ab longinqua obsidione;

deinde Romani ea a castris vendiderunt ne populi ea hostiliter raperent. Romani ea a castris 'bona Porsennae' appellaverunt.

Romani auctionem 'bona Porsennae' appellaverunt gratiam doni. tutulus non significavit Romanos fortunas Porsennae cepisse. Romani potestatem non habuerunt.

Porsenna non voluit vidi duxisse exercitum contra romanos frustra, itaque postquam bellum Porsenna mittit filium, Arruntem, cum parte exercitus oppugnatum Ariciam.

primo, Aricini inexpectato impetu mirati sunt, deinde auxilia, et a Latinis populis et a Cumis, fecerunt tantum spei ut Aricini auderent pugnam intrare.

Etrusci tam ferociter pugnaverunt ut funderent Aricinos ipso incursu:

Cumanae cohortes, arte in loco vis, se paululum verterunt et Etruscos ab tergo oppugnaverunt.

Ita Etrusci, prope iam victores, victi sunt.

minima pars exercitus, duce amisso, sine armis, Romam revenerunt, quod nullum locum tutum proprius erat.

Romani Etruscos bene acceperunt et Etruscos cum hospitibus diviserunt.

postquam Etrusci sanati sunt, alii domos profecti sunt, nuntii hospitalium Romanorum: multi alii Romae remanserunt.

locus ad habitandum datum Etruscis quem postquam appellarunt Tuscum.

Livy AUC 2.14 Tier 2

abhorrens huic huic tam pacatae profectioni regis Etrusci ab urbe, mos traditus ab antiquis manet usque ad nostram aetatem, inter cetera sollemnia, vendendi bona regis Porsennae.

necesse est originem cuius moris aut natam esse inter bellum neque omissam in pace,

aut crevisse a mitiore principio quam hic titulus prae se ferat vendendi bona hostiliter.

proximum vero est ex iis quae traduntur, Porsennam discedentem ab Ianiculo castra opulenta dono Romanis dedisse,

(castra opulenta) convecto ex propinquis ac commeatu fertilibus arvis Etruriae,

(Romanis) tum inopi urbe ab longinqua obsidione;

deinde, ne populo immisso hostiliter diriperentur, ea venisse, appellataque bona Porsennae,

gratiam muneris magis quam significante titulo auctionem regiae fortunae quae ne in potestate quidem populi Romani esset.

Porsenna, bello Romano omisso, ne adductus exercitus frustra in ea loca videretur, mittit filium Arruntem cum parte copiarum oppugnatum Ariciam.

primo necopinata res Aricinos perculerat; deinde arcessita auxilia et a Latinis populis et a Cumis fecere tantum spei ut auderent decernere acie.

proelio inito, Etrusci adeo impetu concitato se intulerant ut funderent Aricinos ipso incursu:

Cumanae cohortes, usae arte adversus vim, declinavere paululum, conversis signis ab tergo adortae sunt hostes praelatos.

ita Etrusci prope iam victores in medio caesi (sunt).

pars perexigua, duce amisso, inermes, et fortuna et specie supplicum, Romam delati sunt, quia nullum perfugium propius erat.

ibi (Etrusci) benigne excepti divisique in hospita.

volneribus curatis, alii profecti (sunt) domos, nuntii hospitalium beneficiorum (Romanorum): caritas Romae urbisque multos tenuit.

locus ad habitandum datus his quem deinde appellarunt Tuscum.

Livy AUC 2.14 Segmented Reader

Huic tam pacatae profectioni ab urbe regis Etrusci
abhorrens mos traditus
ab antiquis usque ad nostram aetatem
inter cetera sollemnia manet,
bona Porsennae regis vendendi.
Cuius originem moris necesse est
aut inter bellum natam esse
neque omissam in pace,
aut a mitiore crevisse principio
quam hic prae se ferat titulus bona hostiliter vendendi.
Proximum vero est ex iis quae traduntur
Porsennam discedentem ab Ianiculo
castra opulenta,
convecto ex propinquis
ac fertilibus Etruriae arvis commeatu,
Romanis dono dedisse,
inopi tum urbe ab longinqua obsidione;
ea deinde,
ne populo immisso diriperentur hostiliter,
venisse,
bonaque Porsennae appellata,
gratiam muneris
magis significante titulo quam auctionem fortunae regiae
quae ne in potestate quidem populi Romani esset.
Omisso Romano bello Porsenna,
ne frustra in ea loca exercitus adductus videretur,
cum parte copiarum
filium Arruntem Ariciam oppugnatum mittit.
Primo Aricinos res necopinata perculerat;
arcessita deinde auxilia
et a Latinis populis et a Cumis
tantum spei fecere,

ut acie decernere auderent.
Proelio inito,
adeo concitato impetu se intulerant Etrusci
ut funderent ipso incursu Aricinos:
Cumanae cohortes arte adversus vim usae
declinavere paululum,
effuseque praelatos hostes conversis signis
ab tergo adortae sunt.
Ita
in medio prope iam victores
caesi Etrusci.
Pars perexigua,
duce amisso,
quia nullum propius perfugium erat,
Romam inermes
et fortuna et specie supplicum
delati sunt.
Ibi benigne excepti
divisique in hospitia.
Curatis volneribus,
alii profecti domos,
nuntii hospitalium beneficiorum:
multos Romae hospitum urbisque caritas tenuit.
His locus ad habitandum datus
quem deinde Tuscum vicum appellarunt.

Livy AUC 2.14 Liber Ipse

Huic tam pacatae profectioni ab urbe regis Etrusci abhorrens mos traditus ab antiquis usque ad nostram aetatem inter cetera sollemnia manet, bona Porsennae regis vendendi. Cuius originem moris necesse est aut inter bellum natam esse neque omissam in pace, aut a mitiore crevisse principio quam hic prae se ferat titulus bona hostiliter vendendi. Proximum vero est ex iis quae traduntur Porsennam discedentem ab Ianiculo castra opulenta, convecto ex propinquis ac fertilibus Etruriae arvis commeatu, Romanis dono dedisse, inopi tum urbe ab longinqua obsidione; ea deinde, ne populo immisso diriperentur hostiliter, venisse, bonaque Porsennae appellata, gratiam muneris magis significante titulo quam auctionem fortunae regiae quae ne in potestate quidem populi Romani esset. Omisso Romano bello Porsenna, ne frustra in ea loca exercitus adductus videretur, cum parte copiarum filium Arruntem Ariciam oppugnatum mittit. Primo Aricinos res necopinata perculerat; arcessita deinde auxilia et a Latinis populis et a Cumis tantum spei fecere, ut acie decernere auderent. Proelio inito, adeo concitato impetu se intulerant Etrusci ut funderent ipso incursu Aricinos: Cumanae cohortes arte adversus vim usae declinavere paululum, effuseque praelatos hostes conversis signis ab tergo adortae sunt. Ita in medio prope iam victores caesi Etrusci. Pars perexigua, duce amisso, quia nullum propius perfugium erat, Romam inermes et fortuna et specie supplicum delati sunt. Ibi benigne excepti divisique in hospitia. Curatis volneribus, alii profecti domos, nuntii hospitalium beneficiorum: multos Romae hospitum urbisque caritas tenuit. His locus ad habitandum datus quem deinde Tuscum vicum appellarunt.

Livy AUC 2.14 Questions

1. Translate *huic tam...regis vendendi*.

2. What does Livy think is inconsistent about the way things ended with Porsenna?

3. *cuius originem...hostiliter vedendi*, what reasoning doe Livy give for why the king's goods would be sold. Quote the Latin that supports your answer.

4. *proximum...obsidione*, explain why Porsenna may have left the goods. Quote the Latin that supports your response.

5. *ea deinde...Romani esset*, why were the goods sold, and why were they called the kings goods?

6. Identify *Arruntem*.

7. Locate *Ariciam*.

8. *omisso...mitit*, explain why Porsenna had his forces attack Aricia.

9. Identify *Cumis*.

10. Identify *Latinis*.

11. Translate *primo Aricinos...decernere auderent*.

12. *proelio...caesi Etrusci*, outline how the battle turns against the Etruscans. Quote the Latin that supports your response.

13. *pars perexigua...in hospitia,*describe how different the scene is when this group of Etruscans arrived from their previous siege. Quote the Latin that supports your response.

14. *curatis volneribus...apellarunt*, explain why some of the Etruscans stayed in Rome. Quote the Latin that supports your response.

15. Identify any stylistic features of this passage that help convey Livy's message.

Companion Texts for Paper 1 Practice:

Paper 1 Practice 1.

From Ovid Heroides, Dido to Aeneas:

7.1-22

accipe, Dardanide[1], moriturae carmen Elissae[2];

    quae legis, a nobis ultima verba legis:

sic ubi fata vocant, udis abiectus in herbis

    ad vada Maeandri[3] concinit albus olor.[4]

nec quia te nostra sperem prece posse moveri,

    adloquor — adverso movimus ista deo;

sed merita et famam corpusque animumque pudicum   5

    cum male perdiderim, perdere verba leve est.

certus es ire tamen miseramque relinquere Dido,

    atque idem venti vela fidemque ferent?

certus es, Aenea,[5] cum foedere solvere naves,

    quaeque ubi sint nescis, Itala regna sequi?   10

nec nova Carthago,[6] nec te crescentia tangunt

    moenia nec sceptro tradita summa tuo?

facta fugis, facienda petis; quaerenda per orbem

---

[1] Dardanidus, i (m): Dardanian, Trojan

[2] Elissa, ae (f): Dido, Queen of Carthage

[3] Meander, i (m): a river in Phrygia

[4] olor, oloris (m): swan

[5] *Aeneas, Aeneae* (m): Leader of the Trojan refugees

[6] *Carthago, Carthaginis*, (f): The city Dido founded in North Africa

altera, quaesita est altera terra tibi.

ut terram invenias, quis eam tibi tradet habendam?   15

    quis sua non notis arva tenenda dabit?

scilicet alter amor tibi restat et altera Dido;

    quamque iterum fallas altera danda fides.

quando erit, ut condas instar Carthaginis urbem

    et videas populos altus ab arce tuos?   20

omnia ut eveniant, nec te tua vota morentur,

    unde tibi, quae te sic amet, uxor erit?

1. *sic ubi…albus olor* (lines 1-2). Analyze the couplet for signs that Dido will be dead soon. No need to quote the Latin. [2]

2. *nec quia…leve est* (lines 3-6). Outline Dido's thoughts on writing this letter to Aeneas. No need to quote the Latin. [2]

3. *certus es…regna sequi* (lines 7-10). Outline how Dido emphasizes the betrayal she feels. No need to quote the Latin. [3]

4. *nec nova…summa tuo* (lines 11-12). List the three things that Dido expects should have caused Aeneas to want to stay. No need to quote the Latin. [3]

5. *facta fugis…tenenda dabit* (lines 13-16). List two things that Dido thinks Aeneas will try to no avail. Quote the Latin that supports your response. [4]

6. Translate *scilicet alter…uxor erit* (lines 17-22). [16]

Extension: Identify stylistic choices throughout this passage that enhance our understanding of Dido's emotions.

Paper 1 Practice 2.

From Ovid Heroides, Dido to Aeneas:

7.23-40

uror, ut inducto ceratae sulpure taedae,

    ut pia fumosis addita tura focis.

Aeneas oculis semper vigilantis inhaeret;   25

    Aenean animo noxque quiesque refert.

ille quidem male gratus et ad mea munera surdus,

    et quo, si non sim stulta, carere velim;

non tamen Aenean, quamvis male cogitat, odi,

    sed queror infidum questaque peius amo.   30

parce, Venus, nurui, durumque amplectere fratrem,

    frater Amor,[7] castris militet ille tuis!

aut ego, quae coepi, (neque enim dedignor) amorem,

    materiam curae praebeat ille meae!

fallor, et ista mihi falso iactatur imago;   35

    matris ab ingenio dissidet ille suae.

te lapis et montes innataque rupibus altis

    robora, te saevae progenuere ferae,

aut mare, quale vides agitari nunc quoque ventis,

    qua tamen adversis fluctibus ire paras.   40

---

[7] *Amor, Amoris* (m): Cupid

1. *uror, ut…tura focis* (lines23-24). Identify what Dido compares herself to. No need to quote the Latin. [2]

2. *Aeneas oculis…quiesque refert* (lines 25-26). Describe Dido's state of mind within this couplet. Quote the Latin that supports your response. [3]

3. *ille quidem…peius amo* (lines 27-30). Outline Dido's ambivalent feelings towards Aeneas. No need to quote the Latin [3].

4. *parce, Venus…ille tuis* (lines 31-32). Describe Dido's relationships within these lines. Quote the Latin that supports your answer. [4]

5. *aut ego…ille meae* (lines 33-34). Identify Dido's confession in this couplet. No need to quote the Latin. [2]

6. Translate *fallor, et…ire paras* (lines 35-40). [16]

Extension: Identify stylistic features within this passage that Ovid uses to highlight Dido's longing for Aeneas.

Paper 1 Practice 3.

From Ovid Heroides, Dido to Aeneas:

7.41-60

quo fugis? obstat hiemps. hiemis mihi gratia prosit!

    adspice, ut eversas concitet Eurus[8] aquas!

quod tibi malueram, sine me debere procellis;

    iustior est animo ventus et unda tuo.

non ego sum tanti — quid non censeris inique? —   45

    ut pereas, dum me per freta longa fugis.

exerces pretiosa odia et constantia magno,

    si, dum me careas, est tibi vile mori.

iam venti ponent, strataque aequaliter unda

    caeruleis Triton[9] per mare curret equis.   50

tu quoque cum ventis utinam mutabilis esses!

    et, nisi duritia robora vincis, eris.

quid, quasi nescires, insana quid aequora possint,

    expertae totiens tam male credis aquae?

ut, pelago suadente viam, retinacula solvas,   55

    multa tamen latus tristia pontus habet.

nec violasse fidem temptantibus aequora prodest;

    perfidiae poenas exigit ille locus,

praecipue cum laesus amor, quia mater Amorum

    nuda Cytheriaci[10] edita fertur aquis.   60

---

[8] *Eurus, i* (m): East wind

[9] *Triton, Tritonis* (m): Son of Neptune and deity of the sea

[10] *Cytheriacus, a, um:* of or belonging to Cythera, the island near which Venus is said to have been born

1. *quo fugis…unda tuo* (lines 41-44). List three things Dido reveals about the storm. No need to quote the Latin. [3]

2. *non ego…longa fugis* (lines 45-46). List two things Dido believes about Aeneas' departure. No need to quote the Latin. [2]

3. *exerces pretiosa…vile mori* (lines 47-48). Identify what Dido believes Aeneas is doing and identify what she believes the result of his actions will be. Support your response by quoting from the Latin text. [4]

4. *iam venti…vincis eris* (lines 49-52). Outline What Dido wished of Aeneas. Quotation of the Latin is not needed. [3]

5. *quid, quasi…credis aquae* (lines 53-54) Identify what trait Dido thinks Aeneas must have and Identify the evidence she offers for said trait. No need to quote the Latin. [2]

6. Translate *ut, pelago…fertur aquis* (lines 55-60). [16]

Extension: How do the literary qualities of the selection help convey Dido's message? Quote precise evidence from the text that supports your response.

Paper 1 Practice 4.

From Ovid Heroides, Dido to Aeneas:

7.61-80

perdita ne perdam, timeo, noceamve nocenti,

    neu bibat aequoreas naufragus hostis aquas.

vive, precor! sic te melius quam funere perdam.

    tu potius leti causa ferere mei.

finge, age, te rapido — nullum sit in omine pondus! —   65

    turbine deprendi; quid tibi mentis erit?

protinus occurrent falsae periuria linguae,

    et Phrygia[11] Dido fraude coacta mori;

coniugis ante oculos deceptae stabit imago

    tristis et effusis sanguinolenta comis.   70

quid tanti est ut tum 'merui! concedite!' dicas,

    quaeque cadent, in te fulmina missa putes?

da breve saevitiae spatium pelagique tuaeque;

    grande morae pretium tuta futura via est.

haec minus ut cures, puero parcatur Iulo!   75

    te satis est titulum mortis habere meae.

quid puer Ascanius,[12] quid di meruere Penates?

    ignibus ereptos obruet unda deos?

sed neque fers tecum, nec, quae mihi, perfide, iactas,

    presserunt umeros sacra paterque tuos.   80

---

[11] *Phrygius, a, um*: Trojan, Phrygian

[12] *Ascanius, i* (m): Aeneas' son with his deceased wife Creusa

1. *perdita ne…hostis aquas* (lines 61-62). List two things Dido fears. No need to quote the Latin.[2]

2. *vive, precor…ferere mei* (lines 63-64). Identify the two results of Aeneas surviving his flight from Carthage . Quote the Latin that supports your response. [4]

3. *finge, age…coacta mori* (lines 65-68). Describe what Aeneas must imagine. No need to quote the Latin. [3]

4. *coniugis ante…comis* (lines 69-70). Describe what Aeneas will see. No need to quote the Latin. [2]

5. *quid tanti…via est* (lines 71-74). Outline Dido's request to Aeneas. No need to quote the Latin. [3]

6. Translate *haec minus…paterque tuos* (lines 75-80). [16]

Extension: How is Ovid playing with language in such a way as to make Dido either more pitiable or to help the reader better empathize with her? Quote the precise evidence from the text that supports your answer.

Paper 1 Practice 5.

From Ovid Heroides, Dido to Aeneas:

7.81-97

omnia mentiris, neque enim tua fallere lingua

    incipit a nobis, primaque plector ego.

si quaeras, ubi sit formosi mater Iuli —

    occidit a duro sola relicta viro!

haec mihi narraras — sat me monuere! merentem   85

    ure; minor culpa poena futura mea est.

nec mihi mens dubia est, quin te tua numina damnent.

    per mare, per terras septima iactat hiemps.

fluctibus eiectum tuta statione recepi

    vixque bene audito nomine regna dedi.   90

his tamen officiis utinam contenta fuissem,

    et mihi concubitus fama sepulta foret!

illa dies nocuit, qua nos declive sub antrum

    caeruleus subitis conpulit imber aquis.

audieram vocem; nymphas ululasse putavi —   95

    Eumenides[13] fati signa dedere mei!

exige, laese pudor, poenas! violate Sychaei ...[14]

    ad quas, me miseram, plena pudoris eo.

---

[13] *Eumenis, Eumenidis* (f): The furies

[14] *Sychaeus, i* (m): Dido's former husband, killed by her brother

1. *omnia mentiris…plector ego* (lines 81-82). Outline Dido's accusations against Aeneas.No need to quote the Latin. [3]

2. *si quaeras…mea est* (lines 83-86). Outline the way Dido reveals her disgust with Aeneas. No need to quote the Latin. [3]

3. *nec mihi…iacta hiemps* (lines 87-88). Identify what Dido believes about Aeneas' current situation. Quote the Latin to support your response. [4]

4. *fluctibus eiectum…regna dedi* (lines 89-90). Identify what Dido did for Aeneas. No need to quote the Latin to support your answer. [2]

5. *his tamen…imber aquis* (lines 91-94). List Dido's regrets. No need to quote the Latin. [2]

6. Translate *illa dies…pudoris eo* (lines 93-98). [16]

Extension: Discuss how Ovid's writing style reinforces the resentment that Dido feels.

Paper 1 Practice 6.

From Ovid Heroides, Dido to Aeneas:

7.99-124

est mihi marmorea sacratus in aede Sychaeus

  (oppositae frondes velleraque alba tegunt).   100

hinc ego me sensi noto quater ore citari;

  ipse sono tenui dixit 'Elissa, veni!'

nulla mora est, venio, venio tibi debita coniunx;

  sum tamen admissi tarda pudore mei.

da veniam culpae! decepit idoneus auctor;   105

  invidiam noxae detrahit ille meae.

diva parens seniorque pater, pia sarcina nati,

  spem mihi mansuri rite dedere viri.

si fuit errandum, causas habet error honestas;

  adde fidem, nulla parte pigendus erit.   110

durat in extremum vitaeque novissima nostrae

  prosequitur fati, qui fuit ante, tenor.

occidit internas coniunx mactatus ad aras,

  et sceleris tanti praemia frater habet;

exul agor cineresque viri patriamque relinquo,   115

  et feror in dubias hoste sequente vias.

adplicor his oris fratrique elapsa fretoque

  quod tibi donavi, perfide, litus emo.

urbem constitui lateque patentia fixi

  moenia finitimis invidiosa locis.   120

bella tument; bellis peregrina et femina temptor,

  vixque rudis portas urbis et arma paro.

mille procis placui, qui me coiere querentes

　　nescio quem thalamis praeposuisse suis.

1. *est mihi…alba tegunt* (lines 99-100). Describe Sychaeus' tomb. No need to quote the Latin. [2]

2. *hinc ego…pudore mei* (lines 101-104). Describe two details from this selection that show Dido feels guilty about her relationship with Aeneas. Quote the Latin that supports your response. [4]

3. *da veniam…pigendus erit* (lines 105-110). List three reasons why Dido felt Aeneas could be trusted. No need to quote the Latin. [3]

4. *durant in…frater habet* (lines 111-114). Identify what Dido feels about her life and identify the first event she cites as evidence. No need to quote the Latin. [2]

5. *exul agor…litus emo* (lines 115-118). List three things that Dido experienced fleeing her homeland. No need to qoute the Latin. [3]

6. Translate *urbem constitui…praepuisse suis* (lines 119-124).

Extension: In this selection Dido is expressing remorse for her relationship with Aeneas. How does Ovid help get across her suffering in this passage through things like word choice, poetic techniques, and the vividness of his writing?

Paper 1 Practice 7.

From Aulus Gellius' *Noctes Atticae* **5.14 1-8**

Apion, qui "Plistonices" appellatus est, litteris homo multis praeditus rerumque
Graecarum plurima atque varia scientia fuit. eius libri non incelebres feruntur,
quibus omnium ferme, quae mirifica in Aegypto visuntur audiunturque, historia
comprehenditur. sed in his, quae vel audisse vel legisse sese dicit, fortassean vitio
5   studioque ostentationis sit loquacior — est enim sane quam in praedicandis
doctrinis sui venditator -; hoc autem, quod in libro Aegyptiacorum* quinto
scripsit, neque audisse neque legisse, sed ipsum sese in urbe Roma vidisse oculis
suis confirmat.

"in circo maximo," inquit, "venationis amplissimae pugna populo dabatur. eius
10   rei, Romae cum forte essem, spectator," inquit, "fui. multae ibi saevientes ferae,
magnitudines bestiarum excellentes, omniumque invisitata aut forma erat aut
ferocia. sed praeter alia omnia leonum," inquit, "immanitas admirationi fuit
praeterque omnis ceteros unus.

*Aegyptiacus, a, um: Egyptian

1. *Apion, qui…scientia fuit* (lines 1-2). List two details about who Apion was. No need to quote the Latin. [2]

2. *eius libri…historia comprehenditur* (lines 3-4). Describe Apion's works. Quote the Latin that supports your answer. [4]

3. *sed in…sui venditator* (lines 4-6). List three details about Apion and his works. No need to quote the Latin. [3]

4. *hoc autem…suis confirmat* (lines 6-8). Outline the thing that makes this account different from Apion's other works. No need to quote the Latin. [3]

5. *in circo…populo dabatur* (line 9). Identify the spectacle and why it was occuring. No need to quote the Latin. [2]

6. Translate *eius rei…ceteros unus* (lines 9-12). [16]

Extension: Analyze the selction for stylistic features that serve to show Apion's importance or reliability. Support your response by quoting precise evidence from the text.

Paper 1 Practice 8.

From Aulus Gellius' *Noctes Atticae* **5.14 9-14**

is unus leo corporis impetu et vastitudine terrificoque fremitu et sonoro, toris

comisque cervicum fluctuantibus animos oculosque omnium in sese converterat.

introductus erat inter compluris ceteros ad pugnam bestiarum datus servus viri

consularis; ei servo Androclus nomen fuit. hunc ille leo ubi vidit procul, repente,"

5 inquit, "quasi admirans stetit ac deinde sensim atque placide tamquam

noscitabundus ad hominem accedit. tum caudam more atque ritu adulantium

canum clementer et blande movet hominisque se corpori adiungit cruraque eius

et manus prope iam exanimati metu lingua leniter demulcet. homo Androclus

inter illa tam atrocis ferae blandimenta amissum animum recuperat, paulatim

10 oculos ad contuendum leonem refert. tum quasi mutua recognitione facta laetos,"

inquit, "et gratulabundos videres hominem et leonem."

1. *is unus…sese converterat* (lines 1-2). List three reasons that the lion attracted attention. No need to quote the Latin. [3]

2. *introductus erat…nomen fuit* (lines 3-4). Identify two things we learn about Androclus. Quote the Latin that supports your answer. [4]

3. *hunc ille…hominem accedit* (lines 4-6) List three of the lion's actions. NO need to quote the Latin. [3]

4. *tum caudam…blande movet* (lines 6-7). Outline the surprising way the lion is described. No need to quote the Latin. [2]

5. *hominisque se…leniter demulcet* (lines 7-8). Outline what the lion does. No need to quote the Latin. [2]

6. Translate *homo Androclus…et leonum* (lines 8-11). [16]

Extension: Examine the text for stylistic features meant to help convey the wondrous nature of the story that is unfolding.

Paper 1 Practice 9.

From Aulus Gellius' *Noctes Atticae* **5.14 15-20**

> ea re prorsus tam admirabili maximos populi clamores excitatos dicit
>
> accersitumque a Caesare Androclum quaesitamque causam, cur illi atrocissimus
>
> leo uni parsisset. ibi Androclus rem mirificam narrat atque admirandam. "cum
>
> provinciam," inquit, "Africam proconsulari imperio meus dominus obtineret, ego
>
> 5   ibi iniquis eius et cotidianis verberibus ad fugam sum coactus et, ut mihi a
>
> domino, terrae illius praeside, tutiores latebrae forent, in camporum et arenarum
>
> solitudines concessi ac, si defuisset cibus, consilium fuit mortem aliquo pacto
>
> quaerere. tum sole medio," inquit, "rabido et flagranti specum quandam nanctus
>
> remotam latebrosamque in eam me penetro et recondo. neque multo post ad
>
> 10 eandem specum venit hic leo debili uno et cruento pede gemitus edens et
>
> murmura dolorem cruciatumque vulneris commiserantia."atque illic primo
>
> quidem conspectu advenientis leonis territum sibi et pavefactum animum dixit.

1. *ea re…uni parsisset* (lines 1-3). Outline what happens to Androclus after the surprising event. No need to quote the Latin. [3]

2. *ibi Andoclus…dominus obtineret* (lines 3-4). Outline two things we learn about Androclus. No need to quote the Latin. [2]

3. *ego ibi…latebrae forent* (lines 4-6). List three reasons Androclus ran away from the *dominus*. No need to quote the Latin. [3]

4. *in camporum…pacto quaerere* (lines 6-8). Outline Androclus' intentions. Quote the Latin that supports your answer. [4]

5. *tum sole…et recondo* (lines 8-9). List two things Androclus did. No need to quote the Latin [2]

6. Translate *neque multo…animum dixit* (lines 9-12). [16]

Extension: How does Gellius portray Androclus and the lion as similar in this section.

Paper 1 Practice 10.

From Aulus Gellius' *Noctes Atticae* **5.14 21-25**

"sed postquam introgressus," inquit, "leo, uti re ipsa apparuit, in habitaculum

illud suum, videt me procul delitescentem, mitis et mansues accessit et sublatum

pedem ostendere mihi et porrigere quasi opis petendae gratia visus est. ibi,"

inquit, "ego stirpem ingentem vestigio pedis eius haerentem revelli

5   conceptamque saniem volnere intimo expressi accuratiusque sine magna iam

formidine siccavi penitus atque detersi cruorem. illa tunc mea opera et medella

levatus pede in manibus meis posito recubuit et quievit, atque ex eo die

triennium totum ego et leo in eadem specu eodemque et victu viximus. nam, quas

venabatur feras, membra opimiora ad specum mihi subgerebat, quae ego ignis

10   copiam non habens meridiano sole torrens edebam."

1. *sed postquam…mansues accessit* (lines 1-2). Explain why the lion did not seem to be looking for food. No need to quote the Latin. [2]

2. *et sublatum…visus est* (Lines 2-3). Outline the interaction between the lion and Androclus. No need to quote the Latin. [3]

3. *ibi, inquit…detersi cruorem* (lines 3-6). List three things Androclus did to help the lion. No need to quote the Latin. [3]

4. *illa tunc…et quievit* (lines 6-7). Explain why we know the lion was comforted. Quote the Latin that supports your response. [4]

5. *atque ex…victu viximus* (lines 7-8). Describe Androclus' living situation. No need to quote the Latin that supports your answer. [2]

6. Translate *atque ex…torrens edebam* (lines 7-10). [16]

Extension: Analyze Gellius' stylistic choices in terms of how they help convey the relationship between Androclus and the lion.

Paper 1 Practice 11.

From Aulus Gellius' *Noctes Atticae* 5.14 26-30

"sed ubi me," inquit, "vitae illius ferinae iam pertaesum est, leone in venatum

profecto reliqui specum et viam ferme tridui permensus a militibus visus

adprehensusque sum et ad dominum ex Africa Romam deductus. is me statim rei

capitalis damnandum dandumque ad bestias curavit. intellego autem," inquit,

5   "hunc quoque leonem me tunc separato captum gratiam mihi nunc beneficii et

medicinae referre."

haec Apion dixisse Androclum tradit eaque omnia scripta circumlataque tabula

populo declarata atque ideo cunctis petentibus dimissum Androclum et poena

solutum leonemque ei suffragiis populi donatum. "postea," inquit, "videbamus

10   Androclum et leonem loro tenui revinctum urbe tota circum tabernas ire, donari

aere Androclum, floribus spargi leonem, omnes ubique obvios dicere: 'hic est leo

hospes hominis, hic est homo medicus leonis.' "

1. *sed ubi…reliqui specum* (lines 1-2). Identify when and why Androclus left the cave. No need to quote the Latin. [2]

2. *et viam…Romam deductus* (lines 2-3). Outline the events that brought Androclus back to his *dominus*. No need to quote the Latin. [3]

3. *is me…bestias curavit* (lines 3-4). Outline the punishment. No need to quote the Latin. [2]

4. *intellego autem…medicinae referre* (lines 4-6). Outline Androclus' thoughts why he and the lion are in the situation they are now. Quote the Latin that supports your response. [4]

5. *haec Apion…populi donatum* (lines 7-9). Outline the outcome for Androclus sharing this story with the Roman people. No need to quote the Latin. [3]

6. Translate *postea, inquit…medicus leonis* (lines 9-12). [16]

Extension: What does Gellius' plain story telling style contribute to the story?

This glossary that follows was first generated with Collatinus 11. Collatinus 11 is a free and open tool developped by Yves Ouvrard and Philippe Verkerk and it can be downloaded from http://outils.biblissima.fr/en/collatinus/index.php. Note on using the glossary: This glossary includes the letter j, so every consonantal -I is a -j instead. I then edited entries to make them more useful for students.

While generally I would prefer a curated glossary that included all of the forms, I intentionally did not do that with this glossary as the dictionary skills needed for paper 1 will be better reinforced without a curated glossary.

ā, ăb, ābs, prép. + abl. : by (agent), from (departure, cause, remote origin/time); after (reference);

ā, interj. : ah! alas! ha! ah me!

ăbăvus, i, m. : Great-greatgrandfather, quartus pater

ābdĭtum, i, n. : hidden places, abstruse matters

ābdĭtus, a, um : hidden, concealed, secreted, secret

ābdo, ere, didi, ditum : to put away, remove; and abdere se, to go away, betake one's self

ābdūco, ere, duxi, ductum : to lead away, carry off; to detach, attract away, entice, seduce, charm; to withdraw;

ăbĕo, ire, ii, itum : to depart, go away; to go off, go forth; to pass away, die, disappear; to be changed;

ăbhŏrrēns, entis : +Abl. = which is at the opposite of

ăbhŏrrĕo, ere, horrui, - : to abhor, shrink back; to be averse to, shudder at; to differ from; to be inconsistent with;

ābĭto, ĕre, intr. : to go away, depart

ābstĭnĕo, ere, tinui, tentum : to withhold, keep away/clear; to abstain, fast; to refrain (from); to avoid; to keep hands of;

ābsŭm, esse, afui : to be away/absent/distant/missing; to be free/removed from; to be lacking; to be distinct;

ābsūmo, ere, sumpsi, sumptum : to spend, waste, squander, use up; to take up (time); to consume; to exhaust, wear out;

ăc, conj. coord. : and, and also, and besides;

āccēdo, ere, cessi, cessum : to come near, approach; to agree with; to be added to (w/ad or in + ACC); to constitute;

āccēndo, ere, di, sum : to set on fire, to kindle, light; to inflame

āccēnsus, i, m. : One who attends another of higher rank, an attendant, follower; hence, a state officer who attended one of the highest magistrates

āccĭdo, ere, cidi : to fall upon/down/to/at or near, to descend, alight; to happen, occur; to happen to (DAT);

āccĭngo, ere, cinxi, cinctum : to gird on or about, to surround; to equip, provide (with); to get ready, prepare (for);

āccĭo, ire, acciui, accitum : to call or summon, to fetch; to invite; (w/mortum) to commit suicide;

āccĭpĭo, ere, cepi, ceptum : to take, grasp, receive, accept, undertake; to admit, let in, hear, learn; to obey;

Āccĭus, i : a Roman poet who wrote tragedies.

āccōmmŏdo, are : to adapt, adjust to, fit, suit; to apply to, fasten on; to apply/devote oneself to;

āccūsātĭŏ, onis, f. : accusation, inditement; act/occasion of accusation; rebuke, reproof;

āccūsātŏr, oris, m. : accuser, prosecutor at trial; plaintiff; informer;

āccūso, are : to accuse, blame, find fault, impugn; to reprimand; to charge (w/crime/offense);

ācĕr, cris, cre : sharp, bitter, pointed, piercing, shrill; sagacious, keen; severe, vigorous;

Ăchāĭa, ae, f. : The province of Achaia, in the northern part of the Peloponnesus

Ăchīllēs, m. : Achilles, Greek hero; (other Greeks); (typifying great warrior);

ăcĭēs, ei, f. : sharpness, sharp edge, point; battle line/array; sight, glance; pupil of eye;

ācrĭtĕr, adv. : sharply, vigilantly, fiercely; severely, steadfastly; keenly, accurately;

āctŭm, i, n. : sharply, pointedly; acutely;

ăcŭo, ere, ui, ūtum : to make sharp, pointed, to sharpen, whet.

ăcūtus, a, um : sharp, sharpened, pointed/tapering; severe; glaring; acute, wise; high-pitched;

ăd, prép. + acc. : to, up to, towards; near, at; until, on, by; almost; according to; about w/NUM;

āddo, ere, didi, ditum : to add, insert, bring/attach to, to say in addition; to increase; to impart; to associate;

āddūco, ere, duxi, ductum : to lead up/to/away; to bring up/to; to persuade, induce; to lead, bring; to contract, tighten;

āddūctus, a, um : contracted, drawn together; frowning, grave; compressed, terse; strict, severe;

ădĕdo, ere, ēdi, ēsum : to begin to eat, to bite, to nibble at, to gnaw, verb finite

ădĕo, adv. : to such a degree/pass/point; precisely, exactly; thus far; indeed

ădĕo, ire, ii, itum : to go to or to approach a person or thing

ādfĕcto, are : to aim at, to desire, aspire, try, lay claim to; to try to control; to feign, pretend;

ādfĕctus, a, um : endowed with, possessed of; minded; affected; impaired, weakened; emotional;

ādfĕro, fers, ferre, adttuli att-, adlatum all- : to bring to, to carry, convey; to report, bring word, allege, announce; to produce, cause;

ādfĭcĭo, ere, feci, fectum : to affect, make impression; to move, influence; to cause (hurt/death), to afflict, weaken;

ādfĭrmo, are : to affirm/assert (dogmatically/positively); to confirm, ratify, restore; to emphasize;

ādflŭo, ere, fluxi, fluctum : to flow on/to/towards/by; to glide/drift quietly; to flock together, throng; to abound;

ādfŏr, aris, ari, atus sum : to speak to, to accost, address one, to pray to the gods, to bid farewell to the dead at the burial, to take the last adieu

ādgnōsco, ere, oui, itum : to recognize, realize, discern; to acknowledge, claim, admit to/responsibility;

ādgrĕdĭŏr, eris, i, gressus sum : approach, advance; attack, assail; undertake, seize (opportunity)

ădhāerĕo, ere, haesi, haesum : to adhere, stick, cling/cleave to; to hang on; to be attached/concerned/involved;

ădĭmo, ere, emi, emptum : to withdraw, to take away, to carry off; cto astrate; to deprive, steal, seize; to annul; to rescue;

ădītus, us, m. : approach, access; attack; entrance; chance, opportunity, means, way; beginning;

ādjūnctus, a, um : Joined, added to, connected with a thing

ādjūngo, ere, iunxi, iunctum : to add, attach, join to, to add to, to support; to apply to; to harness, yoke; to direct; to confer;

ādmīrābĭlĭs, e : admirable, wonderful; strange, astonishing, remarkable; paradoxical, contrary;

ādmīrātĭŏ, onis, f. : wonder, surprise, astonishment; admiration, veneration, regard; marvel;

ādmīrŏr, aris, ari, atus sum : to wonder at, to be astonished at, to regard with admiration, to admire

ādmŏnĕo, ere, monui, monitum : to admonish, remind, prompt; to suggest, advise, raise; to persuade, urge; to warn,

ādno, are : to swim to/towards, to approach by swimming; to sail to/towards; to brought by sea (goods);

ădŏrĭŏr, iris, iri, adortus sum : to rise up for the purpose of going to some one, something, of undertaking something great, difficult, hazardous

ādrĭgo, ere, rexi, rectum : to water (plants), to moisten the soil around;

ādrŏgāns, antis : arrogant

ādrŏgo, are : - to ask, question; to arrogate to one's self, to claim, make undue claim; to confer (upon); - to adopt (an adult) as one's son (esp. at his instance);

ādsērvo, are : to keep, guard, preserve; to watch, observe; to keep in custody; to save life of, to rescue;

ādsĭdŭē, adv. : continually, constantly, regularly;

ādsĭdŭus, a, um : constant, regular; unremitting, incessant; ordinary; landowning, first-class;

ādsĭmĭlo, ādsĭmŭlo, are : to make, like, to consider as similar, to compare

ādsŭm, esse, adfui : to be near, to be present, to be in attendance, to arrive, appear; to aid (w/DAT);

ādtōllo, ere : to raise/lift up/towards/to a higher position; to erect, build; to exalt; to extol, exalt;

ădŭlēscēns, entis, m. : "young, youthful; ""minor"" (in reference to the younger of two having same name);"

ădŭlēscēntĭa, ădŏlēscēntĭa, ae, f. : youth, young manhood; characteristic of being young, youthfulness; the young;

ădŭlēscēntŭlus, i, m. : very youthful, quite young;

ădŭltĕr, era, erum : - impure/adulterated; mixed/crossbred (plant); adulterous, unchaste; of adulterer; - forged/counterfeit; debased (coinage); [~ clavis => skeleton/false key];

ădŭltĕrĭŭm, i, n. : adultery; blending/mixing of different strains/ingredients; contamination;

ădūmbrātus, a, um : Delineated only in semblance, counterfeited, feigned, false

ădūmbro, are : to sketch out, to silhouette, outline, represent; to shade, screen, obscure; to feign;

ādvĕnĭo, ire, ueni, uentum : to come to, to arrive; to arrive at, to reach, be brought; to develop, set in, to arise;

ādvērsus, a, um : facing, opposite, against, towards; contrary to; face to face, in presence of;

ādvērsŭs, prép. + acc. adv. : turned toward, opposite, in front of

ādvērto, (aduorto) is, ere, uerti, uersum : to turn/face to/towards; to direct/draw one's attention to; to steer/pilot (ship);

ādvŏcātus, i, m. : counselor, advocate, professional pleader; witness, supporter, mediator;

ādvŏco, are : to call, summon, invite, convoke, call for; to call in as counsel; to invoke the Gods;

ădўtŭm, i, n. : innermost part of a temple, sanctuary, shrine; innermost recesses/chamber;

aedēs, f. : temple, shrine; tomb; apartment, room; house (pl.), abode, dwelling; household;

aedĭfĭcĭŭm, ii, n. : building; edifice, structure;

aedĭs, f. : aedes, aedis, a building for habitation., fire-place, hearth;

aemŭla, ae, f., cf. aemulus : envious, jealous, grudging, (things) comparable/equal (with/to);

aemŭlus, a, um : envious, jealous, grudging, (things) comparable/equal (with/to);

Āenēās, ae, m. : Aeneas

āenĕus, a, um : copper, of copper (alloy); bronze, made of bronze, bronze-colored; brazen;

āēnum, i, n. : a bronze vessel

āēnus, a, um : copper, of copper (alloy); bronze, made of bronze, bronze-colored; brazen;

āequē, adv. : equally, justly, fairly; in same/like manner/degree, just as; likewise, also;

āequo, are : to level, make even/straight; to equal; to compare; to reach as high or deep as;

āequŏr, oris, n. : level/smooth surface, plain; surface of the sea; sea, ocean;

āequum, i, n. : -I. level ground, a plain, an eminence - II. subst., equitable conduct toward others, fairness, equity, et, according to greater equily

āequus, āecus, a, um : level, even, equal, like; just, kind, impartial, fair; patient, contented;

āēr, aeris, m. : air (one of 4 elements); atmosphere, sky; cloud, mist, weather; breeze; odor;

āerātus, a, um : covered/decorated with/made of brass/bronze; with bronze fittings (ship);

āĕrĭus, a, um : of/produced in/existing in/flying in air, airborne/aerial; towering, airy;

ăĕs, aeris, n. : money, pay, fee, fare; copper/bronze/brass, base metal; (w/alienum) debt; gong;

Aesŏnĭus, a, um : Aesonian

āestus, us, m. : agitation, passion, seething; raging, boiling; heat/fire; sea tide/spray/swell;

āetās, atis, f. : lifetime, age, generation; period; stage, period of life, time, era;

āethēr, (aethera) eris, m : upper air; ether; heaven, sky; sky (as a god); space surrounding a deity;

āethĕra, cf. aether : upper air; ether; heaven, sky; sky (as a god); space surrounding a deity;

āethĕrĭus, a, um : ethereal, heavenly, divine, celestial; of the upper atmosphere; aloft; lofty;

āevŭm, i, n. : time, time of life, age, old age, generation; passage/lapse of time; all time;

āffīnĭs, e : relation (by marriage); neighbor; accomplice;

Āfrĭca, ae, f. : Africa (North); (Roman province); Libya (Carthagenian); the continent;

āfrĭcŭm, i, n. : African wind

Āfrĭcus, a, um : African

Ăgămēmnōn, onis, m. : Agamemnon

ăgĕr, agri, m. : field, ground; farm, land, estate, park; territory, country; terrain; soil;

āggĕr, eris, m. : rampart (or material for); causeway, pier; heap/pile/mound; dam/dike; mud wall;

ăgĭlĭs, e : agile, nimble, quick, swift; alert (mind), active; energetic, busy; rousing;

ăgĭtātŏr, oris, m. : driver, charioteer; one who drives (animals);

ăgĭto, are : to stir/drive/shake/move about; to revolve; to live; to control, ride; to consider, pursue;

āgmĕn, inis, n. : stream; herd, flock, troop, crowd; marching army, column, line; procession;

ăgo, ere, egi, actum : to drive/urge/conduct/act; to spend (time w/cum); to thank (w/gratias); deliver

ăgrēstĭs, e : countryman, peasant; rube, rustic, bumpkin;

ăgrēstĭs, m. : a countryman, rustic, farmer, peasant

Ājāx, ācis, m., npr. : the name of two Greeks renowned for their bravery.

ălăcrĭtās, atis, f. : eagerness, enthusiasm, ardor, alacrity; cheerfulness, liveliness;

ālbum, i, n. : White color, white

ālbus, a, um : white, pale, fair, hoary, gray; bright, clear; favorable, auspicious,

ālĕs, itis, f. : winged, having wings; swift/quick; [ales deus => Mercury; ales puer => Cupid];

ălĭā, adv. : in another way, in a different manner

ălĭās, adv. : at/in another time/place; previously, subsequently; elsewhere; otherwise;

ălĭēno, are : to avoid (with antipathy); to cause to feel disgust; to be insane/mad; to be different;

ălĭēnum, i, n. : The property of a stranger, a foreign, province

ălĭēnus, a, um : foreign; unconnected; another's; contrary; unworthy; averse, hostile; mad;

ălĭēnus, i, m. : One not belonging to one's house, family, country

ălĭō, adv. : to another place, to another, elsewhere, to some other place, to another subject, had a very different purpose, in one way ... in another; hither ... thither, each in a different way, one in one way ... another in another, negative, quam, nisi, for nothing else

ălĭquā, adv. : Somewhere, somewhither

ălĭquăm, adv. : largely, to a large extent, a lot of; [~ multi/multum => fair number/amount];

ălĭquāmdĭū, ălĭquāndĭū, adv. : for some time, for a considerable time/distance (travel), for a while;

ălĭquāndŏ, adv. : sometime (or other), at any time, ever; finally; before too late; at length;

ălĭquī, quă, quŏd, adj. : in some way/extent;

ălĭquis, a, id, pron. : Somebody or other

ălĭquō, adv. : to some place/person (or other); in some/any direction/quarter; some/anywhere;

ălĭquŏt, dét. : some, several; a few; not many; a number (of); more than one;

ălĭtĕr, adv. : otherwise, differently; in any other way [aliter ac => otherwise than];

ālĭum, ii, n. : garlic

ălĭus, a, ud, pron. : the_one ... the_other (alius ... alius);

ālmus, a, um : nourishing, kind, propitious; of a nurse/breast, providing nurture, fostering;

ălo, ere, ui, altum (alitum) : to feed, nourish, rear, nurse, suckle; to cherish; to support, maintain, develop;

ālsus, a, um : chilly, cold, cool.

āltăr, cf. altare : altar (usu. pl.), fitting for burnt offerings; burnt offering; high altar;

āltāre, n. : altar (usu. pl.), fitting for burnt offerings; burnt offering; high altar;

āltē, adv. : high, on high, from above, loftily; deep, deeply; far, remotely; profoundly;

āltĕr, era, erum : - one (of two); second/another; former/latter; [unus et ~=> one or two/other]; - second/further/next/other/latter/some person/thing (PRONominal ADJ); either;

āltŭm, i, n. : deeply, deep; high, on high, from above;

āltus, a, um : high; deep/profound; shrill; lofty/noble; deep rooted; far-fetched; grown

ālvus, i, f. : belly/paunch/stomach; womb; bowel; bowel movement; hull (ship); beehive;

ămāns, antis : loving/fond/affectionate; beloved/dear to; friendly/kind; having love/

ămārus, a, um : bitter, brackish, pungent; harsh, shrill; sad, calamitous; ill-natured,

ămātŏr, oris, m. : lover

ămātōrĭus, a, um : of love or lovers, amatory; inducing love (potions); amorous, procuring love;

āmbāgēs, f. : circuit; roundabout way; long story, details; riddle; ambiguity; lie; mystery;

āmbĭgŭē, adv. : ambiguously, equivocally; with uncertain meaning/outcome; unreliably;

āmbĭo, ire, ii, itum : to go round, visit in rotation, inspect; to solicit, canvass; to circle, embrace;

āmbĭtĭōsē, adv. : ingratiatingly, earnestly; ambitiously, presumptuously; ostentatiously;

āmbĭtĭōsus, a, um : ambitious, eager to please/for advancement/favor; showy; winding, twisting;

āmbĭtus, us, m. : circuit, edge, extent; orbit, cycle; canvass, bribery; circumlocution; show;

āmbo, ambae, o, pl. : both

ămēns, entis : insane, demented, out of one's mind; very excited, frantic, distracted;

ămīca, ae, f. : female friend; girl friend, sweetheart; patron; mistress, concubine; courtesan;

ămīcĭo, ire, icui et ixi, ictum : clothe, cover, dress; wrap about; surround; veil; clothe with words;

ămīcĭtĭa, ae, f. : friendship, bond between friends; alliance, association; friendly relations;

ămīcus, a, um : friendly, dear, fond of; supporting (political), loyal, devoted; loving;

ămīcus, i, m. : friend

āmītto, ere, misi, missum : to lose; to lose by death; to send away, to dismiss; to part with; to let go/slip/fall, to drop;

āmnĭs, m. : river (real/personified), stream; current; (running) water; the river Ocean;

ămo, are : to love, like; to fall in love with; to be fond of; to have a tendency to;

ămŏr, oris, m. : love; affection; the beloved; Cupid; affair; sexual/illicit/homosexual passion;

ămŏvĕo, ere, moui, motum : to move/take/put away, to remove, steal; to banish, cause to go away; to withdraw, retire;

āmplēctŏr, eris, i, amplexus sum : to wind or twine round a person or thing, to surround, encompass, encircle

āmplēxus, us, m. : clasp, embrace, surrounding; sexual embrace; coil (snake); circumference;

āmplus, a, um : great, large, spacious, wide, ample; distinguished, important, honorable;

ăn, conj. : - can it be that (introduces question expecting negative answer/further question); - whether; (utrum ... an = whether ... or); or; either;

Ānchīsēs, ae, m., npr. : Son of Capys, father of Aeneas, who bore him forth from burning Troy upon his shoulders

āncīlla, ae, f. : slave girl; maid servant; handmaid; (opprobrious of man); nun (selfdescribed);

Āndrŏgĕus, i : son of the Cretan king Minos, whom the Athenians and Megarians slew; on account of which the enraged father made war upon them

Āndrŏmăchē, f., npr. : a daughter of king Eeuml;tion, and wife of Hector.

ānguĭs, m. : snake, serpent; dragon; (constellations) Draco, Serpens, Hydra;

ănĭma, ae, f. : soul, spirit, vital principle; life; breathing; wind, breeze; air (element);

ănĭmo, are : to animate, give/bring life; to revive, refresh; to rouse, animate; to inspire; to blow;

ănĭmōsus, a, um : courageous, bold, strong, ardent, energetic, noble; stormy (wind/sea), furious;

ănĭmus, i, m. : mind; intellect; soul; feelings; heart; spirit, courage, character, pride; air;

ānnus, i, m. : year (astronomical/civil); age, time of life; year's produce; circuit, course;

āntĕ, prép. +acc. : in front/presence of, in view; before (space/time/degree); over against,

āntĕquăm, conj. sub. : before, sooner than; until;

āntēs, ium, m. : rows, ranks

āntīqui, orum, m. : the ancients, esp. the ancient writers, old

āntīquum, i, n. : antiquity, the things of olden times

āntīquus, a, um : old/ancient/aged; time-honored; simple/classic; venerable; archaic/outdated;

ānxĭus, a, um : anxious, uneasy, disturbed; concerned; careful; prepared with care;

Āŏnĭus, a, um : of or belonging to Aonia, i.e. Bœotia (purely poet.), Aonian, Bœotian

ăpĕrĭo, ire, ui, apertum : to uncover, open, disclose; to explain, recount; to reveal; to found; to excavate; to spread out;

ăpēx, icis, f. : point, top, summit; cap, crown

ăpĭs, f. : bee; swarm regarded as a portent; Apis, sacred bull worshiped in Egypt;

ăpīscŏr, eris, i, aptus sum : to reach after, in order to take, seize, get possession of

Ăpŏllō, inis, m. : Apollo; (Roman god of prophecy, music, poetry, archery, medicine);

Ăpŏllōnĭa, ae, f. : The name of several celebrated towns.

Ăpŏllōnis, ĭdis, f. : Apollonis

Ăpŏllōnĭus, ii, m. : a distinguished rhetorician in Rhodes

āppārĕo, ere, ui, itum : it is apparent/ evident/ clear/ certain/ visible/ noticeable/ found; it appears;

ăppăro, are : to prepare, fit out, to make ready, to equip, provide; to attempt; to organize (project);

ăppēllo, are : to drive to or toward, to go to in order to accost, to make a request, admonish

Ăppĭus, a, um : of Appius; Appius, i, m., Appius

ăppōno, ere, posui, positum : to place near, to set before/on table, to serve up; to put/apply/add to; to appoint/assign;

ăppŏsĭtus, a, um : placed, situated at, near to, contiguous to, bordering upon;, dat.

ăpprŏbo, are : to approve, commend, endorse; to prove; to confirm; to justify; to allow; to make good;

āptē, adv. : closely, fitly, suitably, rightly, fitly, suitably, properly, duly, rightly, opportunely, becomingly

ăpto, are : to adapt, fit, apply, adjust, accommodate; to put on, to fasten; to prepare, furnish;

ăptus, a, um : suitable, adapted; ready; apt, proper; tied, attached to; dependent on (w/ex);

ăpŭd, ăpŭt, prép. + acc. : or aput, at, by, near, among; at the house of; before, in the presence/writings/view of;

ăqua, ae, f. : water; sea, lake; river, stream; rain, rainfall (pl.), rainwater; spa; urine;

āra, ae, f. : altar, structure for sacrifice, pyre; sanctuary; home; refuge, shelter;

ărātrŭm, i, n. : plow;

Ărātus, i, m. : A Greek poet of Soli, in Cilicia, who fl., author of an astronomical poem, entitled

ărbĭtrĭŭm, i, n. : arbitration; choice, judgment, decision; sentence; will, mastery, authority;

ărbĭtrŏr, aris, ari, atus sum : to make a decision, give judgment or sentence; to believe

ārbŏr, oris, f. : tree; tree trunk; mast; oar; ship; gallows; spearshaft; beam; squid?;

ărcĕo, ere, ui : to ward/keep off/away; to keep close, confine; to prevent, hinder; to protect; to separate;

ărcēsso, ere, iui, itum : to send for, summon, indict; to fetch, import; to invite; to invoke; to bring on oneself;

ărcus, us, m. : bow, arc, coil, arch; rainbow; anything arched or curved;

ārdēns, entis : glowing, fiery, hot, ablaze, sparkling, gleaming, fiery, Burning, ardent, impassioned

ārdĕo, ere, arsi, arsurus : to be on fire; to burn, blaze; to flash; to glow, sparkle; to rage; to be in a turmoil/love;

ārdŭus, a, um : steep, high, lofty, towering, tall; erect, rearing; uphill; arduous, difficult;

ārĕo, ēre, arui, intr. : to be dry

Ārgēus, a, um : Argive, Grecian, Argiva

Ārgīvus, a, um : of Argos, Argive

ārgŭo, ere, ui, utum : to prove, argue, allege; to disclose; to accuse, complain of, charge, blame, convict;

Ărīcĭa, ae, f. : an ancient town of Latium, in the neighborhood of Alba Longa, upon the Appian Way, La Riccia;

Ărīcīni, orum, m. : the inhabitanls of Aricia

Ărīcīnus, a, um : pertaining to Aricia, Arician

ărĭēs, etis, m. : ram (sheep); battering ram; the Ram (zodiac); large unidentified marine animal;

ārma, orum, n. pl. : Implements of war, arms, both of defence and offence

ārmāti, orum, m. : armed men, soldiers = miles

ārmātus, a, um : armed, equipped; defensively armed, armor clad; fortified; of the use of arms;

ārmātŭs, us, m. : armor, armed soldiers

ārmēntŭm, i, n. : herd (of cattle); a head of cattle, individual bull/horse; cattle/horses (pl.);

ārmĭgĕr, era, erum : bearing arms, armed; warlike, martial, of war/fighting; producing armed men;

ārmĭgĕr, eri, m. : one who bears arms, An armor-bearer, shield-bearer

ārmĭpŏtēns, pŏtentis : powerful in arms, valiant, warlike;

ārmo, are : to equip, fit with armor; to arm; to strengthen; to rouse, stir; to incite war; to rig (ship);

ārmus, i, m. : inct., the shoulder where it is fitted to the shoulder-blade, the fore quarter, the shoulder of an animal, umerus

ăro, are : to plow, till, cultivate; to produce by plowing, grow; to furrow, wrinkle;

Ārrūns, untis, m. : Arruns

ārs, artis, f. : skill/craft/art; trick, wile; science, knowledge; method, way; character (pl.);

ārtĭfĭcĭŭm, ii, n. : art/craft/trade; skill/talent/craftsmanship; art work; method/trick;

ārtus, a, um : close, firm, tight; thrifty; dense, narrow; strict; scarce, critical; brief;

ārtus, us, m. : the muscular strength in the joints; hence, in gen., strength, power; the limbs

ārvŭm, i, n. : female external genitalia (rude);

ārx, arcis, f. : citadel, stronghold, city; height, hilltop; Capitoline hill; defense, refuge;

ās, assis, m. : penny, copper coin; a pound; one, whole, unit; circular flap/valve; round

Āscănĭus, i, m. : son of Æneas and Creüsa, king of Lavinium, and founder of Alba Longa

āscēndo, ere, ascendi, ascensum : to climb; to go/climb up; to mount, scale; to mount up, embark; to rise, ascend, move upward;

Āscrāeus, a, um : Ascrœan; subst. m. Hesiod

Āsĭa, ae, f. : Asia (Roman province formed from Pergamene); Asia Minor; the East;

āspĕr, era, erum : rough/uneven, coarse/harsh; sharp/pointed; rude; savage; pungent; keen; bitter;

Āspĕr, pri, m. : a Latin grammarian

āspĕro, are : to roughen; to sharpen, point, tip; to enrage, make fierce/violent; to grate on; to aggravate;

āspĭcĭo, ere, spexi, spectum : to look/gaze on/at, see, observe, behold, regard; to face; to consider, contemplate;

āspōrto, are : to bear, carry, take off, away

āst, conj. : but, on the other hand/contrary; but yet; at least; in that event; if further;

āstrŭm, i, n. : star, heavenly body, planet/sun/moon; the stars, constellation; sky, heaven;

ăsȳlŭm, i, n. : place of refuge, asylum, sanctuary; place for relaxation/recuperation, retreat;

ăt, conj. coord. : but, but on the other hand; on the contrary; while, whereas; but yet; at least;

ătăvus, i, m. : the father of a great-great-grandfather, great-great-grandmother

Ătāx, ăcis, m. : a small river in, Aude

ātĕr, tra, trum : - black, dark; dark-colored (hair/skin); gloomy/murky; unlucky; sordid/squalid; - deadly, terrible, grisly (esp. connected with underworld); poisonous;

ātquĕ, conj. coord. : and, as well/soon as; together with; and moreover/even; and too/also/now; yet;

Ătratīnus, i, m. : Atratinus (surnom romain)

Ătrida, ae, m. : male descendant of Atreus; Atrides, absol. usu. for Agamemnon; in plur. Atridae, the Atrides, i. e. Agamemnon and Menelaus

Ătrīdēs, ae, m. : a male descendant of Atreus; Atrides, absol., Agamemnon; the Atrides, Agamemnon and Menelaus

ātrĭŭm, i, n. : atrium, reception hall in a Roman house; auction room; palace (pl.), house;

āttĕnŭo, are : to make thin, weak; to thin, attenuate; to weaken, enfeeble; to lessen, diminish.

āttīcē, f. : espèce d'ocre

Ăttīcus, a, um : of, pertaining to Attica, Athens, Attic, Athenian, sincere, firm, the Athenians

Ăttīcus, i, m. : Athénian

āttŏnĭtus, a, um : astonished, fascinated; lightning/thunder-struck, stupefied, dazed; inspired;

āttŏno, are, ŭi, ĭtum : to thunder at;to stun, stupefy

āttŭlo, ĕre : to bring to

āuctĭŏ, onis, f. : auction; public sale; property put up for sale at auction/the catalog/proceeds;

āucto, are : to increase, enlarge much

āuctŏr, oris, m. : seller, vendor; originator; historian; authority; proposer, supporter; founder;

āuctus, a, um : abundant, ample, richer in

āudācĭa, ae, f. : boldness, daring, courage, confidence; recklessness, effrontery, audacity;

āudācĭtĕr, adv. : boldly, audaciously, confidently, proudly, fearlessly; impudently, rashly;

āudāx, acis : bold, daring; courageous; reckless, rash; audacious, presumptuous; desperate;

āudĕo, ere, ausus sum : to intend, be prepared; to dare/have courage (to go/do), act boldly, venture, risk;

āudĭo, ire, iui, itum : to hear, listen, accept, agree with; to obey; to harken, pay attention; to be able to hear;

āudītus, us, m. : hearing; listening; act/sense of hearing; hearsay;

āugĕo, ere, auxi, auctum : to increase, enlarge, augment; to spread; to honor, promote, raise; to exalt; to make a lot

āugūstus, a, um : sacred, venerable; majestic, august, solemn; dignified; worthy of honor (Ecc);

Āugūstus, i, m. : August (month) (mensis understood); abb. Aug.; renamed from Sextilis in 8 BC;

āura, ae, f. : breeze, breath (of air), wind; gleam; odor, stench; vapor; air (pl.), heaven;

āurātus, a, um : gilded, overlaid/adorned with gold, golden, gold mounted/embroidered/bearing;

āurĕus, a, um : of gold, golden; gilded; gold bearing; gleaming like gold; beautiful, splendid;

āurĕus, i, m. : the standard gold coin of Rome, a gold piece, s., d., shekels

āurĭfĕr, fera, ferum : gold-bearing, producing/yielding gold (mine/country); bearing golden fruit;

āurĭs, f. : "ear; hearing; a discriminating sense of hearing, ""ear"" (for); pin on plow;"

āuro, āre : to overlay with gold, to gild, finite verb

āurŭm, i, n. : gold (metal/color), gold money, riches;

āuspĭcĭŭm, ii, n. : divination (by birds); omen; beginning; auspices (pl.); right of doing

āusŭs, us, m. : a hazard, attempt, having dared

āut, conj. coord. : or, or rather/else; either...or (aut...aut) (emphasizing one);

āutĕm, conj. coord. : but (postpositive), on the other hand/contrary; while, however; moreover, also;

Āutŏmĕdōn, ontis, m. : A son of Diores and charioteer of Achilles

āuxĭlĭŭm, ii, n. : help, assistance; remedy/antidote; supporting resource/force; auxiliaries

ăvārus, a, um : avare

ăvārus, i, m. : avaricious, greedy; stingy, miserly, mean; covetous, hungry for;

ăvē, interj. : hail!, formal expression of greetings;

ăvērsus, a, um : turned/facing away, w/back turned; behind, in rear; distant; averse; hostile;

ăvĭa, ae, f. : - grandmother; rooted prejudice, old wives tale; - unidentified plant; groundsel ; (also called senecio, erigeron);

ăvĭs, f. : bird; sign, omen, portent;

ăvĭtus, a, um : ancestral, of one's ancestors, family; of/belonging to a grandfather;

āvĭŭm, i, n. : pathless region (pl.), wild waste, wilderness, desert; lonely/solitary places;

āvĭus, a, um : out of the way, unfrequented, remote; pathless, trackless, untrodden; straying;

ăvus, i, m. : grandfather; forefather, ancestor;

āxĭs, m. : - axle, axis, pole; chariot; the sky, heaven; north pole; region, clime; - Indian quadruped; (spotted deer?); - plank, board;

Bācchus, i, m. : Bacchus, god of wine/vine; the vine, wine;

Bājāe, arum, f. pl. : the region of Baiœ, the Baian territory

bālbus, a, um : stammering, stuttering, lisping, suffering from a speech defect; fumbling;

Bālbus, i, m. : Balbus

bārba, ae, f. : beard/ whiskers; large unkempt beard (pl.); [Jovis ~ => shrub Anthyllis barba];

bārbărĭcus, a, um : outlandish; foreign, strange; barbarous, savage; of uncivilized world/people;

bārbātus, a, um : bearded, having a beard; (like the men of antiquity); (as sign of) adult;

bārbŭla, ae, f. : A little beard

Bāttĭădēs, ae, m. : an inhabitant of Cyrene, the poet Callimachus, a native of Cyrene

bēllo, are : to fight, wage war, struggle; to take part in war/battle/fight (also animals/games);

bēllŭm, i, n. : war, warfare; battle, combat, fight; (at/in) (the) war(s); military force,

bēllus, a, um : pretty, handsome, charming, pleasant, agreeable, polite; nice, fine, excellent;

bĕnĕ, adv. : well, very, quite, rightly, agreeably, cheaply, in good style; better; best;

bĕnĕfĭcĭŭm, ii, n. : kindness, favor, benefit, service, help; privilege, right;

bĕnĕfĭcus, a, um : comp., sup., generous, liberal, beneficent, obliging, favorable.

bĕnīgnē, adv. : kindly, benevolently, obligingly; courteously, cheerfully; freely, generously;

bĕnīgnus, a, um : kind, favorable, obliging; kindly, mild, affable; liberal, bounteous;

bēs, bessis, m. : two thirds of any whole; [ex bese => in ratio of 2/3; or 8, 2/3 of 12];

bēstĭa, ae, f. : beast, animal, creature; wild beast/animal, beast of prey in arena;

bĭpēnnĭs, e : -I. having two wings, two-winged -II. having two edges, two-edged

bĭs, adv. : twice, at two times, on two occasions, in two ways

blāndīmēntŭm, i, n. : blandishment, coaxing/wheedling behavior, cajolery; favors; charm, delight;

blāndītĭa, ae, f. : flattery, caress, compliment; charm (pl.), flatteries, enticement, courtship;

blāndus, a, um : flattering, coaxing; charming, pleasant; smooth, gentle; alluring, attractive;

bŏnus, a, um : good, honest, brave, noble, kind, pleasant, right, useful; valid; healthy;

bōs, bouis, m. : ox; bull; cow; ox-ray; cattle (pl.); (ox-like animals); [luca ~ => elephant];

brācchĭŭm, ii, n. : arm; lower arm, forearm; claw; branch, shoot; earthwork connecting forts;

brāchĭŭm, ii, n. : arm; lower arm, forearm; claw; branch, shoot; earthwork connecting forts;

brĕvī, adv. : in a short time; shortly, briefly; in a few words; [in brevi => in brief];

brĕvĭs, e : short catalog, summary document;

Brīsēis, ĭdis, f. : Hippodamia, daughter of Brises, and slave of Achilles, from whom she was taken by Agamemnon

brūma, ae, f. : winter, winter cold/weather; winter solstice; shortest day; sun position then;

bŭbŏ, onis, m : horned or eagle owl (esp. as bird of ill omen);

cădo, ere, cecidi, casum : to fall, sink, drop, plummet, topple; to be slain, die; to end, cease, abate; to decay;

caecus, a, um : blind; unseeing; dark, gloomy, hidden, secret; aimless, confused, random; rash;

Caecus, i, m. : agnomen of Appius Claudius Crassus, as being blind

caedēs, f. : murder/slaughter/massacre; assassination; feuding; slain/victims; blood/gore;

caedo, ere, cecidi, caesum : to chop, hew, cut out/down/to pieces; to strike, smite, murder; to slaughter; to sodomize;

Caelĭus, i, m. : an orator, contemporary with Crassus

caelo, are : to carve, make raised work/relief; to engrave, emboss; to chase, finish; to embroider;

caelŭm, cōelum, i, n. : - chisel; engraving tool; burin; - heaven, sky, heavens; space; air, climate, weather; universe, world; Jehovah;

caerŭla, orum, n. : the sea, the blue surface of the sea, Neptune

caerŭlus, a, um : blue, cerulean; deep/sky/greenish-blue, azure; of river/sea deities; of sky/

caesĭus, a, um : gray, gray-blue, steel-colored; having gray/gray-blue/steel-colored eyes;

cālcĭtro, are, intr. : to strike with the heels, to kick

cāllĭdus, a, um : crafty, sly, cunning; wise, expert, skillful, clever, experienced, ingenious;

Cāllīmăchus, i, m. : A distinguished Greek poet and grammarian of Cyrene, who lived in Alexandria in the reign of Ptolemy Philadelphus

Cālpūrnĭus, a, um : the name of the very distinguished Calpurnian

Cālpūrnĭus, i, m. : Calpurnius

cāmpēstĕr, tris, tre : level, even, flat, of level field; on open plain/field; plain-dwelling; Campus Martius

cāmpēstrĭs, tris, tre. : of or pertaining to a level field, even, flat, level, champaign

cāmpus, i, m. : plain; level field/surface; open space for battle/games; sea; scope; campus;

cāmus, i, m. : A muzzle

cāndŏr, oris, m. : whiteness; snow; radiance, bright light; heat, glow; beauty; purity; kindness;

cānĕo, ere, ui, - : to be/become covered in white; to be hoary, be white/gray (with age);

cāno, ere, cecini, cantum : to sing, celebrate, chant; to crow; to recite; to play (music)/sound (horn); to foretell;

cāntus, us, m. : song, chant; singing; cry (bird); blast (trumpet); poem, poetry; incantation;

cānus, a, um : white, gray; aged, old, wise; hoary; foamy, white-capped; white w/snow/frost;

cāpīllus, i, m. : hair; hair of head; single hair; hair/fur/wool of animals; hair-like fiber;

cāpĭo, ere, cepi, captum : taking/seizing; [usus ~ => getting ownership by continued possession];

Cāpĭtōlĭŭm, ii, n. : Capitol; Capitoline Hill in Rome;

cāptīva, ae, f. : a female captive, woman prisoner

cāptīvo, āre : to take captive

cāptīvus, a, um : caught, taken captive; captured (in war), imprisoned; conquered; of captives;

cāptīvus, i, m. : a captive in war, a captive, prisoner

cāpto, are : to try/long/aim for, desire; to entice; to hunt legacy; to try to catch/grasp/seize/reach;

cāptŭs, us, m. : A taking, seizing; that which is taken, grasped

cāpŭlus, i, m : sepulcher, tomb, scacophagus; halter for catching/fastening cattle, lasso;

cāpŭt, itis, n. : heading; chapter, principal division; [~ super pedibus => head over heels];

cārdō, inis, m. : hinge; pole, axis; chief point/circumstance; crisis; tenon/mortise; area;

cārĕo, ere, ui, iturus : to be without/absent from/devoid of/free from; to miss; to abstain from, lack, lose;

cārīna, ae, f. : keel, bottom of ship, hull; boat, ship, vessel; voyage; half walnut shell;

cārĭōsus, a, um : decayed, rotten.

cārītās, atis, f. : charity; love, affection, esteem, favor; dearness; high price;

cārmĕn, minis, n. : song/music; poem/play; charm; prayer, incantation, ritual/magic formula;

cārnĭfĕx, icis, m. : tormenting, torturing; murderous, killing; deadly;

cārpo, ere, carpsi, carptum : - to seize/pick/pluck/gather/browse/tear off; to graze/crop; to tease/pull out/card (wool); - to separate/divide, tear down; to carve; to despoil/fleece; to pursue/harry; to consume/ erode;

Cāssāndra, ae, f. : Cassandra (A Priam's daughter)

Cāstālĭa, ae, f. : a fountain on Parnassus, sacred to Apollo and the Muses

Cāstālĭus, a, um : of Castaliea, fountain on Parnassus, sacred to Apollo and the Muses

cāstīmōnĭa, ae, f. : chastity, abstinence, ceremonial purity/purification; morality, moral purity;

cāstra, orum, n. pl. : camp, military camp/field; army; fort, fortress; war service; day's march;

cāstrēnsĭs, e : of/connected with camp or active military service; characteristic of soldiers;

cāstro, āvi, ātum : To deprive of generative power, to emasculate, castrate, geld

cāstrum, i, n. : any fortified place; a castle, fort, fortress

cāsus, cāssus, us, m. : - fall, overthrow; chance/fortune; accident, emergency, calamity, plight; fate; - grammatical case; termination/ending (of words);

cātĕrva, ae, f. : crowd/cluster; troop, company, band of men/followers/actors; flock/herd/swarm;

cāusa, ae, f. : for sake/purpose of (preceded by GEN.), on account/behalf of, with a view to;

cāutē, adv. : cautiously; with security/precautions, without risk; circumspectly, carefully;

cāutēs, f. : rough pointed/detached rock, loose stone; rocks (pl.), cliff, crag; reef;

cāutus, a, um : cautious

cāvĕo, ere, caui, cautum : to beware, avoid, take precautions/defensive action; to give/get surety; to stipulate;

cāvo, are : to hollow out, make concave/hollow; to excavate; to cut/pierce through; to carve in relief;

cāvus, a, um : - hollow, excavated, hollowed out; concave; (of waning moon); enveloping; - sunken; deep, having deep channel; tubular; having cavity inside

cēdo, ere, cessi, cessum : to be in motion, move, walk, go along.

cĕlĕbro, are : to celebrate/perform; to frequent; to honor/glorify; to publicize/advertise; to discuss/bandy;

cēlsus, a, um : high, lofty, tall; haughty; arrogant/proud; prominent, elevated; erect; noble;

cēnsōrĭus, a, um : of/belonging to/dealt with by/having been a censor, censorial; austere, moral;

cēntŭm, num. : one hundred;

cēra, ae, f. : wax, beeswax; honeycomb; wax-covered writing tablet, letter; wax image/seal;

Cĕrēs, eris, f. : Ceres (goddess of grain/fruits); wheat; bread; food;

cērĕus, a, um : waxed, waxen, of/like wax; wax colored/pale yellow; pliant/soft; easily moved;

cērno, ere, creui, cretum : to sift, separate, distinguish, discern, resolve, determine; to see; to examine; to decide;

cēro, are : to cover, overlay, smear with wax, to wax, part. pass.

cērtāměn, inis, n. : contest, competition; battle, combat, struggle; rivalry; (matter in) dispute;

cērtē, adv. : surely, certainly, without doubt, really; at least/any rate, in all events;

cērtō, adv. : certainly, definitely, really, for certain/a fact, truly; surely, firmly

cērto, are : to decide something by a contest, to fight, struggle, contend, combat

cērtus, a, um : fixed, settled, firm; certain; trusty/reliable; sure; resolved, determined;

cērvīx, icis, f. : neck (sg/pl.), nape; severed neck/head; cervix, neck (bladder/uterus/jar/land);

cēsso, are : to be remiss/inactive; to hold back, leave off, delay, cease from; to rest; to be free of;

cētěrā, adv. : as for the rest, otherwise

cētěri, ae, a pl. : the_others (pl.). the_remaining/rest, all the_rest

cētěrum, i, n. : the rest

cētěrus, a, um : the other, that which exists besides, can be added to what is already named of a like kind with it; the other part, the remainder, the rest, for the rest

cēu, conj. coord. : as, in the same way/just as; for example, like; (just) as if; as (if) it were;

cībus, i, m. : food; fare, rations; nutriment, sustenance, fuel; eating, a meal; bait;

Cĭcěrō, onis, m. : Cicero; (gens Tullia cognomen; M. Tullius Cicero, Roman orator and statesman);

cĭcūta, ae, f. : the hemlock given to criminals as poison;

cĭeo, ere, ciui, citum : - to move, set in motion; to excite/rouse/stir up; to urge on; to summon/muster/call up;

cīngo, ere, cinxi, cinctum : to surround /encircle /ring; to enclose; to beleaguer; to accompany; to gird, equip; ring

cĭnĭs, eris, m. : ashes; embers, spent love/hate; ruin, destruction; the grave/dead, cremation;

cĭnnăbăr, ăris, n. : red pigment, red color

cĭo, īre : to put in motion

cĭrcŭlus, cīrclus, i, m. : circle; orbit, zone; ring, hoop; belt, collar; company; cycle; circumference;

cīrcŭm, adv. : around, about, among, near (space/time), in neighborhood of; in circle around;

cīrcŭmăro, are : to plow around, to surround with a furrow;

cīrcŭmdo, are, dedi, datum : to surround; to envelop, post/put/place/build around; to enclose; to beset; to pass around;

cīrcŭmfěro, fers, ferre, tuli, latum : to carry/hand/pass/spread/move/take/cast around (in circle); to publicize; to divulge;

cīrcūmfūndo, ere, fudi, fusum : to pour/drape/crowd around; to cause (water) to go round/part; to surround; to distribute;

cīrcūmspēcto, are : to look about with attention, precaution, desire, to cast a look around, to search around;, to look about one's self, attentively, anxiously, after something, to look all around upon something

cīrcus, i, m. : race course; circus in Rome, celebration of games; circle; orbit;

cĭtātus, a, um : quick, rapid, speedy, swift, in haste, at full speed, at full gallop

cĭtō, are : to urge on, encourage; to promote, excite; to summon; to set in motion; to move (bowels)

cīvĭs, m. : fellow citizen; countryman/woman; citizen, free person; a Roman citizen;

cīvĭtās, atis, f. : community/city/town/state; citizens; citizen rights/citizenship;

clādēs, f. : - defeat, reverse; casualties, slaughter/carnage/devastation; ruins; - disaster, ruin, calamity; plague; pest, bane, scourge (cause of disaster);

clăm, adv. : without knowledge of, unknown to; concealed/secret from; (rarely w/ABL);

clāmo, are : to proclaim, declare; to cry/shout out; to shout/call name of; to accompany with shouts;

clāmŏr, oris, m. : - shout, outcry/protest; loud shouting (approval/joy), applause; clamor/noise/ - war-cry, battle-cry; roar (thunder/surf); cry of fear/pain/mourning; wailing;

clārus, a, um : clear, bright, gleaming; loud, distinct; evident, plain; illustrious, famous;

Clāudĭa, Clōdĭa, ae, f. : Claudia

Clāudĭus, ii, m. : Claudius; Roman gens; (Ti. C. Nero Germanicus, Emperor, 41-54 AD); the_Lame;

clāudus, a, um : limping, lame; defective/crippled/imperfect; uneven/halting/wavering/uncertain;

clāustrŭm, clōstrum, orum, n. : monastery, cloister (often pl.);

clĭpĕum, i, n. : The round brazen shield of Roman soldiers

clĭpĕus, clỹpĕus, i, m. : round/embossed shield (usu. bronze); disk of sun; vault of sky; meteorite;

Clōdĭus, a, um : Claudian, Clodian, a branch of the Via Cassia, an aqueduct begun by the emperor Caligula, and finished by the emperor Claudius

clōdus, a, um : limping, halting, lame.

Clōelĭa, ae, f. : name of a Roman, a Roman maiden, who, when a hostage to Porsenna, with several companions, swam back to Rome

Clūsīnus, a, um : pertaining to Clusium, of Clusium, cold baths

Clūsĭum, ii, n. : one of the oldest and most important towns of Etruria, the residence of Porsenna, previously called, Chiusi

Clūsĭus, ii, m. : a cognomen of Janus, whose temple was closed in peace

Cn, npr. : Gnaeus (Roman praenomen); (abb. Cn.)

coactus, a, um. : see cogo

Cŏclēs, itis, m. : one-eyed person; Horatius (who kept Etruscans from Subician bridge);

cŏepĭo, ere, coepi, coeptum : to begin, commence, initiate; (rare early form, usu. shows only PERFDEF);

cōgĭto, are : to think; to consider, reflect on, ponder; to imagine, picture; to intend, look forward to;

cōgnātus, a, um : related, related by birth/position, kindred; similar/akin; having affinity

cōgnĭtŏr, ōris, m. : one who has made himself familiar with a case in law;

cōgnĭtus, a, um : known, acknowledged, approved., dat..

cōgnōmĕn, inis, n. : surname, family/3rd name; name (additional/derived from a characteristic);

cōgnōsco, ere, noui, cognitum : to become acquainted with/aware of; to recognize; to learn, find to be; to inquire/examine;

cōgo, ere, egi, actum : to collect/gather, round up, restrict/confine; to force/compel; to convene; to congeal;

cŏhāerĕo, ere, haesi, haesum : - to stick/cling/hold/grow together, adhere; to embrace; to touch, adjoin, be in - to be consistent/coherent; to be connected/bound/joined/tied together; to be in

cŏhĭbĕo, ere, bui, bitum : to hold together, contain; to hold back, restrain, curb, hinder; to confine; to repress;

cŏhōrs, chōrs, ortis, f. : - court; enclosure/yard/pen, farmyard; attendants, retinue, staff; circle; - cohort, tenth part of legion (360 men); armed force; band; ship crew;

cŏlĕus, i, m. : a leather bag, a sack for holding liquids.

cōllābŏr, eris, i, lapsus sum : to collapse, fall down/in ruin; to fall in swoon/exhaustion/death; to slip/slink (meet)

cōllĭgo, are : to bind, tie, fasten together, to connect, bind, tie up

cōllĭgo, ere, legi, lectum : to bind/tie/pack together/up, connect, unite/unify; to fetter/bind; to immobilize, stop;

cōllīna, ae, f. : hilly land

cōllīno, ere, lēvi, lĭtum : to besmear, to cover over, defile, pollute

cōllīnus, a, um : of or pertaining to a hill, found, growing on a hill, hilly, hill-

Cōllīnus, a, um : of/belonging to/pertaining to hills; found/growing on hill ; hilly, hill

cōllĭs, m. : hill, hillock, eminence, hill-top; mound; high ground; mountains (pl.)

cōllŭm, i, n. : neck; throat; head and neck; severed head; upper stem (flower); mountain ridge;

cŏlo, ere, colui, cultum : - to live in (place), inhabit; to till, cultivate, promote growth; to foster, maintain; to embellish;

cŏlŏr, oris, m. : color; pigment; shade/tinge; complexion; outward appearance/show; excuse/

cŏlŭbĕr, bri, m. : snake; serpent; (forming hair of mythical monsters);

cŏlūmba, ae, f. : pigeon; dove; (term of endearment); (bird of Venus/symbol of love/gentleness);

cŏma, ae, f. : hair;

cŏmāns, antis : hairy; long-haired; flowing (beard); plumed; leafy; w/foliage; w/radiant train;

cŏmēs, itis, m. : comrade, companion, associate, partner; soldier/devotee/follower of another;

cŏmĭs, e : courteous/kind/obliging/affable/gracious; elegant, cultured, having good taste;

cŏmīssātĭŏ, cŏmēssātĭo, cŏmīsātĭo, cŏmmīsātĭo, ionis, f. : carousing, merry-making, feasting, revelry; Bacchanal procession/rioting ;

cŏmĭtātus, a, um : accompanied, attended.

cŏmĭtĕr, adv. : courteously/kindly/civilly, readily; in friendly/sociable manner; w/good will;

cŏmĭtĭum, i, n. : place in Forum where comitia were held; comitia (pl.), assembly; elections;

cŏmĭto, are : to join as an attendant, guard/escort; to accompany, follow; to attend (funeral); to occur;

cŏmĭtŏr, aris, ari : to join as an attendant, guard/escort; to accompany, follow; to attend (funeral)

cŏmmăcŭlo, are : to stain deeply, pollute, defile; to contaminate, defile morally; to sully (reputation);

cŏmmĕātus, us, m. : supplies/provisions; goods; voyage; passage; convoy/caravan; furlough/leave;

cŏmmēndo, are : to entrust, give in trust; to commit; to recommend, commend to; to point out, designate;

cŏmmĕo, are : to go to, visit, travel; to pass; to resort to; to go to and fro, come and go; to communicate;

cŏmmĭnŭs, cŏmĭnŭs, adv. : hand to hand (fight), in close combat/quarters; close at hand; in presence of;

cŏmmĭtto, ere, misi, missum : to bring together, unite/join, connect/attach; to put together, construct; to entrust; to forfeit;

cŏmmŏdo, are : to lend, hire; to give, bestow, provide; to put at disposal of, oblige; to make fit, adapt

cŏmmŏdŭm, i, n. : just, a very short time before; that/this very minute; even now, at this

cŏmmŏdus, a, um : - suitable, convenient, obliging; opportune/timely; favorable/lucky; - standard, full weight/size/measure; desirable, agreeable; good (health/news);

cōmmŏvĕo, ere, moui, motum : - to shake/stir up, agitate; to displace, disturb, trouble/worry, upset; to jolt; - to waken; to provoke; to move (money/camp); to produce; to cause, start (war); to raise

cōmmūnālĭs, e : belonging to the community

cōmmūne, n. : that which is common, publicity, the sole credit for common achievements, A community, state, for common use, for all, for a common object, for the general advantage, equally upon patricians and plebeians, halves!, in general, all, commonplaces

cōmmūnĭco, are : to share; to share/divide with/out; to receive/take a share of; to receive; to join with;

cōmmūnĭo, ire, iui, itum : community, mutual participation; association; sharing; fellowship; communion;

cōmmūnĭs, e : - common/joint/public; general/universal; [Doctor Communis => St.Thomas - ordinary; sociable, courteous obliging; related, having something in common; cases;

cōmo, ere, compsi, comptum : to be furnished/covered with hair; to clothe/deck with hair/something hair-like;

cōmŏedĭa, ae, f. : comedy (as form of drama/literature; comedy (work/play);

cōmpăr, aris : equal, equal to; like, similar, resembling; suitable, matching, corresponding;

cōmpārĕo, ere, ui, - : to appear/come in sight; to be visible/present/in evidence/clearly stated

cōmpăro, are : - to prepare; to provide; to compose; to collect, get together/hold of; to raise (force); - to place together, match, couple, pair; to set/pit against; to treat as equal; - to set up/establish/institute; to arrange, dispose, settle; to buy, acquire, secure;

cōmpēllo, are : to accost one.

cōmpēllo, ere, puli, pulsum : to drive together (cattle), round up; to force, compel, impel, drive; to squeeze; to gnash;

cōmplēctŏr, eris, i, complexus sum : to embrace, hug; to welcome; to encircle, encompass; to attain; to include, bring in, involve

cōmplĕo, ere, pleui, pletum : - to fill (up/in); to be big enough to fill; to occupy space, crowd; to furnish/supply/man; to satisfy;

cōmplēxus, us, m. : - surrounding, encompassing, encircling; clasp, grasp, hold, embrace; - sexual intercourse (w/Venerius/femineus); hand-to-hand fighting;

cōmpōno, ere, posui, positum : - to compare; to place/put/add/collect together, collate; to match (up); to store/hoard; - to construct, build; to arrange, compile, compose, make up; to organize, order;

cōmpŏsĭtum, i, n. : according to agreement, by agreement, in concert

cōmpŏsĭtus, a, um : Well-arranged, ordered, constituted, orderly, regular

cōmprĕhēndo, cōmprēndo, ere, prehendi, prehensum : - to catch/seize/grasp firmly; to arrest; to take hold/root/fire, ignite; to conceive - to embrace; to include/cover/deal with (in speech/law); to express (by term/symbol);

cōmprĭmo, ere, pressi, pressum : - to press/squeeze together, fold, crush; to hem/shut/keep/hold in; to copulate (male);

cōmptus, a, um : - adorned/decorated, dressed/arranged/brushed (hair), smart; ornate/ - elegant (writing/writers), neat, in order, polished, smoothed;

cōnātus, us, m. : attempt, effort; exertion, struggle; impulse, tendency; endeavor, design;

cōncēdo, ere, cessi, cessum : to relinquish/give up/concede; to depart; to pardon; to submit, allow/grant/permit/condone;

cōncēsso, are : to cease/desist temporarily, leave off; to rest;

cōncēssus, us, m. : permitted/ allowable/ allowed/ granted; lawful; relinquished; permitting/

cōncīdo, ere, cidi, cisum : to cut up, cut through, cut away, cut to pieces, to bring to ruin, destroy

cōncĭdo, ere, cidi, intr. : - to fall down/faint/dead/victim/to earth/short, to collapse; to drop, subside; to decline; to decay;

cōncĭlĭŭm, ii, n. : a collection of people, an association, gathering, union, meeting, assembly; close conjunction; sexual union;

cōncītātus, a, um : prompt, rapide

cōncĭto, are : rapidly;

cōncōrdĭs, e : Plur. neutr., of the same mind, united, agreeing, concordant, harmonious

cōncōrdo, are : to agree, be united, be of one mind, harmonize, to be consistent, be in harmony, agree

cōncōrs, cordis : agreeing, concurring; like-minded; united, joint, shared; peaceful, harmonious;

cōncūrro, ere, curri, cursum : - to run/assemble/knock/snap together; to agree, fit, concur; to coincide; to make same - to charge, fight/engage in battle; to come running up/in large numbers; to rally;

cōncūrsus, us, m. : - running to and fro/together, collision, charge/attack; assembly/crowd; - encounter; combination, coincidence; conjunction, juxtaposition; joint right;

cōncŭtĭo, ere, cussi, cussum : - to shake/vibrate/agitate violently; to wave, brandish; (sound) strike (the ear);

cōndēnsus, a, um : very dense, close, thick

cōndĭcĭŏ, onis, f. : - agreement/contract; terms, proposal/option/alternative; situation; - marriage (contract); spouse, bride; relation of lover/mistress; paramour;

cōndo, ere, didi, ditum : to put/insert (into); to store up/put away, preserve, bottle (wine); to bury/inter; - to build/found, make; to shut (eyes); to conceal/hide/keep safe; to put together, - to restore; sheathe (sword); to plunge/bury (weapon in enemy); to put out of sight;

cōnfěro, ferre, tuli, latum : to bring together, carry/convey; to collect/gather, compare; to unite, add; to direct - to discuss/debate/confer; to oppose; to pit/match against another; to blame; to bestow;

cōnfērtus, a, um : - crowded/pressed together/thronging; in close order (troops); dense/compact;

cōnfīdo, ere, confisus sum : to have confidence in, rely on, trust (to); to believe, be confident/assured;

cōnfīgo, ere, i : - to fasten/nail together, construct; to set/cover with studs/points; to drive in - to pierce through, transfix; to strike down, pierce with a weapon;

cōnfītěŏr, eri, fessus sum : to acknowledge, confess, own, avow (an error, mistake, or a fact previously denied or doubted)

cōnflīgo, ere, flixi, flictum : to clash, collide; to contend/fight/combat; to be in conflict/at war; to argue/disagree;

cōnflo, are : to forge; to refine, purify; to inflame;

cōnfūndo, ere, fudi, fusum : - to pour/mix/mass/bring together; to combine/unite/blend/merge; to spread over, - to upset/confuse; to blur/jumble; to bring disorder/ruin; to disfigure; to bewilder, dismay;

cōnfūsus, a, um : - mixed together /jumbled /disordered; in disorder; indistinct; inarticulate; blushing;

cōngěro, ere, gessi, gestum : thief;

cōngrědĭŏr, eris, i, essus sum : to go, come, or meet with one, esp. with the access. idea of intention, in a friendly or hostile sense

cōnĭcĭo, ere, jēci, jectum : To throw or bring together, to unite

cōnjĭcĭo, ere, ieci, iectum : - to throw/put/pile together; to conclude, infer/guess; to assign, make go; to classify - to throw/cast/fling (into area); to devote/pour (money); to thrust, involve; to insert;

cōnjūnctĭŏ, ionis, f. : - union; mutual love/familiarity, match, fellowship; joint occurrence/ - conjunction (word); combination; compound proposition; association/affinity;

cōnjūnctus, a, um : United, connected;, bordering upon, near

cōnjūngo, ere, iunxi, iunctum : - to connect, join/yoke together; to marry; to connect/compound (words) (w/ - to unite (sexually); to place/bring side-by-side; to juxtapose; to share; to add; to associate;

cōnjūnx, iugis, f. : yoked together; paired; linked as a pair; spouse

cōnjūrātĭŏ, onis, f. : conspiracy, plot, intrigue; alliance; band of conspirators; taking joint oath;

cōnjūrātus, i, m. : conspiring; leagued;

cōnjūrō, are : to swear/act together, join in an oath/plot; to conspire, plot; to form alliance/league;

cōnŏr, aris, ari : to undertake, endeavor, attempt, try, venture, presume

cōnscělěrātus, a, um : wicked, depraved; criminal; (person/actions);

cōnscělěro, are : to stain, pollute with guilt, to dishonor, disgrace by wicked conduct;, verb finit

cōnsěděo, ēre, intr. : int., être assis avec / être assis ensemble

cōnsēnsus, us, m. : agreed upon;

cōnsēntĭo, ire, sensi, sensum : - to join/share in sensation/feeling; to be in agreement/harmony; to be of the same - to act together; to plot, conspire, combine; to coincide; to be in conjunction (planets);

cōnsěquŏr, eris, i, cutus sum : To follow, follow up, press upon, go after, attend, accompany, pursue any person or thing (class. in prose and poetry); constr. with acc. or absol.

cōnsěro, ere, erui, ertum : to connect, entwine, tie, join, fit, bind into a whole

cōnsěro, ere, seui, situm : to sow, plant (field/crops/seeds/tree), set; to breed; to sow/strew plentifully/thickly

cōnsīdo, ere, sedi, sessum : - to sit down/be seated; to hold sessions, sit (judge), try; to alight; to subside/sink - to encamp/bivouac; to take up a position; to stop/stay, make one's home, settle;

cōnsīlĭŭm, ii, n. : - debate/discussion/deliberation/consultation; advice/counsel/suggestion; - decision/resolution; intention/purpose/policy/plan/action; diplomacy/ - deliberative/advisory body; state council, senate; jury; board of assessors;

cōnsīsto, ere, stiti : - to stop/stand/halt/cease; to pause, linger; to stop spreading/flowing; to take a - to stand together/fast; to consist of/be reckoned in; to rest/depend upon; to be/make a stand; to stay, remain (fixed), stand still/erect/upright; to correspond to;

cōnspēctus, a, um : visible, in full view, Striking, distinguished, eminent, noteworthy, remarkable, signal, glaring

cōnspĭcĭo, ere, spexi, spectum : looking/ observing/ discerning, action of looking; (augury);

cōnstĭtŭo, ere, tui, tutum : - to set up/in position, erect; to place/dispose/locate; to (call a) halt; to plant - to decide/resolve; to decree/ordain; to appoint, post/station (troops); to settle - to establish/create/institute; to draw up, arrange/set in order; to make up, form;

cōnsto, are, constiti : it is agreed/ evident/ understood/correct/well known (everyone knows/agrees);

cōnsŭētūdō, dinis, f. : - habit/custom/usage/way; normal/general/customary practice, tradition/ - experience; empirical knowledge; sexual/illicit intercourse, intimacy,

cōnsŭl, m. : consul (highest elected Roman official - 2/year); supreme magistrate elsewhere;

cōnsŭlātus, us, m. : consulship/consulate; (term of) office of consul; actions/acts as consul;

cōnsŭlo, ere, sului, sultum : - to ask information/advice of; to consult, take counsel; to deliberate/consider; - to decide upon, adopt; to look after/out for (DAT), pay attention to; to refer to;

cōnsūmo, ere, sumpsi, sumptum : - to burn up, destroy/kill; to put end to; to reduce/wear away; to annul; to extinguish - to devour/swallow up/consume/eat/use up/exhaust/expend; to spend; to squander/waste;

cōntērrĕo, ere, ŭi, ĭtum : to terrify greatly, to frighten.

cōntīngo, ĕre : to wet, moisten

cōntīngo, ere, tigi, tactum : it happens, it turns out; (PERF) it came to pass;

cōntĭnŭō, adv. : - immediately, forthwith, at once, without delay/intermission; continuously;

cōntĭnŭo, are : to make continuous (space/time); to put in line, join (in succession), connect, - to bridge (gap); to extend/prolong/draw out/last/renew; to keep on; to do without pause

cōntĭnŭus, a, um : incessant/unremitting, constantly repeated/recurring; successive, next in - continuous, connected/hanging together; uninterrupted; indivisible; lasting;

cōntrā, adv. : against, facing, opposite; weighed against; as against; in resistance/reply - contrary to, not in conformance with; the reverse of; otherwise than;

cōntrārĭum, ii, n. : in opposite directions

cōntrārĭus, a, um : - opposite, contrary, in contradiction; antithetical; opposed/hostile/adverse;

cōntŭmēlĭōsus, a, um : insulting, outrageous, humiliating; rude, insolent, abusive; reproachful ;

cōntūndo, ere, tudi, tusum : to quell /crush /outdo /subdue utterly; to bruise/beat; to pound to pieces/powder/pulp;

cōnvēcto, āre : to bear, carry, bring together in abundance

cōnvēho, ere, vexi, vectum : to carry, bear, bring together

cōnvēllo, ere, uulsi, uulsum : - to shatter, batter, convulse, shake violently; to heave up, set in motion; - to pull/pluck/tug/tear up/at dislodge, uproot; to wrench, strain, dislocate

cōnvĕnĭēns, entis : - fitting; appropriate; comfortable; internally consistent, harmonious;

cōnvēnĭo, ire, ueni, uentum : it agrees/came together/is agreed/asserted; [bene ~ nobis=>we're on good

cōnvērro, ere, verri, versum : to sweep, brush together, to sweep, clear away

cōnvērto, ere, uerti, uersum : to convert; to change, alter; to refresh; to turn;

cōnvīcĭŭm, i, n. : noise (angry), chatter/outcry/clamor/bawling; noise source; noisy - reprimand/reproach/reproof; abuse/jeers/mockery/insults; object of shame;

cōnvīnco, ere, uici, uictum : - to conquer, establish; to convince; to overcome, demonstrate, prove clearly; to grant;

cōnvīvĭŭm, ii, n. : banquet/feast/dinner party; guests/people at party; dining-club; living

cōnvōlvo, ere, volvi, vŏlūtum : to roll together, roll up, roll round

cōpĭa, ae, f. : an abundance

cŏr, cordis, n. : heart; mind/soul/spirit; intellect/judgment; sweetheart; souls/persons (pl.);

cōrăm, prép. et adv. : in the presence of, before; (may precede or follow object); personally ;

cōrdus, a, um : lateborn, produced late in the season, the second crop of hay, after-math

Cŏrīnna, ae, f. : A celebrated Greek poetess of Tanagra, contemporary with Pindar

cōrnū, us, n. : horn; hoof; beak/tusk/claw; bow; horn/trumpet; end, wing of army; mountain top;

Cŏrŏebus, i, m. : son of Mygdon of Phrygia, who freed Cassandra. and fought for Priam against the Greeks before Troy

cōrpŭs, oris, n. : - body; person, self; virility; flesh; corpse; trunk; frame(work); collection/ - substantial/material/concrete object/body; particle/atom; corporation, guild;

cōrrēpo, ere, psi, ptum, intr. : to creep, slink to a place, to creep, creep

cōrrĭpĭo, ere, ripui, reptum : - to seize/ grasp/ snatch up, lay hold of; to sweep off; to carry away; to appropriate - to censure/reproach/rebuke/chastise; to shorten/abridge; to hasten (upon); to catch

cōrrŏbŏro, are : to strengthen, harden, reinforce; to corroborate; to mature; to make powerful, fortify;

Cōrsĭcus, a, um : Corsican

cŏrūscus, a, um : vibrating /waving/ tremulous /shaking; flashing, twinkling; brilliant ;

cŏthūrnus, i, m. : a high Grecian shoe.

cŏtīdĭē, adv. : daily, every day; day by day; usually, ordinarily, commonly;

crātēr, ēris, m. : a vessel in which wine was mingled with water, a mixing-vessel, bowl

crēbĕr, bra, brum : thick/crowded/packed/close set; frequent/repeated, constant; numerous/abundant;

crēbrō, adv. : frequently/repeatedly/often, one after another, time after time; thickly

crēdībĭlĭs, e : credible/ trustworthy/ believable/ plausible/ convincing/likely/probable;

crēdo, ere, didi, ditum : - to trust, entrust; to commit/consign; to believe, trust in, rely on, confide; to suppose; sure;

crēsco, ere, creui, cretum : - to come forth/to be; to arise/spring (from); to be born; to become visible/great; grow - to thrive, increase (size/number/honor), multiply; to ascend; to attain, be promoted;

Crēusa, ae, f. : A daughter of king Creon, of Corinth, married to Jason, and on that account put to death by Medea by means of a charmed offering

crīmĕn, inis, n. : - indictment/charge/accusation; blame/reproach/slander; verdict/judgment ;

crīnĭs, m. : hair; lock of hair, tress, plait; plume (helmet); tail of a comet;

crīsta, ae, f. : a tuft on the head of animals;, the comb of a cock, his crest rises, he carries his head high, he is conceited

crūdēlĭs, e : cruel/hardhearted/unmerciful/severe, bloodthirsty/savage/inhuman; harsh/bitter;

crŭēnto, are : - to stain/spot/mark with blood; to cause to bleed, wound; to pollute with blood-guilt;

crŭēntus, a, um : - bloody/bleeding/discharging blood; gory; blood red; polluted w/blood-guilt;

crūx, crucis, f. : cross; hanging tree; impaling stake; crucifixion; torture/torment/trouble/

cŭbĭcŭlŭm, i, n. : - bedroom; sleeping chamber/apartment/suite; (as scene of marital/other sex); sepulcher

cŭbĭto, are : to recline, lie down, take rest, sleep; to lie down often; to lie/sleep (sexual);

cūlmĕn, inis, n. : height/peak/top/summit/zenith; roof, gable, ridge-pole; head, chief;

cūltē, adv. : elegantly.

cūltus, a, um : cultivated/tilled/farmed (well); ornamented, neat/well groomed; polished/

cŭm, conj. : when, while; since, because, as

cŭm, quŏm, quŭm, prép. + abl. et adv. : with, together/jointly/along/simultaneous with, amid; supporting; attached;

Cūmāe, arum, f. pl. : an ancient colony of the Chalcidians, in Campania, on the sea-coast, renowned on account of its Sibyl

Cūmānus, a, um : pertaining to Cumae

cŭmŭlo, are : - to heap/pile up/high, gather into a pile/heap; to accumulate, amass; to load/fill - to increase/augment/enhance; to perfect/finish up; (PASS) to be made/composed of;

cŭmŭlus, i, m. : - heap/pile/mound/aggregate/mass/accumulation; wave (water); surplus, increase; speech;

cūncti, ae, a : altogether (usu. pl.), in a body; every, all, entire; total/complete; whole of

cūnctŏr, aris, ari : to delay, impede, hold up; to hesitate, tarry, linger; to be slow to act; to dawdle; to doubt

cūnctus, cf. cuncti : altogether (usu. pl.), in a body; every, all, entire; total/complete; whole of

cŭpĭdĭtās, atis, f. : enthusiasm/eagerness/passion; (carnal) desire; lust; greed/usury/fraud;

cŭpīdō, dinis, f. (m.) : to desire/love/wish/longing (passionate); to lust; to greed, appetite; to desire for gain;

Cŭpīdo, ĭnis, m. : the god of love, Cupid, son of Venus

cŭpīdus, a, um : eager/passionate; longing for/desirous of (with gen.); greedy; wanton/

cŭpĭo, ere, i(u)i, itum : to wish/long/be eager for; to desire/want, covet; to desire as a lover; to favor, wish

cūr, adv. : why, wherefore; for what reason/purpose?; on account of which?; because;

cūra, ae, f. : - concern, worry, anxiety, trouble; attention, care, pains, zeal; cure, - office/task/responsibility/post; administration, supervision; command (army);

cūrātus, a, um : carefully regarded, anxious

cūro, cŏiro, are : to arrange/see/attend to; to take care of; to provide for; to worry/care about; to heal/ - to undertake; to procure; to regard w/anxiety/interest; to take trouble/interest; to desire;

cūrro, ere, cucurri, cursum : to run/trot/gallop, hurry/hasten/speed, move/travel/proceed/flow swiftly/quickly;

cūrrus, us, m. : chariot, light horse vehicle; triumphal chariot; triumph; wheels on plow; cart;

cūrsus, us, m. : running; lesson

cūrvo, are : to bend/arch, make curved/bent; to form a curve; to make stoop/bow/yield; to influence;

cūrvus, a, um : curved/bent/arched; crooked; morally wrong; stooped/bowed; winding; w/many

cūspĭs, idis, f. : point/tip (spear), pointed end; spit/stake; blade; javelin/spear/lance; sting;

cūstōdĭa, ae, f. : - protection, safe-keeping, defense, preservation; custody, charge; prisoner;

cūstōdĭo, ire, iui or ii, itum : to guard/protect/preserve, watch over, keep safe; to take heed/care, observe;

cūstōs, odis, m. : - guard; sentry/watch; guardian/protector/keeper; doorkeeper/watchman/janitor; shoot;

Cўbĕlē, f. : Cybèle

Cўthĕrēa, ae, f. : Venus

Cўthĕrēus, a, um : of Cythera, Cytherean

Dănăē, f. : daughter of Acrisius, and mother of Perseus by Zeus

Dănăi, orum, pl. : the Greeks

Dănăus, a, um : belonging to Danaus;, Greek, Grecian

Dārdăni, orum, m. : a people in Upper Moesia, the modern Servia

Dārdănĭa, ae, f. : the city Dardania, in Troas

Dārdănĭdēs, ae, m. : son or descendant of Dardanus

Dārdănis, ĭdis, f. : Dardanian, Trojan,

Dārdănus, i, m. : -I. The son of Jupiter and Electra of Arcadia, founder of the city Dardania, in Troas, and ancestor of the royal race of Troy

dăto, are : to give away, administer

dē, prép. + abl. : down/away from, from, off; about, of, concerning; according to; with regard to;

dĕa, ae, f. : goddess;

dēbĕo, ere, ui, itum : to owe; to be indebted/responsible for/obliged/bound/destined; to ought, must, should;

dĕcĕm, adj. num. : ten; (ten men);

dĕcērno, ere, creui, cretum : to decide/settle/determine/resolve; to decree/declare/ordain; to judge; to vote for;

dĕcĕt, impers. : It is seemly, comely, becoming,; it beseems, behooves, is fitting, suitable, proper

dĕcĭdo, ere, cidi : to fall/drop/hang/flow down/off/over; to sink/drop; to fail, fall in ruin; to end up; to die;

dĕcĭpĭo, ere, cepi, ceptum : to cheat /deceive /mislead /dupe /trap; to elude/escape notice; to disappoint/frustrate/

dēclīnĭs, e : turning aside

dēclīno, are : to decline/conjugate/inflect (in the same manner/like); to change word form, modify;

dĕcŏr, oris, m. : beautiful; pleasing to the senses;

dĕcŏro, are : to adorn/grace, embellish/add beauty to; to glorify, honor/add honor to; to do credit

dĕcōrum, i, n. : Absol., decorated, ornamented, adorned; elegant, fine, beautiful, handsome, Sup.

dĕcōrus, a, um : - beautiful/good looking/handsome/comely; adorned; graceful/elegant (non- - honorable, noble; glorious, decorated; decorous, proper, decent, fitting;

dĕcūrro, ere, curri, cursum : to run/hurry/rush/flow/slope down; to hasten; to travel downstream; to come to land/end (army);

dĕcŭs, oris, n. : glory/splendor; honor/distinction; deeds; dignity/virtue; decorum; grace/

dēdĭcātus, a, um : dévoué (seult. au superlatif)

dēdĭco, are : to give out (tidings, a notice); to affirm, declare, announce (any thing);

dēdĭtus, a, um : devoted/attached to, fond of; devoted/directed/given over (to) (activity);

dēdo, ere, dedidi, deditum : to give up/in, surrender; to abandon/consign/devote (to); to yield, hand/deliver over;

dēdūco, ere, duxi, ductum : - to lead/draw//pull/bring/stretch down/away/out/off; to escort; to eject/evict - to divert/draw (water); to draw (sword); to spin; to deduct/reduce/lessen; to describe; - to launch/bring downstream (ship); to remove (force); to entice; to found/settle

dēfĕndo, ere, fendi, fensum : - to defend/guard/protect, look after; to act/speak/plead/write for defense; - to repel, fend/ward off, avert/prevent; to support/preserve/maintain; to defend

dēfēnsŏr, oris, m. : defender/protector; supporter/champion/apologist; defendant; defense advocate;

dēfĕro, fers, ferre, tuli, latum : to honor; to export (medieval usage);

dēfĭcĭo, ere, feci, fectum : to fail/falter; to run short/out; to grow weak/faint; to come to end; to revolt/rebel, - to pass away; to become extinct, die/fade out; to subside/sink; to suffer eclipse, wane;

dēgĕnĕr, eneris : - degenerate/base; inferior to ancestors; ignoble, unworthy, untrue, - low-born, of/belonging to inferior stock/breed/variety; soft/weak; softened;

dēgĕnĕro, are : - to be inferior to ancestors/ unworthy; to deteriorate/decline; to lower oneself;

dēĭcĭo, ere, ieci, iectum : - to throw /pour/ jump/ send/ put/push/force/knock/bring down; to cause to fall/drop; - to overthrow, bring down, depose; to kill, destroy; to shoot/strike down; to fell - to unhorse; to let fall; to shed; to purge/evacuate bowel; to dislodge/rout; to drive/throw

dēīncĕps, adv. : following, next in succession;

dĕīndĕ, dĕin, adv. : then/next/afterward; thereon/henceforth/from there/then; in next position/

dēlābŏr, beris, bi, lapsus sum : to drop, descend; to sink; to fall/fail/lose strength; to flow down; to be carried downstream

dēlēctātĭŏ, onis, f. : straining/effort/tenesmus; inclination/futile straining to void bowels/bladder;

dēlēcto, are : - to delight, please, amuse, fascinate; to charm, lure, entice; to be a source of - (PASS) to be delighted/glad, take pleasure; (w/INF) to enjoy (being/doing);

dēlēctŏr, aris, āri : to delight, charm

dēlĕo, ere, evi, etum : to erase, wipe/scratch/remove (letters/marks), wipe/blot out, expunge, delete; to abolish; to annul;

dēlĭcĭāe, arum, f. pl. : pleasure/delight/fun (usu. pl.), activity affording enjoyment, luxuries; - ornaments/decorations; erotic verse; charms

dēlĭcĭum, ii, n. : delight, pleasure, charm, allurement; deliciousness, luxuriousness, voluptuousness, curiosities of art; sport, frolics

dēlĭgo, ere, legi, lectum : to choose out, to select

dēlūbrŭm, i, n. : shrine; temple; sanctuary ;

dēmĕrĕo, ere, merui, meritum : to oblige/please, win favor of; to earn/merit, deserve (well of); to lay under

dēmĭgro, are : to emigrate; migrate; to depart/remove/withdraw/go away (from situation/local/thing);

dēmītto, ere, misi, missum : - to drop, let fall; to sink; to send/cast/go/flow/float/slope down; to flow/shed/let - to bend/stoop/bow/sag; to lower (eyes); to let (clothes/hair/beard) hang down; to absorb (tree);

dēmo, ere, dempsi, demptum : to take/cut away/off, remove, withdraw; to subtract; to take away from;

dēmŭm, adv. : - finally, at last; at length, in the end, eventually; [tum demum => only - other possibilities being dismissed; only/alone, and no other/nowhere else;

dēnĭquĕ, adv. : finally, in the end; and then; at worst; in short, to sum up; in fact, indeed;

dēns, dentis, m. : tooth; tusk; ivory; tooth-like thing, spike; destructive power, envy, ill will;

dēnso, are : to make thick, thicken, press, pack, close

dēnsus, a, um : - thick/dense/solid; (cloud/shadow); crowded/thick_planted/packed/covered - frequent, recurring; terse/concise (style); harsh/horse/thick (sound/voice);

dēpāsco, (or) is, ere, paui, pastum : to cull, select; to prune away, remove; to destroy, waste; to lay waste;

dēpāscŏr, eris, i, pastus sum : to feed down, feed off

dēpello, ere, puli, pulsum : - to drive/push out//off/away/aside, repel; to expel; to remove, wean; to banish utterly; to dismiss;

dēpĕrĕo, ire : to perish/die; to be lost/totally destroyed; to be much in love with/love to

dēpōno, ere, posui, positum : - to put/lay down/aside/away; to let drop/fall; to give up; to resign; to deposit/entrust; - to lift off; to take off (clothes); to have (hair/beard/nails) cut; to shed (tusks);

dēpōsco, ere, depoposci, - : to demand peremptorily; to ask for earnestly; to require; to request earnestly; to challenge;

dēprĕcŏr, aris, ari : to avert by prayer; to entreat/pray/beg; to intercede/beg pardon/mercy/relief/exemption

dēprĕhēndo, ere, di, sum : to seize/catch; to catch napping/redhanded; to surprise/pounce on; to arrest; to intercept;

dēprēndo, ere, di, sum : to seize/catch; to catch napping/redhanded; to surprise/pounce on; to arrest; to intercept;

dēscrībo, ere, scripsi, scriptum : to describe/draw, mark/trace out; to copy/transcribe/write; to establish (law/right)

dēsĕro, ere, ui, desertum : to undo or sever (one's connection with another); to leave, forsake, abandon, desert, give up;

dēsērtum, i, n. : desert places, deserts, wastes.

dēsērtus, a, um : deserted; esp. of places, desert, solitary, waste

dēsērvĭo, īre, intr. : to serve zealously, be devoted to, subject to

dēsĭdĭa, ae, f. : - idleness, slackness; inactivity; remaining in place; leisure; indolence, - ebbing; subsiding; (process of); retiring ;

dēsĭdĭōsus, a, um : slothful, indolent, lazy

dēsĭlĭo, ere, silui, sultum : to leap/jump down, dismount, alight; to jump headlong, venture heedlessly;

dēsĭno, ere, sii, situm : to stop/end/finish, abandon/leave/break off, desist/cease; to come to/at end/close;

dēsīsto, ere, destiti, destitum : to stop/cease/desist (from); to give up, leave/stand off; to dissociate oneself;

dēstĭtŭo, ere, destitui, destitutum : - to fix/set (in position), set up, make fast; to leave destitute/without; to render - to desert/leave/abandon/forsake/leave in lurch; to disappoint/let down; to fail/give

dēsŭēsco, ere, sueui, suetum : to forget/unlearn; to become/be unaccustomed to; to disaccustom; to lay aside custom/habit;

dēsŭētus, a, um : disaccustomed; that has fallen out of use or become unfamiliar;

dēsultŏr, oris, m. : vaulter/leaper (between horses), circus trick rider; fickle person/lover ;

dēsŭm, esse, defui : to be wanting/lacking; to fail/miss; to abandon/desert, neglect; to be away/absent/missing;

dētĭnĕo, ere, tinui, tentum : to detain, hold; to hold off, keep away (from); to hold prisoner; to retain; to occupy; to protract;

dētrăho, ere, traxi, tractum : - to drag/pull/strip/take down/away/off; to remove; to exclude, omit, cut out; to subtract; - to detach, dislodge (troops); to draw (into action); to demolish; to abstract, derive;

dētrēcto, dētrācto, are : to refuse (to undertake/undergo), decline, reject, evade, recoil from;

dētrūdo, ere, trusi, trusum : to push /thrust /drive/ force off/ away/aside/from/down; to expel; to dispossess; to postpone;

dĕus, i, m. : a god, a deity

dēvīncĭo, ire, uinxi, uinctum : to tie/bind up, hold/fix fast; to subjugate; to obligate/ oblige/ constrain; to unite

dēvīnctus, a, um : P. a.,devoted, greatly attached to

dēvŏlvo, ere, ui, utum : to roll/fall down; to roll off; to sink back; to fall into; to hand over, transfer; to deprive;

dēvŏro, are : to devour, consume; to swallow, gulp down; to engulf/ingulf, absorb, drink in;

dēxtĕr, tra, trum : right, on/to the right hand/side; skillful/dexterous/handy;

dēxtră, dēxtĕra, , f. : on the right of; on the right-hand side of;

Dīāna, ae, f. : Diana (virgin goddess of light/moon/hunt); (identified w/Artimis); moon;

dīca, ae, f. : a lawsuit, judicial process, action, to bring an action, to bring a heavy action

dīco, are : to dedicate, consecrate, devote any thing to a deity; to deify

dīco, ere, dixi, dictum : to say, declare, state; to allege, declare positively; to assert; to plead (case); to mean;

dīcto, are : - to dictate (for writing/speaking); to compose; to draw up; to order/prescribe; to fix - to say/declare/assert repeatedly/habitually/often/frequently; to reiterate; to recite;

dīctŭm, i, n. : words/utterance/remark; one's word/promise; saying/maxim; bon mot, witticism;

dĭes, ei, m. et f. : day; daylight; (sunlit hours); (24 hours from midnight); open sky; weather;

dīffĕro, fers, ferre, distuli, dilatum : - to postpone/delay/differ; to put off, keep waiting; to give respite to; differ, - to spread abroad; to scatter/disperse; to separate; to defame; to confound/bewilder;

dīffĭcĭlĭs, e : - difficult, troublesome; hard; hard to please/manage/deal with/carry out;

dīffĭcūltās, atis, f. : difficulty; trouble; hardship/want/distress/poverty ; obstinacy;

dīffŭgĭo, ere : to scatter, disperse, dispel; to flee/run away in different/several directions;

dĭgĭtus, i, m. : finger; toe; finger's breadth, inch; (1/16 of a pes); twig;

dĭgnĭtās, atis, f. : - worth, excellence; fitness/suitability (for task),; honor, esteem, standing;

dĭgno, are : worthily; appropriately/suitably; in a fitting manner; becomingly ;

dĭgnus, a, um : appropriate/suitable; worthy, deserving, meriting; worth (w/ABL/GEN);

dīlēctus, a, um : loved, beloved, dear; Subst. m. a favorite

dīlĭgēns, entis : - careful; diligent, scrupulous; accurate; industrious; assiduous;

dīlĭgēntĕr, adv. : carefully; attentively; diligently; scrupulously; thoroughly/completely/well;

dīlĭgo, ere, lexi, lectum : to value or esteem highly, to love

dīlŭo, ere, dilui, dilutum : to wash (away/off); to dissolve and carry away; to purge/clear/empty (bowels); to drench; to dissipate;

dīmĭcātĭŏ, ionis, f. : fight; instance of a battle/engagement; combat; struggle, conflict; contest;

dīmĭco, are : to fight, battle; to struggle/contend/strive; to brandish weapons; to be in conflict/peril;

dīmĭnŭo, ere, minui, minutum : to shatter; to break; to dash to pieces ; to violate/outrage; to lessen/diminish (Ecc);

dīmītto, ere, misi, missum : - to send away/off; to allow to go, let go/off; to disband, discharge, dismiss - to dissolve (assembly); to part with; to put away; to divorce; to pay off, settle (debt); - to discontinue, renounce, abandon/forsake, forgo, give up (activity); to dispatch;

Dĭŏmēdēs, m. : A son of Tydeus, king of Aetolia, and Deipyle

dīra, orum, n. : fearful things, ill-boding events

dīrāe, arum, f. : ill-boding things, portents, unlucky signs

dīrĭmo, ere, emi, emptum : - to pull/break/take apart; to cleave; to sort (votes); to break up/dissolve (joint - to divide; to separate/cut off/remove; to delay/interrupt temporally/put off/ - to cause to diverge;; to draw a line/boundary; to settle, impose decision on;

dīrĭpĭo, ere, ripui, reptum : to pull/tear apart/to pieces/away; to tear asunder/to shreds; to pull out/off; to divert;

dīrus, a, um : awful/dire/dreadful (omen); ominous/frightful/terrible/horrible; skillful

dīs, dītis : rich

dīscēdo, ere, cessi, cessum : to go/march off, depart, withdraw; to scatter, dissipate; to abandon; to lay down (arms);

dīscēptātŏr, ōris, m. : an umpire, arbitrator, judge

dīscĭdĭŭm, i, n. : separation, divorce, discord; disagreement, quarrel; tearing apart;

dīscīngo, ere, cinxi, cinctum : to ungird, deprive of the girdle

dīscĭplīna, ae, f. : teaching, instruction, education; training; discipline; method, science, study;

dīsco, ere, didici : to learn; to hear, get to know, become acquainted with; to acquire knowledge/skill of/

dīscōrdĭa, ae, f. : disagreement, discord;

dīscōrs, ordis : warring, disagreeing, inharmonious; discordant, at variance; inconsistent;

dīscrīmĕn, inis, n. : crisis, separating line, division; distinction, difference;

dīsērtus, a, um : eloquent; skillfully expressed;

dīssĭmĭlĭs, e : unlike, different, dissimilar;

dĭū, adv. : (for) a long/considerable time/while; long since; [quam diu => as long as];

dīus, a, um : of or belonging to a deity, divine.

dīva, ae, f. : goddess;

dīvēllo, ere, uelli, uulsum : - to alienate/estrange; to compel (persons) to part company, force away; to separate - to tear away/open/apart, tear to pieces/in two; to break up, sunder/disrupt;

dīvērsium, ii, n. : course de chars

dīvērsus, dīvōrsus, a, um : opposite; separate, apart; diverse, unlike, different; hostile;

dīvērto, ere, verti, versum : to turn, go different ways, to part, separate, turn aside, verb. finit.

dīvĕs, itis : rich/wealthy; costly; fertile/productive (land); talented, well endowed;

dīvīdo, ere, uisi, uisum : to divide; to separate, break up; to share, distribute; to distinguish;

dīvīsus, a, um : division;

dīvum, i, n. : the sky, under the open sky, in the open air;

dīvus, a, um : divine; blessed, saint (Latham);

dō, das, dare, dedi, datum : - to give; dedicate; to sell; to pay; to grant/bestow/impart/offer/lend; to devote; to allow; - to surrender/give over; to send to die; to ascribe/attribute; to give birth/produce;

dŏcĕo, ere, cui, ctum : to teach, show, point out;

dŏctus, a, um : learned, wise; skilled, experienced, expert; trained; clever, cunning, shrewd;

dŏcŭmēntum, i, n. : lesson, instruction; warning, example; document; proof;

dŏlēns, dolentis : qui cause de la douleur

dŏlĕo, ere, ui, itum : to hurt; to feel/suffer pain; to grieve; to be afflicted/pained/sorry; to cause pain/grief;

dōlĭum, ii, n. : large earthenware vessel (~60 gal. wine/grain); hogshead (Cas); tun/cask;

Dŏlŏpēs, um, m. pl. : the part of Thessaly formerly inhabited by the Dolopes

dŏlŏr, oris, m. : pain, anguish, grief, sorrow, suffering; resentment, indignation;

dŏlus, i, m. : trick, device, deceit, treachery, trickery, cunning, fraud;

dŏmēstĭcus, a, um : domestic, of the house; familiar, native; civil, private, personal;

dŏmī, adv. : at home

dŏmĭna, ae, f. : mistress of a family, wife; lady, lady-love; owner;

dŏmĭnus, i, m. : owner, lord, master; the Lord; title for ecclesiastics/gentlemen;

Dŏmītĭus, i, m. : Domitius; (Roman gens name);

dŏmĭto, are : to tame, break in, a team

dŏmo, are, ui, itum : to subdue, master, tame; to conquer;

dŏmus, us or **i, f.** : house, building; home, household; (N 4 1, older N 2 1); [domu => at home];

dōnĕc, conj. sub. : while, as long as, until;

dōno, are : To give (alicui aliquod, or aliquem aliqua re => one something as a present); to present, bestow; to grant, vouchsafe, confer; to forgive; give (gifts), bestow;

dōnŭm, i, n. : gift, present; offering;

dōrmĭo, ire, iui, itum : to sleep, rest; to be/fall asleep; to behave as if asleep; to be idle, do nothing;

drăcŏ, onis, m. : dragon; snake;

dŭbĭē, adv. : doubtfully

dŭbĭto, are : to doubt; to deliberate; to hesitate (over); to be uncertain/irresolute;

dŭbĭŭm, ii, n. : doubt; question;

dŭbĭus, a, um : doubtful, dubious, uncertain; variable, dangerous; critical;

dūco, ere, duxi, ductum : to lead, command; to think, consider, regard; to prolong;

dūctus, us, m. : conducting; generalship;

dūlcēdō, inis, f. : sweetness, agreeableness; charm;

dūlcĭs, e : pleasant, charming; sweet; kind, dear; soft, flattering, delightful;

dŭm, conj. sub. : while, as long as, until; provided that;

dŭŏ, ae, o, pl. : two (pl.);

dŭplēx, icis : twofold, double; divided; two-faced;

dŭplĭco, are : to double, bend double; to duplicate; enlarge;

dūro, are : to harden, make hard; to become hard/stern; to bear, last, remain, continue; to endure;

dūrus, a, um : hard, stern; harsh, rough, vigorous; cruel, unfeeling, inflexible; durable;

dūx, ducis, m. : leader, guide; commander, general;

Dўmās, antis, m. : the father of Hecuba

ĕā, adv. : par cet endroit

ĕādĕm, adv. : -I. By the same way -II. masc.

ēccĕ, adv. : behold! see! look! there! Here!

ēcfĕro, cf. effero : to carry out; to bring out; to carry out for burial; to raise;

ĕdāx, acis : greedy, rapacious, voracious, gluttonous; devouring, consuming, destructive;

ēdīco, ere, edixi, edictum : to proclaim, declare; to appoint;

ēdīsco, ere, didici : to learn by heart; to commit to memory; to study; to get to know;

ēdo, edis, edere, edidi, editum : to give out, put forth, bring forth

ĕdo, edis, esse, edi, esum : to eat/consume/devour; to eat away (fire/water/disease); to destroy; to spend money on

ēdŭco, are : to bring up, to rear, to educate

ēdūco, ere : to lead out; to draw up; to bring up, rear;

ēffātum, i, n. : a dialectical proposition, an axiom

ēffĕro, fers, ferre, extuli, elatum : to carry out; to bring out; to carry out for burial; to raise;

ēffŏr, atur, ari, atus sum : to utter; to declare; to speak

ēffrēnātus, a, um : unbridled; unrestrained, unruly, headstrong, violent; freed from/not subject t;

ēffrēno, are : to unbridle, let loose

ēffŭgĭo, ere, fugi, fugiturus : to flee/escape; to run/slip/keep away (from), eschew/avoid; to baffle, escape notice;

ēffūndo, ere, fudi, fusum : - to pour out/away/off; to allow to drain; to shower; to volley (missiles); to send/stream - to shed (blood/tears); to discharge (vomit/urine), debouch, emit; to flow out, - to break out; to bear/yield/bring forth; to expend/use up; to unseat, eject/drop/discard;

ēffūsē, adv. : over a wide area, extensively; freely, in a disorderly manner; lavishly;

ēffūsus, a, um : vaste, large, libre

ĕgēns, entis : needy, poor, in want of; very poor, destitute (of);

ĕgĕo, ere, egui : to need (w/GEN/ABL), lack, want; to require, be without;

ĕgō, mei, pron. : moi, me

ĕgrĕdĭor, eris, i, egressus sum : to go/march/come out; to set sail; to land, disembark; to surpass, go beyond

ĕgrĕgĭus, a, um : singular; distinguished; exceptional; extraordinary; eminent; excellent;

ĕgrēssŭs, us, m. : sortie, départ, débarquement, issue, digression

ēi, interj. : Ah! Woe!, oh dear, alas; (of grief or fear);

ēlābŏr, eris, i, lapsus sum : to slip away; to escape; to elapse

ēlĭcĭo, ere, cui, citum : to draw/pull out/forth, entice, elicit, coax;

ēlĭgo, ere, legi, lectum : to pick out, choose;

ēlŏquēns, entis : eloquent, expressing thoughts fluently/forcefully; articulate, able in speech;;

ēlŏquēntĭa, ae, f. : eloquence;

ēlŏquŏr, eris, i, locutus sum : to speak out, utter

ēmĭnĕo, ere, ui, - : to stand out; to be prominent/preeminent, excel; to project;

ēmītto, ere, misi, missum : to hurl; to let go; to utter; to send out; to drive; to force; to cast; to discharge; to expel; to publish;

ēmŏvĕo, ere, moui, motum : to move away, remove, dislodge;

ēn: behold! see! lo! here! hey! look at this!;

ĕnĭm, conj. : namely (postpos.); indeed; in fact; for; I mean, for instance, that is to say;

Ēnnĭus, i, m. : Ennius

ēnsĭs, m. : sword;

ĕō, adv. : there, to that place; on this account, therefore; to that degree, so far

ĕo, ire, iui, itum : to go (of every kind of motion of animate or inanimate things), to walk, ride, sail, fly, move, pass;

ĕōdĕm, adv. : in the same place

Ĕōus, a, um : Belonging to the morning, morning- ; Belonging to the east, eastern, orient

Ĕōus, i, m. : the morning-star

ĕphĕmĕrĭda, cf. ephemeris : a day-book, diary, ephemeris

ĕqua, ae, f. : mare;

ĕquĕs, itis, m. : horseman/cavalryman/rider; horsemen (pl.), cavalry; equestrian order;

ĕquēstĕr, tris, tre : equestrian, mounted on horse; of/belonging to/consisting of horseman/cavalry;

ĕquus, i, m. : horse; steed;

ĕra, ae, f. : mistress; lady of the house; woman in relation to her servants; Lady;

ērādo, ere, rasi, rasum : to scratch out, scrape off

ērēpo, ere, psi, ptum : I. Neutr., to creep out, crawl forth II. Act. To creep through, To climb

ērgā, prép. + acc. : towards, opposite (friendly);

ērgō, conj. : therefore; well, then, now;

ērĭpĭo, ere, ere, ripui, reptum : to snatch away, take by force; to rescue;

ērro, are : to wander, to wander or stray about, to wander up and down, to rove; to miss the right way, to lose one's self, go astray;

ērro, ōnis, m. : a wanderer, vagabond, vagrant, Of vagabond soldiers

ērrŏr, oris, m. : wandering; error; winding, maze; uncertainty; deception;

ērŭbēsco, ere, bui : to redden, blush, blush at; to blush for shame, be ashamed of;

ĕrus, i, m. : master, owner;

Ēsquĭlīna, ae, f. (porta) : the Esquiline gate

ĕt, conj. adv. : and, and even; also, even; (et ... et = both ... and);

ĕtĭam, adv. : - and also, besides/furthermore, in addition/as well; even, actually; yes/ - now too, as yet, still, even now; yet again; likewise; (particle); (et-iam);

Ĕtrūrĭa, ae, f. : Etruria

Ĕtrūsci, orum, m. : the Etruscans

Ĕtrūscus, a, um : of Etruria, Etruscan

Ēurōpa, ae, f. : Europe;

Ēurōpē, f. : Daughter of the Phoenician king Agenor, sister of Cadmus, and mother of Sarpedon and Minos by Jupiter, who, under the form of a bull, carried her off to Crete

ēurus, i, m. : east (or south east) wind; the east

ēvādo, ere, uasi, uasum : to evade, escape; to avoid;

ēvăgŏr, aris, ari : to wander forth, to roam about; to scatter or spread about, to extend

ēvānēsco, ere, euanui, - : to vanish/disappear; to pass/fade/die (away/out); to lapse; to become weak/void/forgotten;

ēvĕnĭo, ire, ueni, uentum : it happens, it turns out; come out, come forth;

ēvērro, ere, verri, versum : to sweep out

ēvērto, ere, uerti, uersum : to overturn, turn upside down; to overthrow, destroy, ruin;

ēvĭdēns, entis : apparent, visible, evident, manifest, plain, clear.

ēvīnco, ere, uici, uictum : to overcome, conquer, subdue, overwhelm, defeat utterly; to prevail, bring to pass;

ēx, prép. + abl. : out of, from; by reason of; according to; because of, as a result of;

ēxcēdo, ere, cessi, cessum : to pass, withdraw, exceed; to go away/out/beyond; to die;

ēxcēlsum, i, n. : an elevated station, position, in the highest

ēxcēlsus, a, um : lofty/high; tall; exalted; elevated; noble; of high position/rank/reputation;

ēxcīdo, ere, cidi, cisum : to cut down; to perish

ēxcĭpĭo, ere, cepi, ceptum : to take out; to remove; to follow; to receive; to ward off, relieve;

ēxcĭtātus, a, um : lively, vehement, excited, rising

ēxcĭto, are : to wake up, stir up; to cause; to raise, erect; incite; to excite, arouse;

ēxclāmo, are : to exclaim, shout; to cry out, call out;

ēxcūsātĭŏ, ionis, f. : excuse;

ēxcŭtĭo, ere, cussi, cussum : to shake out or off; to cast out; to search, examine;

ēxēmplŭm, i, n. : example, sample, specimen; instance; precedent, case; warning, deterrent; transcription;

ēxĕo,ire, ii, itum : - to come/go/sail/march/move out/forth/away, leave; to pass (away), expire/perish; - to discharge (fluid); to rise (river); to become visible; to issue/emerge/escape; to sprout;

ēxērcĕo, ere, cui, citum : to exercise, train, drill, practice; to enforce, administer; to cultivate;

ēxērcĭtātĭŏ, ionis, f. : exercise, training, practice; discipline;

ēxērcĭto, are : to practice, exercise, train hard, keep at work;

ēxērcĭtus, us, m. : army, infantry; swarm, flock;

ēxhāurĭo, ire, hausi, haustum : to draw out; to drain, drink up, empty; to exhaust, impoverish; to remove; to end;

ēxĭgŭum, i, n. : a little, a trifle. Adv. shortly, briefly; slightly, scantily, sparingly.

ēxĭgŭus, a, um : small; meager; dreary; a little, a bit of; scanty, petty, short, poor;

ēxĭlĭo, ire, ilui, ultum : to spring/leap/burst forth/out, leap up, start up, bound; to emerge into existence;

ēxĭlĭs, e : small, thin; poor;

ēxĭlĭŭm, ii, n. : exile, banishment; place of exile/retreat ; exiles (pl.), those exiled;

ēxĭmo, ere, emi, emptum : to remove/extract, take/lift out/off/away; to banish, get rid of; to free/save/release;

ēxīstĭmo, ēxīstŭmo, are : to value/esteem; to form/hold opinion/view; to think/suppose; to estimate; to judge/consider;

ēxĭtĭŭm, ii, n. : destruction, ruin; death; mischief;

ēxĭtus, us, m. : exit, departure; end, solution; death; outlet, mouth (of river);

ēxōrdĭŏr, iris, iri, exorsus sum : to begin a web, to lay the warp, to weave

ēxōrsa, orum, n. : a beginning, commencement, preamble

ēxpēcto, ĕre : peigner avec soin d'après

ēxpĕdĭo, ire, i(u)i , itum : to disengage, loose, set free; to be expedient; to procure, obtain, make ready;

ēxpĕdītus, a, um : unencumbered; without baggage; light armed;

ēxpēllo, ere, puli, pulsum : to drive out, expel, banish; to disown, reject;

ēxpĕrĭēns, entis : experienced, enterprising, active, industrious, used to

ēxpĕrĭēntĭa, ae, f. : trial, experiment; experience;

ēxpĕrĭŏr, iris, iri, expertus sum : to test, put to the test; to find out; to attempt, try; to prove, experience

ēxpĕto, ere, i, itum : to ask for; to desire; to aspire to; to demand; to happen; to fall on (person);

ēxplĭco, are, ui, itum (aui - atum) : to unfold, extend; to set forth, explain;

ēxpōno, ere, posui, positum : to set/put forth/out; to abandon, expose; to publish; to explain, relate; to disembark;

ēxprēssus, a, um : clearly exhibited, distinct, manifest, clear, plain, express, distinct, real, articulated with precision

ēxprĭmo, ere, pressi, pressum : to squeeze, squeeze/press out; to imitate, copy; to portray; to pronounce, express;

ēxprōmo, ere, prompsi, promptum : to bring/take out (from store), put out; to put to use, put in play; to disclose,

ēxpūgno, are : to assault, storm; to conquer, plunder; to accomplish; to persuade;

ēxsānguĭs, e : bloodless, pale, wan, feeble; frightened;

ēxsĭlĭo, ire, silui, sultum : to spring/leap/burst forth/out, leap up, start up, bound; to emerge into existence;

ēxsĭlĭŭm, ii, n. : exile, banishment; place of exile/retreat ; exiles (pl.), those exiled;

ēxsīsto, ere, stiti : to step out, come forth, emerge, appear, stand out, project; to arise; to come to light;

ēxspēcto, are, aui, atum : to lookout for, await; to expect, anticipate, hope for;

ēxsŭl, ulis, m. : a banished person, wanderer, exile.

ēxsŭlo, are : to be an exile or banished person, to live in exile; to be banished; to be a stranger; to banish, exile (a person);

ēxsūlto, are : to rejoice; to boast; to exalt; to jump about, let oneself go;

ēxsŭpĕro, are : I. Neutr., to mount up, appear above II. Act., to project or tower above any thing, to surmount, rise above, exceed

ēxtēmplō, ēxtēmpŭlō, adv. : immediately, forthwith;

ēxtĕro, ere, trīvi, trītum : to rub out, bring out by rubbing; to remove by rubbing, to rub off, away

ēxtĕrrĕo, ere, terrui, territus : to strike with terror, scare;

ēxtŏllo, ere, extuli, - : to raise; lift up; to extol, advance; to erect (building);

ēxtrā, prép. + acc. : outside of, beyond, without, beside; except;

ēxtrēmum, i, n. : an end, the end

ēxtrēmus, a, um : rear (pl.);

ēxŭvĭae, arum f. pl. : that which is stripped, drawn, taken off, clothing, equipments, arms

ēxŭvĭum, ii, n. : spoils, booty

făbrīlĭs, e : of or belonging to an artificer, of the sculptor, artist, neutr. subst.

făbŭla, ae, f. : story, tale, fable; play, drama; [fabulae! => rubbish!, nonsense!];

făcĭa, ae, f. : portrait

făcĭes, ei, f. : shape, face, look; presence, appearance; beauty; achievement;

făcĭlĭs, e : easy, easy to do, without difficulty, ready, quick, good natured, courteous;

făcĭlĭtās, atis, f. : facility; readiness; good nature; levity; courteousness;

făcĭnĕrōsus, a, um : wicked, criminal; villainous; vicious; (facinosus);

făcĭnŭs, oris, n. : deed; crime; outrage;

făcĭo, ere, feci, factum : to make /build /construct /create /cause/do; to have built/made; to fashion; to work (metal);

făctĭŏ, onis, f. : party, faction; partisanship;

făctŭm, i, n. : fact, deed, act; achievement;

făllāx, acis : deceitful, treacherous; misleading, deceptive; false, fallacious; spurious;

făllo, ere, fĕfĕlli, fālsum (fāllĭtum) : to deceive; to slip by; to disappoint; to be mistaken, beguile, drive away; to fail; cto heat;

fālsē, adv. : by mistake, untruly, erroneously, unfaithfully, wrongly, falsely

fālsum, i, n. : falsehood, fraud

fālsus, a, um : wrong, lying, fictitious, spurious, false, deceiving, feigned, deceptive;

fālx, falcis, f. : sickle. scythe; pruning knife; curved blade; hook for tearing down walls;

fāma, ae, f. : rumor; reputation; tradition; fame, public opinion, ill repute; report, news;

fămēs, f. : hunger; famine; want; craving;

fămĭlĭa, ae, f. : household; household of slaves; family; clan; religious community (Ecc);

fămĭlĭārĭs, e : member of household (family/servant/esp. slave); familiar acquaintance/friend;

fămĭlĭāris, m. : a servant.

fămĭlĭārĭtās, atis, f. : intimacy; close friendship; familiarity;

fāmōsus, a, um : famous, noted, renowned; talked of; infamous, notorious; slanderous, libelous;

fār, farris, n. : husked wheat; grain, spelt; coarse meal, grits; sacrificial meal; dog's bread;

fās, n. indécl. : divine/heaven's law/will/command; that which is right/lawful/moral/allowed;

fāstīgĭŭm, ii, n. : peak, summit, top; slope, declivity, descent; gable, roof; sharp point, tip;

fătĕŏr, eris, eri, fassus sum : to admit, confess (w/ACC); to disclose; to acknowledge; to praise

fātŭm, i, n. : utterance, oracle; fate, destiny; natural term of life; doom, death, calamity;

fātŭs, us, m. : A word, saying

fāucēs, ium, m. pl. : the upper part of the throat, from the root of the tongue to the entrance of the gullet, the pharynx, throat, gullet

fāux, cf. fauces : the upper part of the throat, from the root of the tongue to the entrance of the gullet, the pharynx, throat, gullet

făvĕo, ere, faui, fautum : to favor (w/DAT), befriend, support, back up;

fāx, facis, f. : torch, firebrand, fire; flame of love; torment;

fēlīx, icis : happy; blessed; fertile; favorable; lucky; successful, fruitful;

fēmĭna, ae, f. : woman; female;

fēmĭnĕus, a, um : woman's; female, feminine; proper to/typical of a woman; effeminate, cowardly;

fĕnēstra, fĕstra, ae, f. : window, opening for light; loophole, breach; orifice; inlet; opportunity;

fĕra, ae, f. : wild beast/animal;

fĕrē, adv. : almost; about, nearly; generally, in general; (w/negatives) hardly ever;

fĕrĭo, ire : to rest from work/labor; to keep/celebrate holiday;

fērmēnto, āvi, ātum, 1 : to cause to rise, ferment;, pass., to rise, ferment.

fĕro, fers, ferre, tuli, latum : to bring, bear; to tell/speak of; to consider; to carry off, win, receive, produce; to get;

fĕrōcĭtĕr, adv. : fiercely

fĕrōx, ocis : wild, bold; warlike; cruel; defiant, arrogant;

fĕrrĕus, a, um : iron, made of iron; cruel, unyielding; (blue);

fĕrrŭm, i, n. : iron; any tool of iron; weapon, sword;

fĕrtĭlĭs, e : Fruitful, fertile

fĕrus, a, um : wild, savage; uncivilized; untamed; fierce;

fĕrus, i : wild beast/animal; wild/untamed horse/boar

fĕrvĭdus, a, um : glowing; boiling hot; fiery, torrid, roused, fervid; hot blooded;

fĕssus, a, um : tired, wearied, fatigued, exhausted; worn out, weak, feeble, infirm, sick;

fĕstīno, are : to hasten, hurry;

fīctum, i, n. : a deception, falsehood, fiction, pretences

fīctus, a, um : feigned, fictitious, false, falsehood, false

fĭdēlĭa, ae, f. : an earthen vessel, pot.

fĭdēlĭs, e : faithful/loyal/devoted; true/trustworthy/dependable/reliable; constant/lasting;

fĭdēs, ei, f. : faith, loyalty; honesty; credit; confidence, trust, belief; good faith

fĭdĕs, ium, f. pl. : chord, instrument string; constellation Lyra; stringed instrument (pl.); lyre;

fīdo, is ere, fisus sum : to trust (in), have confidence (in) (w/DAT or ABL);

fīdus, a, um : faithful, loyal; trusting, confident;

fīgo, fīvo, ere, fixi, fixum : to fasten, fix; to pierce, transfix; to establish;

fīlĭa, ae, f. : daughter;

fīlĭus, ii, m. : son;

fīlŭm, i, n. : thread, string, filament, fiber; texture, style, nature;

fīnālĭs, e : of or relating to boundaries

fīndo, ere, fīdi, fissum : to cleave, split, part, separate, divide

fīngo, ere, finxi, fictum : to mold, form, shape; to create, invent; to produce; to imagine; to compose; to devise, - to adapt, transform into; to modify (appearance/character/behavior); to groom;

fīnĭo, ire, iui, itum : to limit, end; to finish; to determine, define; to mark out the boundaries;

fīnĭs, m. f. : boundary, end, limit, goal; (pl.) country, territory, land;

fīo, fieri, factus sum : to happen, come about; to result (from); to take place, be held, occur, arise (event); to develop;

fīrmo, are : to strengthen, harden; to support; to declare; to prove, confirm, establish;

fīrmus, a, um : firm/steady; substantial /solid /secure /safe; strong/robust/sturdy/stout/ - loyal /staunch/true/constant; stable/mature; valid /convincing/well founded;

fīxus, a, um : fixed, fast, immovable, established, settled, fixed, fast

flăgro, are : to be on fire; to blaze, flame, burn; to be inflamed/excited;

flāmma, ae, f. : flame, blaze; ardor, fire of love; object of love;

flāmmo, are : to inflame, set on fire; to excite;

flāvĕo, ēre, intr. : to be golden yellow, gold-colored, to be light yellow, part. pres.

flāvus, a, um : yellow, golden, gold colored; flaxen, blond; golden-haired (Latham);

flāvus, i, m. : gold pieces

flēcto, ere, flexi, flexum : to bend, curve, bow; to turn, curl; to persuade, prevail on, soften;

flĕo, ere, fleui, fletum : to cry for; to cry, weep;

flōrĕo, ere, ui : to flourish, blossom, be prosperous; to be in one's prime;

flōrus, a, um : shining, bright

flōs, oris, m. : flower, blossom; youthful prime;

flūctus, us, m. : wave; disorder; flood, flow, tide, billow, surge; turbulence, commotion;

flūmĕn, inis, n. : river, stream; any flowing fluid; flood; onrush; [adverso ~ => against

flūmĭnĕus, a, um : of or in, belonging to a river, river

flŭo, ere, fluxi, fluxum : to flow, stream; to emanate, proceed from; to fall gradually;

flŭvĭus, i, m. : river, stream; running water;

fōcŭlŭm, i, n. : brazier

fōedo, are : - to defile; to pollute; to soil, stain, make filthy/unclean; to contaminate; to corrupt; - to make (punishment) horrible/barbarous; to mangle/hack/mutilate, ravage (land);

fōedus, a, um : foul, filthy, loathsome, ugly, unseemly, detestable, abominable, horrible

fōedŭs, deris, n. : treaty, league, formal agreement (between states), alliance; peace, amity; - bond/tie (friendship/kinship/hospitality); law/limit (imposed by nature)

fōns, fontis, m. : spring, fountain, well; source/fount; principal cause; font; baptistry;

fōr, aris, fari, fatus sum : to speak, say

fōrās, adv. : out of doors, abroad, forth, out;

fōrēnt, subj. : = essent

fŏrĭs, f. : a door, gate;, the two leaves of a door

fōrma, ae, f. : form, figure, appearance; beauty; mold, pattern;

fōrmīdō, inis, f. : - fear/terror/alarm; religious dread/awe; thing/reason which scares, bogy/ - rope strung with feathers used by hunters to scare game;

fōrmo, are : to form, shape, fashion, model;

fōrmōsus, fōrmōnsus, a, um : beautiful, finely formed, handsome, fair; having fine appearance/form;

fŏro, are : to bore, pierce

fōrs, fortis, f. : chance, hap, luck, hazard. Fors

fōrsĭtăn, adv. : maaybe, perhaps

fōrtāssē, adv. : perhaps, possibly; it may be;

fōrtĕ, adv. : by chance; perhaps, perchance; as luck would have it;

fōrtīs, e : strong, powerful, mighty, vigorous, firm, steadfast, courageous, brave, bold;

fōrtĭtĕr, adv. : strongly; bravely; boldly;

fōrtūna, ae, f. : chance, luck, fate; prosperity; condition, wealth, property;

fōrtūno, are : to make prosperous, fortunate, to make happy, to prosper, bless

fŏrŭm, i, n. : market; forum (in Rome); court of justice;

fŏrus, i, m. : gangway in a ship; row of benches erected for games/circus; cell of bees;

frāctus, a, um : interrupted, irregular, weakened, weak, feeble, faint

frăgŏr, oris, m. : noise, crash;

frāngo, ere, fregi, fractum : to break, shatter, crush; to dishearten, subdue, weaken; to move, discourage;

frātĕr, tris, m. : brother; cousin;

frātērnus, a, um : brotherly/brother's; of/belonging to a brother; fraternal; friendly; of cousin;

frāudo, are : - to cheat/defraud/swindle; to deprive deceitfully; to baffle, make ineffectual; - embezzle, take (money) dishonestly, steal; to violate; to evade;

frēno, are : to brake, curb, restrain, check;

frēnŭm, i, m. : bridle/harness/rein/bit; harnessed horses/team; check/restraint/brake; mastery;

frĕquēns, entis : crowded; numerous, full, frequented, populous; repeated, frequent, constant;

frĕquēnto, are : to frequent; to repeat often; to haunt; to throng; to crowd; to celebrate;

frĕtŭm, i, n. : sea; narrow sea, straits;

frĕtus, a, um : relying on, trusting to, supported by (w/ABL);

frīgĭdus, a, um : cold, cool, chilly, frigid; lifeless, indifferent, dull;

frīgŭs, oris, n. : cold; cold weather, winter; frost;

frōns, ontis, f. : forehead, brow; face; look; front; fore part of anything

frūmēntŭm, i, n. : grain; crops;

frūstrā, adv. : in vain; for nothing, to no purpose;

frūstro, are : to reject; delay; to rob/defraud/cheat; to pretend; to refute (argument); to corrupt/falsify;

frūstrŏr, aris, ari : to deceive, dis appoint, trick, elude, frustrate, failed to obey, dies on their lips, To miss the mark, throw in vain, To make vain, make useless

fŭga, ae, f. : fugue (music);

fŭgĭēns, entis : fleeing, fleeting, receding, fermenting.mdash;—Plur. n, what is hard to obtain, Fleet, rapid, avoiding, averse to

fŭgĭo, ere, fugi : to flee, fly, run away; to avoid, shun; to go into exile;

fŭgĭtīvus, a, um : fleeing away, fugitive;

fŭgĭtīvus, i, m. : fugitive;

fŭgo, are : to put to flight, rout; to chase away; to drive into exile;

fūlgēns, entis : shining, bright, dazzling, glistening, with gleaming helmet, illustrious, glorious

fūlgĕo, ere, fulsi : to flash, shine; to glow, gleam, glitter, shine forth, be bright;

fūndāmēntŭm, i, n. : foundation; beginning; basis;

fūndo, are : to lay the bottom, keel, foundation (of a thing), to found; to establish, found, begin; to confirm;

fūndo, ere, fusi, fusum : to pour, pour out, shed;

fūndus, i, m. : farm; piece of land, estate; bottom, lowest part; foundation; an authority;

fūnĕbrĭs, e : funeral, deadly, fatal; funereal;

fūnŭs, eris, n. : burial, funeral; funeral rites; ruin; corpse; death;

fŭrēns, tis : raging, wild, mad, furious, distracted, inspired

fŭrĭātus, a, um : enraged, maddened

fŭrĭo, āvi, ātum, 1 : to drive mad, to madden, enrage, infuriate, P. a.

fŭrĭōsus, a, um : furious, mad, frantic, wild;

fŭro, ere : to rave, rage; to be mad/furious; to be wild;

fŭrŏr, aris, ari : to rave, rage; to be mad/furious; to be wild

fŭrŏr, oris, m. : madness, rage, fury, frenzy; passionate love;

fūrtīvus, a, um : stolen; secret, furtive;

fŭtūrus, a, um, part. fut. de sum : about to be; future;

Găbīnus, a, um : of or belonging to Gabii, Gabine, leading from Rome to Gabii, quarried at Gabii

Gāĭus, i, m. : Gaius (Roman praenomen); (abb. C.);

gălĕa, ae, f. : helmet;

Gālli, orum, m. : -I. the Gallic nation, the Gauls, both beyond the Rhine and in Upper Italy; afterwards also in Phrygia as -II. the priests of Cybele, so called because of their raving

Gāllĭus, ii, m. : name of a Roman gens

Gāllus, a, um : Gallic

Gāllus, i, m. : -I. a Gaul -II. a priest of Cybele- III.a tributary of the Sagaris of Phrygia and Bithynia, whose water, according to the fable, made those who drank it mad, Kadsha Su, Gouml;kssu -IV. a Roman surname; a Roman poet, a friend of Virgi

gāllus, i, m. : cock, rooster; Gallus, Gallic, of Gaul/the Gauls; class of gladiator w/Gallic armor

Gāngētis, ĭdis, f. : of the Ganges

gārrŭlus, a, um : talkative, loquacious; chattering, garrulous; blabbing; that betrays secrets;

gāza, ae, f. : treasure (royal);

gĕmĭni, orum, m. : twins; as a constellation Gemini

gĕmĭnus, a, um : twin, double; twin-born; both;

gĕmĭtus, us, m. : groan, sigh; roaring;

gĕmma, ae, f. : bud; jewel, gem, precious stone; amber; cup (material); seal, signet; game

gĕmmo, are : To put forth buds, to bud or gem

gĕmo, ere, gemui, gemitum : to moan, groan; to lament (over); to grieve that; to give out a hollow sound (music, hit);

gĕnĕtrīx, tricis, f. : mother, ancestress;

gĕnĭtŏr, oris, m. : father; creator; originator;

gēns, gentis, f. : tribe, clan; nation, people

gĕnŭ, us, n. : knee;

gĕnŭs, eris, n. : - birth/descent/origin; race/family/house/stock/ancestry; offspring/descent;

gĕro, ere, gessi, gestum : to bear, carry, wear; to carry on; to manage, govern; (se gerere = to conduct oneself);

gīgno, gĕno, ere, genui, genitum : to give birth to, bring forth, bear; to beget; to be born (PASSIVE);

glădĭus, i, m. : sword;

glōrĭa, ae, f. : glory, fame; ambition; renown; vainglory, boasting;

grădĭŏr, eris, i, gressus sum, intr. : to take steps, to step, walk, go

grădus, us, m. : step; position;

Grāeci, orum, m. : the Grecians, Greeks

Grāecĭa, ae, f. : Greece;

Grāecus, a, um : Greek; the Greeks (pl.);

Grāii, orum, m. : the Grecians, Greeks

Grājus, a, um : Greek

grāmĕn, inis, n. : grass, turf; herb; plant;

grăphĭŭm, i, n. : stylus, pen used for writing on wax tablets; modern pen (Cal);

grăssŏr, aris, ari : to march on, advance; to roam in search of victims, prowl; to proceed; to run riot

grātēs, -, f. pl. : thanks (pl.); (esp. to gods); thanksgivings; [~es agere => give thanks];

grātĭa, ae, f. : popularity/esteem/credit (w/bona); partiality/favoritism; unpopularity (w/ -favor/goodwill/kindness/friendship; influence; gratitude; thanks (pl.); - agreeableness, charm; grace; [Doctor Gratiae => St. Augustine of Hippo];

grātus, a, um : pleasing, acceptable, agreeable, welcome; dear, beloved; grateful, thankful;

grăvĭs, e : heavy; painful; important; serious; pregnant; grave, oppressive, burdensome;

grăvĭtās, atis, f. : weight; dignity; gravity; importances, oppressiveness; pregnancy; sickness;

grăvĭtĕr, adv. : violently; deeply; severely; reluctantly; [ferre ~ => to be vexed/upset];

grăvo, are : to show/bear with reluctance/annoyance; to be burdened/vexed; to take amiss; to hesitate;

grēssus, us, m. : going; step; the feet (pl.);

gūrgēs, itis, m. : "whirlpool; raging abyss; gulf, the sea; ""flood"", ""stream"";"

hăbĕo, ere, bui, bitum : to have, hold, consider, think, reason; to manage, keep; to spend/pass (time);

hăbĭlĭs, e : handy, manageable; apt, fit;

hăbĭto, are : to inhabit, dwell; to live, stay;

hăbĭtus, a, um : disposed, inclined, Well kept, fleshy, corpulent

hāerĕo, ere, haesi, haesum : to stick, adhere, cling to; to hesitate; to be in difficulties (sticky situation?);

hāesĭto, are, intr. : to stick fast, remain fixed

hāsta, ae, f. : spear/lance/javelin; spear stuck in ground for public auction/centumviral

hāud, hāu, hāut, adv. neg. : not, not at all, by no means; not (as a particle);

Hēctŏr, oris, m. : Hector; (chief Trojan hero);

Hēctŏrĕus, a, um : of or belonging to Hector;, of the Trojans, of the Romans; Hectorean; Trojan; Roman

Hĕcŭba, ae, f. : Hécube (femme de Priam)

Hĕlĭcōnĭus, a, um : of or belonging to Helicon, Heliconian

Hēr, ēris, m. : a Pamphylian, who, according to legend, rose from the dead

Hērēnnĭus, i, m. : Herennius

Hērmīnĭus, ii, m. : Name of an ancient Roman family of Etruscan origin

Hēspĕrĭa, ae, f. : the land of the west, Italy, Spain

Hēspĕrĭus, a, um : western

hĕu, interj. : oh! ah! alas! (an expression of dismay or pain);

hīc, adv. : here, in this place; in the present circumstances;

hīc, haec, hoc, adj. pron. : this; these

hĭēms, hĭēmps, hiemis, m. : winter, winter time; rainy season; cold, frost; storm, stormy weather;

hīnc, adv. : from here, from this source/cause; hence, henceforth;

hīstŏrĭa, ae, f. : history; account; story;

hōc, adv. : -I. neutr. -II. to this place, hither

hŏdĭē, adv. : today, nowadays; at the present time;

Hŏmērus, i, m. : Homer, epic poet

hŏmŏ, minis, m. : man, human being, person, fellow; [novus homo => nouveau riche];

hŏnŏr, oris, m. : honor; respect/regard; mark of esteem, reward; dignity/grace; public office;

hŏnōrātus, a, um : honored, respected; honorable, respectable, distinguished.

hŏnōro, are : to respect, honor;

hŏnōrus, a, um : Worthy of honor, honorable

hōra, ae, f. : hour; time; season; [Horae => Seasons];

Hŏrātĭus, ii, m. : Horatius

hŏrrēndus, a, um : horrible, dreadful, terrible;

hŏrrĕo, ere, horrui, - : to dread, shrink from, shudder at; to stand on end, bristle; to have rough appearance;

hōrrēsco, is ere, horrui, - : to dread, become terrified; to bristle up; to begin to shake/tremble/shudder/shiver;

hōrrĭbĭlĭs, e : awful, horrible, terrible; monstrous; rough;

hōrrĭdus, a, um : wild, frightful, rough, bristly, standing on end, unkempt; grim; horrible;

hōrrŏr, oris, m. : shivering, dread, awe rigidity (from cold, etc);

hōrtŏr, aris, ari : to encourage; to cheer; to incite; to urge; to exhort

hōrtus, i, m. : garden, fruit/kitchen garden; pleasure garden; park (pl.);

hōspĕs, itis, m. : of relation between host and guest; that hosts; that guests; foreign, alien;

hōspĭta, ae, f. : female guest; hostess, wife of host; landlady; stranger, alien;

hōspĭtālĭs, e : of or for a guest; hospitable;

hōspĭtĭŭm, i, n. : hospitality, entertainment; lodging; guest room/lodging; inn;

hōspĭtus, a, um : hospitable/harboring, affording hospitality; received as guest; foreign/alien;

hōstĭa, ae, f. : victim, sacrifice; sacrificial offering/animal;

hōstīle, n. : hostile country, the enemy's land, soil

hōstīlĭs, e : hostile, enemy; of/belonging to an enemy; involving/performed by an enemy;

hōstīlĭtĕr, adv. : in an unfriendly/hostile way, in the manner of an enemy;

hōstĭo, īre : -I. to make even, return like for like, to recompense, requite -II. to strike

hōstĭs, m. : enemy (of the state); stranger, foreigner; the enemy (pl.);

hūc, adv. : here, to this place; to this point;

hŭmĕrus, i, m. : upper arm, shoulder;

hūmī, adv. : on/to the ground;

hŭmo, are : to cover with earth, to inter, bury.

hŭmus, i, f. : ground, soil, earth, land, country;

Hȳpănĭs, m. : A river of European Sarmatia, Boug

Ĭāso, Ĭāsōn, ŏnis, m. : Jason (chef des Argonautes; tyran de Phères)

ĭbĭ, adv. : there, in that place; thereupon;

ĭcĭo, īci, ictum, 3 : to strike, hit, smite, stab, sting

īco, ere, ici, ictum : to hit, strike; to smite, stab, sting; [foedus ~ => conclude/make a treaty, league]);

īctus, us, m. : blow, stroke; musical/metrical beat; measure (music);

Īda, ae, f. : A high mountain in Crete, where the infant Jupiter was hid, watched over by the Curetes, and fed by Amalthea

Īdās, ae, m. : Son of Aphareus, king of Messene, who took part in the Calydonian boar-hunt

Īdē, f. : A high mountain in Crete, where the infant Jupiter was hid, watched over by the Curetes, and fed by Amalthea;, Psiloriti, no.

Īdĕm, eadem, idem, adj. pron. : the same

Īdĕō, adv. : therefore, for the reason that, for that reason;

ĭgĭtŭr, adv., conj. : therefore (postpositive), so/then; consequently; accordingly; well/in that

īgnārus, a, um : ignorant; unaware, having no experience of; senseless; strange;

īgnāvus, a, um : lazy/idle/sluggish; spiritless; cowardly, faint-hearted; ignoble, mean;

īgnĭo, īvi or ii, ītum, 4 : to ignite, set on fire, make red-hot

īgnĭs, m. : fire, brightness; passion, glow of passion;

īgnōro, are : not to know; to be unfamiliar with; to disregard; to ignore; to be ignorant of;

Īlĭăcus, a, um : Homer's Iliad, of Rome

īlĭcĕt, adv. : you may go/off with you; it's over; at once; [~ malam crucem => to Hell with];

īllā, adv. : in that way, in that direction, there

īllĕ, illa, illud, pron. : that; those (pl.); also DEMONST; that person/thing; the well known; the former;

īllĕcĕbra, ae, f. : allurement, enticement, means of attraction; incitement; enticement by magic;

īlli, adv. : in that place, yonder, there

īllīc, adv. : in that place, there, over there;

īllīnc, īllĭm, adv. : there, in that place, on that side; from there;

īllō, adv. : to that place, thither

īllūc, adv. : there, thither, to that place/point;

ĭmāgō, inis, f. : likeness, image, appearance; statue; idea; echo; ghost, phantom;

īmbēllĭs, e : unwarlike; not suited or ready for war;

īmbĕr, bris, m. : rain, shower, storm; shower of liquid/snow/hail/missiles; water (in general);

īmbŭo, ere, bui, butum : to wet, soak, dip; to give initial instruction (in);

īmmānĭtās, atis, f. : brutality, savage character, frightfulness; huge/vast size; barbarity; monster;

īmmĕmŏr, (immemoris) oris : forgetful (by nature); lacking memory; heedless (of obligations/consequences);

īmmēnsus, a, um : immeasurable, immense/vast/boundless/unending; infinitely great; innumerable;

īmmīscĕo, ere, miscui, mixtum : to mix in, mingle; to confuse;

īmmītto, ere, misi, missum : to send in/to/into/against; to cause to go; to insert; to hurl/throw in; to let go/in; allow

īmmŏdēstĭa, ae, f. : want of restraint; immodest

īmmōrtālĭs, e : immortal, god;

īmmūndus, a, um : dirty, filthy, foul; (morally); unclean, impure; untidy/slovenly/squalid; evil;

īmpĕdīmēntŭm, i, n. : hindrance, impediment; heavy baggage (of an army) (pl.);

īmpēllo, ere, puli, pulsum : to drive/persuade/impel; to urge on/action; to push/thrust/strike against; to overthrow;

īmpēndo, ere, pendi, pensum : to expend, spend; devote (to);

īmpĕrĭŭm, ii, n. : command; authority; rule, supreme power; the state, the empire;

īmpĕro, are : to order, command, levy; to rule (over) (w/DAT);

īmpĕs, impĕs (= impetus), impetis, m. : violence, vehemence, force

īmpĕtro, are : to obtain/procure (by asking/request/entreaty); to succeed/achieve/be granted;

īmpĕtus, us, m. : attack, assault, charge; attempt; impetus, vigor; violent mental urge, fury;

īmpĭgĕr, gra, grum : active, energetic;

īmplĕo, ere, eui, etum : to fill up; to satisfy, fulfill; to fill, finish, complete; to spend (time);

īmplĭco, ere, plic(a)ui, plic(i or a)tum : - to implicate; to involve/engage/entangle/embroil; to interweave/fold/twine w/itself; - to interweave/interlace/intertwine; to clasp/grasp ; to unite/join/mix; - (PASS) to be intimately associated/connected/related/bound; to be a tangle/maze;

īmpōrto, are : to bring in, convey; to import; to bring about, cause;

īmprŏbo, are : to disapprove of, express disapproval of, condemn; to reject;

īmprŏbus, a, um : wicked/flagrant; morally unsound; greedy/rude; immoderate; disloyal; shameless;

īmprōvĭdus, a, um : improvident; thoughtless; unwary;

īmprōvīsō, adv. : on a sudden, unexpectedly

īmprōvīsum, i, n. : that which is unforeseen, an emergency, de, unexpectedly, suddenly, ex

īmprōvīsus, a, um : unforeseen/unexpected; [de improviso => unexpectedly/suddenly, without

īmpūbēs, eris : below age of puberty, under age, youthful; beardless; chaste/virgin/celibate;

īmpŭdīcĭtĭa, ae, f. : sexual impurity (often of homosexuality);

īmpŭdīcus, a, um : shameless; unchaste; flaunting accepted sexual code;

īmus, a, um : inmost, deepest, bottommost, last; (inferus); [~ vox => highest treble];

īn, īndŭ, prép. + acc. or + abl. : in, into, on

īnānĕ, n. : an empty space, a void; that which is empty or vain; emptiness, vanity, inanity

īnānĭāe, arum, f. : emptiness

ĭnānĭo, ire, īvi (ĭi), ītum : to make empty, to empty out, evacuate

ĭnānĭs, e : void, empty, hollow; vain; inane, foolish;

īncēndo, ere, cendi, censum : - to set on fire; to set fire to, kindle, burn; to cause to flame/burn; to keep fire - to scorch; to make fiery hot (fever/thirst); to light up; to cause to glow; to intensify;

īncēnsus, a, um : -I. inflamed, burning, hot -II. not estimated, not assessed, unregistered

īncērto, are : to render uncertain;

īncērtus, a, um : uncertain; unsure, inconstant, variable; doubtful;

īncēstē, adv. : impurely, sinfully

īncēstus, a, um : unchaste; unholy, unclean, religiously impure, polluted, defiled, sinful, lewd;

īncĭdo, ere, cidi (in + cado) : to fall into or upon a thing; to fall, light upon;

īncīdo, ere, cidi, cisum (in+caedo) : to cut into, cut open; to inscribe, engrave inscription; to break off;

īncĭpĭo, ere, cepi, ceptum : to begin; to start, undertake;

īncŏlŭmĭs, e : unharmed, uninjured; alive, safe; unimpaired;

īncŏmĭtātus, a, um : unaccompanied;

īncrĕpo, ere, crepitum : to rattle, snap, clash, roar, twang, make noise; to strike noisily;

īncŭmbo, ere, cubui, -cubitum : to lean forward/over/on, press on; to attack, apply force; to fall on (one's sword);

īncūrro, ere, curri, cursum : to run into or towards, attack, invade; to meet (with); to befall;

īncūrsus, us, m. : assault, attack; raid;

īncūrvo, are : to bend, bow, crook, curve, part. pass.;

īncūrvus, a, um : crooked, curved;

īncūso, are : to accuse, blame, criticize, condemn;

īndĕ, adv. : thence, thenceforth; from that place/time/cause; thereupon;

īndĭcĭŭm, ii, n : evidence (before a court); information, proof; indication;

īndĭco, ere, dixi, dictum : to declare publicly; to proclaim, announce; to appoint; to summon

īndīgnĭtās, atis, f. : vileness, baseness, shamelessness; outrageousness; indignity, humiliation;

īndīgnus, a, um : unworthy, undeserving, undeserved; unbecoming; shameful; intolerable; cruel;

īndo, ere, indidi, inditum : to put in or on; to introduce;

īndŏmĭtus, a, um : untamed; untamable, fierce;

īndūco, ere, duxi, ductum : to lead in, bring in (performers); to induce, influence; to introduce;

īndūlgēns, entis : indulgent; kind, mild; gracious; bestowing favor; partial/addicted to (doing);

īndūlgēntĭa, ae, f. : indulgence, remission before God of temporal punishment for sin;

īndūlgĕo, ere, dulsi, dultum : to indulge; to be indulgent/lenient/kind; to grant/bestow; to gratify oneself; to give in to;

īndŭo, ere, indui, indutum : to put on, clothe, cover; to dress oneself in; [se induere => to impale oneself];

īndūstrĭa, ae, f. : industry; purpose/diligence; purposeful/diligent activity; purposefulness

īndūstrĭus, a, um : hard working

īnĕo, ire, ii, itum : to enter; to undertake; to begin; to go in; to enter upon; [consilium ~ => form a plan];

īnērmĭs, e : unarmed, without weapons; defenseless; toothless, without a sting;

īnērmus, a, um : unarmed, without weapons; defenseless; toothless, without a sting;

īnērs, inertis : helpless, weak, inactive, inert, sluggish, stagnant; unskillful, incompetent;

īnērtĭa, ae, f. : ignorance; inactivity; laziness, idleness, sloth;

īnēxspēctātus, īnēxpēctātus, a, um : unexpected

īnfāmĭa, ae, f. : disgrace, dishonor; infamy;

īnfāmĭs, e : notorious, disreputable, infamous;

īnfāns, antis : infant, child

īnfāns, antis, m. : speechless, inarticulate; new born; childish, foolish;

īnfēlīx, icis : unfortunate, unhappy, wretched; unlucky, inauspicious; unproductive (plant);

īnfēnsus, a, um : hostile, bitterly hostile, enraged;

īnfĕri, orum, m. : underworld, spirits of the dead.

īnfĕrĭāe, arum, f. pl. : offerings to the dead (pl.)

īnfĕrĭŏr, oris : lower

īnfĕrĭus, a, um : that is offered, sacrificed

īnfĕro, ferre, tuli, illatum : - to bring/carry in, import; to advance, bring/march/step/move forward; to impel, urge;

īnfĕrus, a, um : below, beneath, underneath; of hell; vile; lower, further down; lowest, last;

īnfēsto, are : to vex (w/attacks), harass, molest; to make unsafe, disturb; to infest; to damage, impair;

īnfēstus, a, um : unsafe, dangerous; hostile; disturbed, molested, infested, unquiet;

īnfĭdus, a, um : writing without faith; writing faithlessly;

īnfĭmum, i, n. : the lowest part, bottom

īnfĭmus, īnfŭmus, a, um : lowest, deepest, furtherest down/from the surface; humblest; vilest, meanest;

īnfīnītus, a, um : boundless, unlimited, endless; infinite;

īnfīrmus, a, um : - fragile/frail/feeble; unwell /sick /infirm; untrustworthy;

īnflāmmo, are : to set on fire, inflame, kindle; to excite;

īnfŭla, ae, f. : band; fillet; woolen headband knotted with ribbons;

īngĕmĭno, are : to redouble; to increase in intensity;

īngĕnĭōsus, a, um : clever, ingenious; naturally suited (to); having natural abilities/talents;

īngĕnĭŭm, ii, n. : nature, innate quality; natural disposition/capacity; character; talent;

īngēns, entis : not natural, immoderate; huge, vast, enormous; mighty; remarkable, momentous;

īngrātus, a, um : unpleasant; ungrateful; thankless;

īnĭcĭo, ere, ieci, iectum : to hurl/throw/strike in/into; to inject; to put on; to inspire, instill (feeling, etc);

īnĭmīcĭtĭa, ae, f.: unfriendliness, enmity, hostility;

īnĭmīco, 1 : to make enemies, to set at variance.

īnĭmīcus, a, um : unfriendly, hostile, harmful;

īnĭmīcus, i, m. : enemy (personal), foe

īnĭtĭŭm, ii, n. : beginning, commencement; entrance; [ab initio => from the beginning];

īnjĭcĭo, ere, ieci, iectum : to hurl/throw/strike in/into; to inject; to put on; to inspire, instill (feeling, etc);

īnjūrĭa, ae, f. : injury; injustice, wrong, offense; insult, abuse; sexual assault;

īnjūrĭus, a, um : unjust, harsh;

īnjūssus, us, m. : without command

īnnŏcēntĭa, ae, f. : harmlessness; innocence, integrity;

īnnŭmĕrus, a, um : innumerable, countless, numberless; without number; immense;

īnŏpĭa, ae, f. : lack, need; poverty, destitution, dearth, want, scarcity;

īnŏps, opis : weak, poor, needy, helpless; lacking, destitute (of), meager;

īnquăm, v. : it is said, one says;

īnquĭnātus, a, um : befouled, polluted.

īnquĭno, are : "to daub; to stain, pollute; to soil; to ""smear"";"

īnquĭt, vb. says

īnsānĭa, ae, f. : insanity, madness; folly, mad extravagance;

īnsānĭo, ere, i : to be mad, act crazily;

īnsānus, a, um : unsound in mind.

īnscĭus, a, um : not knowing, ignorant; unskilled;

īnsēcto, are : to pursue, pass., pursued

īnsēctŏr, aris, ari : to pursue

īnsĕquŏr, eris, i, secutus sum : suivre, poursuivre

īnsĭdĕo, ere, insedi, insessum : to be fixed/stamped in; to adhere to; to grip; to take possession of; to hold/occupy;

īnsĭdĭāe, arum, f. pl. : ambush/ambuscade (pl.); plot; treachery, treacherous attack/device; trap/snare;

īnsĭdĭātŏr, ōris, m. : a soldier lying in ambush

īnsīdo, ere, sedi, sessum : to sit/settle on; to occupy/seize, hold (position); to penetrate, sink in; to merge into;

īnsīgnē, n. : mark, emblem, badge; ensign, honor, badge of honor;

īnsīgnĭo, ire, īvi (ĭi), ītum : to put a mark upon, to mark; to distinguish, marked with some bodily defect, to distinguish one's self

īnsīgnĭs, e : conspicuous, manifest, eminent, notable, famous, distinguished, outstanding;

īnsīmŭlo, are : to make a plausible charge, against a person, to make suspected, charge, accuse, blame, to invent a charge, bear false witness against

īnsŏlēns, entis : haughty, arrogant, insolent; immoderate, extravagant;

īnspīro, are : to inspire; to excite, inflame; to instill, implant; to breathe into; to blow upon/into;

īnstāuro, are : to renew, repeat, restore;

īnsto, are, stiti, staturus : to pursue, threaten; to approach, press hard; to be close to (w/DAT); to stand in/on;

īnstrūmēntŭm, i, n. : tool, tools; equipment, apparatus; instrument; means; document (leg.), deed;

īnstrŭo, ere, struxi, structum : to construct, build; to prepare, draw up; to fit out; to instruct, teach;

īnsŭla, ae, f. : island; apartment house;

īntāctus, a, um : untouched, intact; untried; virgin;

īntāctŭs, us, m. : intangibleness

īntĕgĕr, gra, grum : untouched, entire, whole, complete; uninjured, sound, fresh (troops), vigorous;

īntĕgro, are : to make whole, renew.

īntēllĕgo, īntēllĭgo, ere, lexi, lectum : to understand; to realize;

īntēndo, ere, tendi, tentum : to hold out; to stretch, strain, exert;

īntēntus, a, um : eager/intent, closely attentive; strict; intense, strenuous; serious/earnest;

īntēntŭs, us, m. : a stretching out, extending

īntĕr, prép. + acc. : between, among; during; [inter se => to each other, mutually];

īntērcĕdo, ere, cessi, cessum, ere : to intervene; to intercede, interrupt; to hinder; to veto; to exist/come between;

īntĕrĕā, adv. : meanwhile;

īntērfĭcĭo, ere, feci, fectum : to kill; to destroy;

īntĕrĭŏr, oris : inner, interior; nearer;

īntērrŏgo, are : to ask, question, interrogate, examine; to indict; to go to law with, sue;

īntērrūmpo, ere, rupi, ruptum : to drive a gap in, break up; to cut short, interrupt;

īntĭmātus, a, um : part. de intimo

īntĭmo, āvi, ātum, 1 : to, put, bring into

īntrā, prép. + acc. : within, inside, on the inside; during; under; fewer than;

īntrō, are : within, in; to the inside, indoors;

īntrōdūco, ere, duxi, ductum : to introduce, bring/lead in;

īntŭs, adv. : within, on the inside, inside; at home;

īnūltus, a, um : unpunished, scot-free; acting with impunity; having no recompense, unavenged;

īnūtĭlĭs, e : useless, unprofitable, inexpedient, disadvantageous; harmful, helpless;

īnvādo, ere, uasi, uasum : to enter, attempt; to invade; to take possession of; to attack (with in +acc.);

īnvĕnĭo, ire, ueni, uentum : to come upon; to discover, find; to invent, contrive; to reach, manage to get;

īnvēntŭm, i, n. : invention, discovery;

īnvēstīgo, are : to investigate; to search out/after/for; to track down; to find (by following game trail);

īnvīdĭa, ae, f. : hate/hatred/dislike; envy/jealousy/spite/ill will; use of words/acts to arouse;

īnvĭŏlātus, a, um : Unhurt, inviolate

īnvīto, are : to invite, summon; to challenge, incite; to encourage; to attract, allure, entice;

īnvītus, a, um : reluctant; unwilling; against one's will;

ĭō, interj. : Hurrah! (ritual exclamation of strong emotion/joy); Ho!; Look!; Quick!

Īphĭtus, i, m. : The son of Eurytus and Antiope, one of the Argonauts

īpsĕ, ipsa, ipsum, pron. : himself/herself/itself; the very/real/actual one; in person; themselves (pl.);

īra, ae, f. : anger; ire, wrath; resentment; indignation; rage/fury/violence; bad blood;

īrāscŏr, eris, i, iratus sum : to get angry, fly into a rage; to be angry at (with dat.)

īrātus, a, um : angry; enraged; furious; violent ; raging; angered;

īrrīto, are : to excite; to exasperate, provoke, aggravate, annoy, irritate;

īrrĭtus, a, um : ineffective, useless; invalid, void, of no effect; in vain;

īrrŭo, rui, ere : to rush into; to invade;

ĭs, ea, id, adj. et pron. : he/she/it/they (by GENDER/NUMBER); DEMONST that, he/she/it, they/them;

īstĕ, a, ud, pron. : that, that of yours, that which you refer to; such;

īstō, adv. : thither

ĭtā, adv. : thus, so; therefore;

Ītălĭa, ae, f. : Italy;

ĭtăquĕ, conj. : and so, therefore;

ĭtĕr, ĭtĭnĕr, itineris, n. : journey; road; passage, path; march [route magnum => forced march];

ĭtĕrŭm, adv. : again; a second time; for the second time;

ĭto, āvi, 1, intr. : to go

jăcĕo, ere, cui, citurus : to lie; to lie down; to lie ill/in ruins/prostrate/dead; to sleep; to be situated;

jăcĭo, ere, ieci, iactum : to throw, hurl, cast; to throw away; to utter;

jăctātus, us, m. : a throwing to and fro, a tossing

jācto, are : to throw away, throw out, throw, jerk about; to disturb; to boast, discuss;

jāctūra, ae, f. : loss; sacrifice; expense, cost; throwing away/overboard;

jăm, jāmjăm, adv. : now, already, by/even now; besides; [non ~ => no longer; ~ pridem => long ago];

Jānĭcŭlŭm, i, n. : one of the hills of Rome, on which Janus was said to have built a citadel

jānŭa, ae, f. : door, entrance;

jŭba, ae, f. : mane of a horse; crest (of a helmet);

jŭbăr, aris, n. : radiance of the heavenly bodies, brightness; first light of day; light source;

jŭbĕo, ere, iussi, iussum : to order/tell/command/direct; to enjoin/command; to decree/enact; to request/ask/bid; to pray;

jūcūndē, adv. : agreeably, delight, fully.

jūcūndus, a, um : pleasant/agreeable/delightful/pleasing (experience/person/senses); congenial;

jūdēx, icis, m. : judge; juror;

jūdĭcĭŭm, ii, n. : - trial, legal action/process; court/tribunal; courts; administration of - judgment/sentence/verdict; judging; jurisdiction/authority; opinion/belief;

jūdĭco, are : to judge, give judgment; to sentence; to conclude, decide; to declare, appraise;

jŭgĭs, e : -I. joined together, marred auspices -II. continual, perpetual;, always flowing, perennial

jŭgo, are : to bind to laths, rails

jŭgōsus, a, um : mountainous

jŭgŭm, i, n. : yoke; team, pair (of horses); ridge (mountain), summit, chain;

jŭgus, a, um : belonging together

jūnctūra, ae, f. : a joining, uniting; a juncture, joint

jūnctus, a, um : united, connected, associated, kindred, in a line, following, most attached, the nearest of kin

jūngo, ere, iunxi, iunctum : to join, unite; to bring together, clasp (hands); to connect, yoke, harness;

Jūnō, onis, f. : Juno; (Roman goddess, wife of Jupiter);

Jūnōnĭus, a, um : of or belonging to Juno, Junonian

Jūppĭtĕr, Jūpĭtĕr, Iouis, m. : Jupiter; (Roman chief/sky god); (supreme being); heavens/sky (poetic);

jūrĕ, adv. : by right, rightly, with justice; justly, deservedly;

jūrgĭŭm, i, n. : quarrel/dispute/strife; abuse/vituperation/invective; separation (man+wife);

jūro, are : to swear; call to witness; vow obedience to; [jus jurandum => oath]; to conspire;

jūs, iūris, n. : law; justice - (also soup; sauce;)

jūsta, orum, n. : due ceremonies, formalities, funeral rites, obsequies

jūstĭtĭa, ae, f. : justice; equality; righteousness (Plater);

jūstus, a, um : just, fair, equitable; right, lawful, justified; regular, proper;

jŭvĕnālĭs, e : youthful, young;

jŭvĕncus, i, m. : young bull; young man;

jŭvĕnĭs, m. : youth, young man/woman;

jŭvĕnta, ae, f. : youth;

jŭvĕntūs, tūtis, f. : youth; the age of youth (20-40), young persons; young men, knights;

jŭvo, are, iuvi, iutum : to help, aid, assist, support, benefit;

jūxtā, adv. : near, (very) close to, next to; hard by, adjoining; on a par with; like;

lăbo, are : to slip, slip and fall; to slide, glide, drop; to perish, go wrong;

lăbŏr, eris, i, lapsus sum : to move gently along a smooth surface, to fall, slide; to slide, slip, or glide down, to fall down, to sink (as the beginning of a fall)

lăbŏr, lăbōs, oris, m. : - labor/ toil/ exertion/ effort/ work; task/ undertaking; production; childbirth; wear+tear;

lăbōro, are : to work, labor; to produce, take pains; to be troubled/sick/oppressed, be in distress;

lăcrīma, ae, f. : tear; exuded gum/sap; bit of lead; quicksilver from ore; weeping (pl.); dirge;

lăcrīmo, are : shed tears, weep;

lăetē, adv. : happily

lăeto, are : to be glad/joyful/delighted; to rejoice; to be fond (of), delight in; to flourish (on/in);

lăetŏr, aris, atus sum : to be glad/joyful; to rejoic

lăetus, a, um : - happy/cheerful/joyful/glad; favorable/propitious; prosperous/successful; welcome;

lăeva, ae, f. : the left hand

lăeva, orum, n. : places lying on the left

lăevo, are : to make smooth, to smooth, polish

lăevus, a, um, adj. : unpropitious, unfavorable, harmful; left, on the left hand; from the left;

lămbo, ere : to lick; to lap/lick/suck up, absorb; to wash/bathe; to surround; to fondle/caress ;

lāna, ae, f. : wool; fleece; soft hair; down; trifles;

Lăŏcŏon, Laocoontis, m. : a son of Priam and Hecaba, priest of the Thymbrean Apollo

lăpĭdo, are : to throw stones at; to stone; [lapidat => it rains stones];

lăpĭs, idis, m. : stone; milestone; jewel;

lāpso, are : to slip, slide, stumble, fall;

lāpsus, us, m. : gliding, sliding; slipping and falling;

Lārcĭus, i, m. : Larcius

lārgē, adv. : exceedingly;

lārgītĭŏ, ionis, f. : generosity, lavish giving, largess; bribery; distribution of dole/land;

lārgus, a, um : lavish; plentiful; bountiful;

Lārīsăeus, a, um : of Larissa

Lārs, Lartis, m. : a praenomen of Etruscan origin

lāsso, are : to tire, weary, exhaust, wear out;

lāssus, a, um : tired, weary; languid;

lātē, adv. : widely, far and wide;

lătĕo, ere, latui : to lie hidden, lurk; to live a retired life, escape notice;

lătĕr, ĕris, m. : a brick, tile

Lătīnĭus, ii, m. : a Roman proper name

Lătīnus, a, um : latin

Lătīnus, i, m. : Latin; of Latium; of/in (good/correct/plain) Latin (language); Roman/Italian;

lātus, a, um : wide, broad; spacious, extensive

lătŭs, eris, n. : side; flank;

lāudātus, a, um : extolled, praiseworthy, esteemed, excellent

lāudo, are : to recommend; to praise, approve, extol; to call upon, name; to deliver eulogy on;

lāurus, i, f. : laurel/bay tree/foliage/sprig/branch (medicine/magic); triumph/victory; honor;

lāus, laudis, f. : praise, approval, merit; glory; renown;

lăvo, are : to wash, bathe

lēctus, a, um : chosen, picked, selected; choice, excellent

lēctus, i, m. : chosen, picked, selected; choice, excellent; (pl. as subst = picked men);

Lēda, ae, f. : Leda

Lēdē, f. : the daughter of Thestius, and wife of Tyndarus; she bore by Jupiter, who visited her in the form of a swan, two eggs, from one of which came Pollux and Helen, and from the other Castor and Clytemnestra, in the part of Leda in a pantomime

lēdŏn, i, n. : a shrub in Cyprus from which a, resin was obtained

lēgālĭs, e : of or belonging to the law, legal, according to the, law, pious

lēgātus, i, m. : envoy, ambassador, legate; commander of a legion; officer; deputy;

lĕgēns, entis, m. : a reader

lĕgo, ere, legi, lectum : to read; gather, collect (cremated bones); to furl (sail), weigh (anchor); to pick out

lēna, ae, f. : procuress; brothel-keeper;

lēnĭo, ire, iui, itum : to mitigate, moderate; alleviate, allay, assuage, ease, calm, placate, appease;

lēnĭs, e : gentle, kind, light; smooth, mild, easy, calm;

lēnĭtĕr, adv. : gently/mildly/lightly/slightly; w/gentle movement/incline; smoothly;

lētŭm, i, n. : death; (usu. violent); Death (personified); manner of dying; destruction;

lĕvĭs, e : light, thin, trivial, trifling, slight; gentle; fickle, capricious; nimble;

lēvis, e : smooth, smoothed, not rough

lĕvo, are : - to lift/raise/hold up; to support; to erect, set up; to lift off, remove (load); to comfort; - to lighten, lessen, relieve; to reduce in force/potency; to bring down (cost/prices);

lēvo, are : to make smooth, to smooth, polish

lēx, legis, f. : word; (Greek);

lĭbēntĕr, lŭbēntĕr, adv. : willingly; gladly, with pleasure;

lĭbĕo, v. : it pleases, is pleasing/agreeable; (w/qui whatever, whichever, no matter);

lĭbĕr, bri, m. : book, volume; inner bark of a tree

lībĕr, era, erum : free, unimpeded; void of; outspoken, frank; licentious

Lībĕr, eri, m. : an old Italian deity, who presided over planting and fructification

lībĕri, orum, m. pl. : children

lībĕro, are : to free; acquit, absolve; to manumit; to liberate, release;

lībērtās, atis, f. : freedom, liberty; frankness of speech, outspokenness;

lĭbīdĭnōsus, a, um : lustful, wanton; capricious;

lĭbīdō, lŭbīdō, dinis, f. : desire/longing/wish/fancy; lust, wantonness; will/pleasure; passion/lusts

lībo, are : to take a little (from any thing)

lĭcēntĭa, ae, f. : freedom, liberty; license, disorderliness; outspokenness;

lĭcĕo, v. impers. : to bid on/for, bid, bid at auction; to make a bid;

lĭcĕt, licere, licuit, impers. : although, granted that; (with subjunctive); it is permitted to

līgnĕus, a, um : wooden, wood-; woody, like wood, tough/stringy; [soleae ~ => worn by

līgnŭm, i, n. : the Cross; staff, cudgel, club; gallows/stocks; [~ pedaneum => altar step];

lĭgo, are : to tie, bind, bind together, bind up, bandage, bind fast

līmĕn, inis, n. : threshold, entrance; lintel; house;

līnĕa, ae, f. : string, line (plumb/fishing); [alba ~ => white line at end of race course];

līnĕus, a, um : of flax, lint, flaxen, linen-

līngŭa, ae, f. : tongue; speech, language; dialect;

līno, inere, lēvi (livi), litum : to daub, besmear, anoint, to spread or rub over

lītŏrĕus, a, um : of the seashore;

līttĕra, ae, f. : letter (alphabet); (pl.) letter, epistle; literature, books, records, account;

lītŭs, līttus, oris, n. : shore, seashore, coast, strand; river bank; beach, landing place;

līvĕo, ēre, intr. : to be of a bluish color, black and blue, livid

līvŏr, ōris, m. : bluish color, leaden color, a black and blue spot

lŏco, are : for, in the place of, instead of;

lŏcŭm, cf. locus : - place, territory/locality/neighborhood/region; position/point;

aim point; - part of the body; female genitals (pl.); grounds of proof;

lŏcus, i, m. : - place, territory/locality/neighborhood/region; position/point; aim point; - part of the body; female genitals (pl.); grounds of proof;

lōngāevus, a, um : of great age, aged, ancient

lōngē, adv. : far (off), distant, a long way; by far; for a long while, far (in future/past);

lōngīnquus, a, um : remote, distant, far off; lasting, of long duration;

lōngŭm, adv. : long, a long while

lōngus, a, um : long; tall; tedious, taking long time; boundless; far; of specific length/time;

lŏquāx, acis : talkative, loquacious;

lŏquŏr, eris, i, locutus sum : to speak, tell; to talk; to mention; to say, utter; to phrase

lŭbrĭco, are : to make smooth, slippery, to lubricate

lŭbrĭcum, i, n. : -I. a slippery place, on the slippery -II. Gliding, fleeting

lŭbrĭcus, a, um : slippery; sinuous; inconstant; hazardous, ticklish; deceitful;

lūcēns, entis : brillant, shining

lūcĕo, ere : - to shine, emit light (heavenly body); to dawn; to cause to shine; to be clear/evident; - to be bright/resplendent; to be visible, show up; [lucet => it is (becoming)

lūcĭfĕr, era, erum : light-bringing, bringing safety

Lūcĭfĕr, eri, m. : Lucifer (planet Venus), day

Lūcrētĭus, ii, m. : Lucretius

lūctŏr, aris, ari : to wrestle; to struggle; to fight (against)

lūcus, i, m. : grove; sacred grove;

lūdo, ere, lusi, lusum : to play, mock, tease, trick;

lūdus, i, m. : game, play, sport, pastime, entertainment, fun; school, elementary school;

lūmĕn, inis, n. : light; lamp, torch; eye (of a person); life; day, daylight;

lūna, ae, f. : moon; month;

lūno, are : to bend like a half-moon, crescent, to crook like a sickle, verb. finit.;

lŭpātus, a, um : furnished with wolf's teeth, iron prickles

lūstro, are : to purify cermonially (w/procession), cleanse by sacrifice, expiate; to through

lūstrŭm, i, n. : - bog/morass/slough, muddy place; forest/wilderness/wilds, haunt of wild - den (usu. pl.) of vice/iniquity, place of debauchery; brothel; 4 years;

lūx, lucis, f. : light, daylight, light of day; life; world; day; [prima luce => at daybreak];

lūxŭrĭōsē, adv. : Wantonly, immoderately, excessively

lūxŭrĭōsus, a, um : luxuriant, exuberant; immoderate; wanton, luxurious, self-indulgent;

Lȳcōris, ĭdis, f. : a freedwoman of the senator Volumnius Eutrapelus, the mistress of Cornelius Gallus, and afterwards of Marc Antony

Lȳdĭus, a, um : Lydian

lȳra, ae, f. : lyre; lyric poetry/inspiration/genius; Lyra/the Lyre (constellation); lute/

māctĕ, interj. : well done! good! bravo! (VOC of mactus, N implied) (macte S, macti P);

mācto, are : to magnify, honor; to sacrifice; to slaughter, destroy;

māctus, a, um : glorified, worshipped, honored, adored

mădĕo, ere : to be wet (w/tears/perspiration), to be dripping/sodden;

Māenās, adis, f. : the priestesses of Bacchus, Bacchantes

Māeŏnĭdēs, ae, m. : Homer

Māeŏnis, ĭdis, f. : Maeonis (femme de Méonie, Arachné, Omphale)

māestus, a, um : sad/unhappy; mournful/gloomy; mourning; stern/grim; ill-omened/inauspicious;

măga, ae, f. : masc., a Magian, a learned man and magician

măgĭs, măgĕ, adv. : to greater extent, more nearly; rather, instead; more; (forms COMP w/DJ);

māgnĭfĭcus, a, um : splendid/ excellent/ sumptuous/ magnificent/ stately; noble/ eminent; proud/

māgnus, a, um : - large/great/big/vast/huge; much; powerful; tall/long/broad; extensive/ - great (achievement); mighty; distinguished; skilled; bold/confident; proud;

măgus, a, um : magic, magical

măgus, i, m. : magic, magical;

māla, ae, f. : cheeks, jaws;

mălē, adv. : badly, ill, wrongly, wickedly, unfortunately; extremely;

mălĕdīco, ere, dixi, dictum : to speak ill/evil of, revile, slander; to abuse, curse;

mălĕdīctŭm, i, n. : insult, reproach, taunt;

mālo, mauis, malle, malui : to prefer; to incline toward, wish rather;

mălŭm, adv. interj. : see 1 malus

mălŭm, i, n. : apple; fruit; lemon; quince; hurt;

mălŭm, i, n. : evil, mischief; disaster, misfortune, calamity, plague; punishment; harm/hurt

mălus, a, um : bad, evil, wicked; ugly; unlucky;

māndo, are : to entrust, commit to one's charge, deliver over; to commission; to order, command;

māndo, ere, mandi, mansum : to chew, masticate

mānĕ, adv. : in the morning; early in the morning;

mānĕo, ere, mansi, mansum : to remain, stay, abide; to wait for; to continue, endure, last; to spend the night

Mānēs, ium, m. pl. : The deified souls of the departed, the ghosts or shades of the dead, the gods of the Lower World, infernal deities, manes

mănĭpŭlus, i, m. : maniple, company of soldiers, one third of a cohort; handful, bundle;

māno, are : to flow, pour; to be shed; to be wet; to spring;

mănŭs, us, f. : hand, fist; team; gang, band of soldiers; handwriting; (elephant's) trunk;

Mārcĭus, a, um : of or belonging to a Marcius, Marcian

Mārcĭus, i, m. : Marcius

mărcus, i, m. : a large hammer

Mārcus, i, m. : Marcus (Roman praenomen); (abb. M.);

mărĕ, n. : sea; sea water;

mārgō, ginis, f. : margin, edge, flange, rim, border; threshold; bank, retaining wall; gunwale;

mărītus, a, um : of or belonging to marriage, matrimonial, conjugal, nuptial, marriage-

mărītus, i, m. : a maried man, husband;

Mārs, Martis, m. : Mars, Roman god of war; warlike spirit, fighting, battle, army, force of arms;

Mārtĭus, a, um : March (month/mensis understood); abb. Mart.; of/belonging to Mars;

Mārtĭus, i, m. : (sc. mensis) March, the month of March, the Ides of March

mās, maris, m. : male; masculine, of the male sex; manly, virile, brave, noble; masculine;

māsso, 1 : to chew

mātĕr, tris, f. : mother, foster mother; lady, matron; origin, source, motherland, mother city;

mātĕrĭa, ae, f. : - wood (building material), lumber, timber; woody branch/growth/part of tree; matter;

mātĕrĭes, ei, f. : - wood (building material), lumber, timber; woody branch/growth/part of tree; matter;

mātĕrĭo, are : to build of wood

mātĕrnus, a, um : maternal, motherly, of a mother;

mātrĭmōnĭum, ii, n. : marriage; matrimony;

mātrōna, ae, f. : wife; matron;

māxĭmē, māxŭmē, adv. :especially, most greatly

mēcŭm, pron. contr. : with me

mĕdĭcātus, a, um : healed, cured

mĕdĭco, are : to heal, cure

mĕdĭcŏr, aris, ari : to heal, cure

mĕdĭŭm, ii, n. : middle, center; medium, mean; midst, community, public; publicity;

mĕdĭus, a, um : middle, middle of, mid; common, neutral, ordinary, moderate; ambiguous;

mēĭo, ĕre, intr. : to make water

mĕl, mellis, n. : honey; sweetness; pleasant thing; darling/honey; [luna mellis => honeymoon];

mĕlĭŭm, i, n. : a dog's collar

mĕmbrŭm, i, n. (généralement au plur) : member, limb, organ; (esp.) male genital member; apartment, room; section;

mĕmĭni, isse, impér. memento : to remember, recollect, to think of, be mindful of, not to have forgotten, to bear in mind

mĕmŏrātus, a, um : memorable, renowned, celebrated

mĕmŏro, are : to remember; to be mindful of (w/GEN/ACC); to mention/recount/relate, remind/speak of;

Mĕnāndĕr, dri, m. : a celebrated Greek comic poet, whom Terence took as his model

Mĕnāndrŏs, i, m. : a celebrated Greek comic poet, whom Terence took as his model

Mĕnĕlāus, i, m. : Son of Atreus, brother of Agamemnon, and husband of Helen

mēns, entis, f. : mind; reason, intellect, judgment; plan, intention, frame of mind; courage;

mēnsa, ae, f. : table; course, meal; banker's counter;

mēnta, ae, f. : mint

mēntĭŏr, iris, iri, titus sum : to lie, cheat, deceive

mēntŭm, i, n. : chin; projecting edge (architecture);

mĕo, are : go along, pass, travel;

mĕrĕŏr, eris, eri, meritus sum : to deserve, merit, to be entitled to, be worthy of

mĕrĕtrīx, icis, f. : courtesan, kept woman; public prostitute; harlot;

mĕrītō, adv. : deservedly; rightly;

mĕrito, are : To earn, gain

mĕrītŭm, i, n. : merit, service; value, due reward;

mĕrītus, a, um : deserving, guilty, unoffending, Due, deserved, fit, just, proper, right

mĕtāllĭcus, a, um : of or belonging to metal, metallic

Mĕtēllus, i, m. : Metellus

mētŏr, aris, ari : to measure, mete; to measure off, mark out

mĕtŭēns, entis : fearing, afraid, fearful, timid, apprehensive, anxious, anxiously, more god-fearing

mĕtŭo, ere, ui, utum : to fear; to be afraid; to stand in fear of; to be apprehensive, dread;

mĕtus, us, m. : fear, anxiety; dread, awe; object of awe/dread;

mĕum, i, n. : mine, my property, my daughter, it is my affair, my concern, my duty, my custom

mĕus, mea, meum : my (personal possession); mine, of me, belonging to me; my own; to me;

mĭcāns, antis : twinkling, sparkling, glittering, gleaming, flashing, glowing

mĭco, are, micui : to vibrate, quiver, twinkle; to tremble, throb; beat (pulse); to dart, flash, glitter;

mīlĕs, itis, m. : soldier; foot soldier; soldiery; knight (Latham); knight's fee/service;

mīlĭtārĭs, e : military man; soldier, warrior;

mīlĭtĭa, ae, f. : military spirit; courage, bravery; the soldiery/military; any difficult work;

mīlĭto, are : to serve as soldier, perform military service, serve in the army; to wage/make war;

mīlle, n. ia, ium : thousand; a thousand; [mille passuum => thousand paces = a mile];

mīna, ae, f. : -I. A Greek weight of a hundred Attic drachmas, a mina -II. adj., smooth, smooth-bellied, with no wool on the belly

mĭnācĭtĕr, adv. : menacingly; in a threatening manner;

mĭnāe, arum, f. pl. : threats (pl.), menaces; warning signs, evil omens/prognostications; pinnacles;

Mĭnērva, ae, f. : Minerva, Roman goddess of wisdom;

mĭnĭmē, adv. : least of all, in the smallest degree, least, very little

mĭnĭmus, a, um. : least, smallest

mĭnīstĕr, tra, trum : that is at hand, that serves, ministers, that further, promote; promotive

mĭnīstĕrĭŭm, i, n. : office, attendance, service, employment, body of helpers; occupation, work;

mĭnīstra, ae, f. : a female attendant, maid-servant; a female assistant, minister

mĭnīstro, are : attend (to), serve, furnish; supply;

mĭnĭtābūndus, a, um : threatening;

mĭnĭum, ii, n. : native cinnabar, Red-lead, minium

mĭnŭs, adv. : less; not so well; not quite;

mīrācŭlŭm, i, n. : wonder, marvel; miracle, amazing act/event/object/sight; amazement; freak;

mīrŏr, aris, ari : to wonder, marvel at, to be astonished, amazed at, to admire

mīscēo, ere, ui, mixtum : to mix, mingle; to embroil; to confound; to stir up;

mĭsĕr, a, um : poor, miserable, wretched, unfortunate, unhappy, distressing;

mĭsĕrābĭlĕ, adv. : pitiably, wretchedly

mĭsĕrābĭlĭs, e : wretched, miserable, pitiable;

mĭsĕrē, adv. : wretchedly, desperately;

mĭsĕrĭa, ae, f. : misery, distress, woe, wretchedness, suffering;

mītĭs, e : mild, meek, gentle, placid, soothing; clement; ripe, sweet and juicy;

mītto, ere, misi, missum : to send, throw, hurl, cast; to let out, release, dismiss; to disregard;

mŏdĭcē, adv. : with moderation, moderately; modestly; in a proper manner; also, in an ordinary manner, meanly, poorly

mŏdĭcus, a, um : moderate; temperate, restrained; small (Bee);

mŏdĭum, ii, n. : the Roman corn-measure, a measure, peck, to measure one's money by the peck, a peck

mŏdĭus, i, m. : peck; Roman dry measure; (about 2 gallons/8000 cc);

mŏdŏ, adv. : but, if only; but only;

mŏdus, i, m. : manner, mode, way, method; rule, rhythm, beat, measure, size; bound, limit;

mōlēs, f. : - large mass; rock/boulder; heap/lump/pile, bulk; monster; mole/jetty/dam/dike; embankment;

mŏlēstē, adv. : annoyingly; in a vexing/annoying/distressing/tiresome manner;

mŏlēsto, are : to trouble, annoy, molest.

mŏlēstus, a, um : annoying; troublesome; tiresome; [molestus esse => to be a worry/nuisance];

mōlĭŏr, iris, iri, itus sum : To set one's self or one's powers in motion, to make exertions, exert one's self, to endeavor, struggle, strive

mōllĭo, ire, iui, itum : to soften, mitigate, make easier; to civilize, tame, enfeeble;

mōllĭs, e : - soft (cushion/grass); flexible/supple/loose/pliant; mild/tolerable; easy; - weak; cowardly; unmanly; effeminate; womanish; pathic; tender (women/youths); - tender, gentle; smooth, relaxing; languid (movement); amorous (writings);

mŏnĕo, ere, ui, itum : to remind, advise, warn; to teach; to admonish; to foretell, presage;

mōns, montis, m. : mountain; huge rock; towering heap;

mōnstro, are : to show; to point out, reveal; to advise, teach;

mōnstrŭm, i, n. : monster; portent, unnatural thing/event regarded as omen/sign/portent;

mŏra, ae, f. : delay, hindrance, obstacle; pause;

mōrdĕo, ere, momordi, morsum : to bite; to sting; to hurt, pain; vex; to criticize, carp at; to eat, consume; to bite/cut into;

mŏrĭŏr, eris, i, mortuus sum : to die

mŏrŏr, aris, ari : to delay, tarry, stay, wait, remain, linger, loiter

mōrs, mortis, f. : death; corpse; annihilation;

mōrsus, us, m. : bite, sting; anguish, pain; jaws; teeth;

mōrtālĭs, e : mortal, transient; human, of human origin;

mōrtālĭs, m. et f. : a man, mortal, human being, plur., mortals, men, mankind

mōrtŭus, a, um : dead, deceased; limp;

mōrtŭus, i, m. : a dead person, dead man

mōrum, i, n. : a mulberry; a blackberry

mōs, moris, m. : custom, habit; mood, manner, fashion; character (pl.), behavior, morals;

mŏto, are : to keep moving, move about, Pass.

mŏvĕo, ere, moui, motum : to move, stir, agitate, affect, provoke, disturb; [movere se => dance];

mū, interj. : to mutter, make a muttering

Mūcĭa, orum, n. : a festival kept by the Asiatics in commemoration of the good government of Q. Mucius Scaevola, the Mucius festival

Mūcĭus, a, um : of or belonging to a Mucius, Mucian

Mūcĭus, i, m. : Mucius

mŭcrŏ, onis, m. : sword, sword point, sharp point;

mūgĭo, ir, iui, itum : to low, bellow; to make a loud deep noise;

mūgītus, us, m. : lowing, bellowing; roaring, rumble;

mŭlĭĕbrĭs, e : feminine, womanly, female; woman's; womanish, effeminate;

mŭlĭĕr, f. : woman; wife; mistress;

mūlta, mūlcta, ae, f. : fine; penalty; penalty involving property (livestock, later money);

mūlti, orum, m. : beaucoup de gens, la multitude, abondant, prolixe, actif, acharné, pressant

mūltĭplēx, icis : - having many twists/turns; having many layers/thicknesses, many deep; complex; versatile;

mūltō, adv. : much, by much, a great deal, very; most; by far; long (before/after);

mūltŭm, adv. : much, greatly, plenty, very; more; most;

mūltum, i, n. : a lot

mūltus, a, um : much, many, great; large, intense, assiduous; tedious;

mūnīmēntŭm, i, n. : fortification, bulwark; defense, protection;

mūnĭo, ire, iui, itum : to fortify; to strengthen; to protect, defend, safeguard; to build (road);

mūnŭs, eris, n. : service; duty, office, function; gift; tribute, offering; bribes (pl.);

mŭrĭa, ae, f. : brine, pickle

mūrus, i, m. : wall, city wall;

mūs, muris, m. : mouse;

Mūsa, ae, f. : muse (one of the goddesses of poetry, music, etc.); sciences/poetry (pl.);

mūstum, i, n. : new, unfermented wine, must

mūstus, a, um : fresh, young; unfermented/ partially fermented (wine);

mūto, are : to move, to move away or from its place; to alter, change a thing; to interchange, exchange;

Mȳrmĭdŏnes, um, m. : the Myrmidons, a people of Phthiotis, Thessaly, about Phthia and Larissa Cremaste, under the sway of Achilles, fem.

mȳrtum, i, n. : the fruit of the myrtle, a myrtle-berry

mȳrtus, i, m. : myrtle, myrtle-tree;

Nāevĭus, a, um : of or belonging to a Naevius, Naevian

năm, conj. : for, on the other hand; for instance;

nāmque, conj. : for indeed, for truly, for

Năpē, : a name

nārro, are : to tell, tell about, relate, narrate, recount, describe;

nāscŏr, eris, i, natus sum : to be born, to be begotten

Nāso, ōnis, m. : amplif., a Roman family name in the Otacilian, Octavian, Ovidian, and Voconian, the poet

nāsus, i, m. : nose; sense of smelling;

nāta, ae, f. : a daughter;

nătĭs, f. : the rump, buttocks

năto, are : to swim; float;

nātūra, ae, f. : nature; birth; character;

nātūrālĭs, e : physical/natural scientist; physicist; natural philosopher;

nātūrālĭtĕr, adv. : naturally, conformably to nature, by nature

nātus, a, um : born;

nātus, i, m. : son,

nāvĭgĭŭm, i, n. : vessel, ship;

nāvĭgo, are : to sail; to navigate;

nāvĭs, f. : ship; [navis longa => galley, battleship; ~ oneraria => transport/cargo ship];

nāvo, are : to do with zeal; [operam navare => do one's best];

nāvus, a, um : busy, diligent, assiduous, active.

nē, adv. : that not, lest; (for negative of IMP);

nē, conj. sub. + subj. : que (verbes de crainte et d'empêchement), de ne pas (verbes de volonté), de peur que, pour que [... ne ... pas]

nĕc, adv. : nor, and..not; not..either, not even;

nĕcēssĕ, adj. : necessary, essential; unavoidable, compulsory, inevitable; a natural law; true;

nĕcēssĭtās, atis, f. : need/necessity; inevitability; difficult straits; poverty; obligation; bond;

nĕco, are : to kill/murder; to put to death; to suppress, destroy; to kill (plant); to quench/drown

nĕcŏpīnātus, a, um : unexpected

nēcto, ere, nex(u)i, nexum : to tie, bind;

nĕglēctus, a, um : P. a., neglected, slighted, disregarded, despised, Sup.

nĕglēgēns, nĕclĕgēns, entis : heedless, neglectful, careless; unconcerned, indifferent; slovenly; unruly;

nĕglēgo, nĕclĕgo, nĕglĭgo, ere, lexi, lectum : to disregard, neglect, ignore, regard of no consequence; to do nothing about;

nĕgo, are : to deny, refuse; to say ... not;

nēmŏ, nullius, nt. nihil, nil (rart. neminis), pron. : nobody

nēmpĕ, adv. : truly, certainly, of course;

nĕo, ere, nēvi, nētum : to spin.

Nĕŏptŏlĕmus, i, m. : The son of Achilles, also called Pyrrhus

nĕpōs, otis, m. : grandson/daughter; descendant; spendthrift, prodigal, playboy; secondary shoot;

Nēptūnus, i, m. : Neptune; sea;

nēquăm, adj. : wicked/licentious/depraved; bad/vile; naughty/roguish; worthless/useless;

nĕquĕ, conj. coord. : nor [neque..neque=>neither..nor; neque solum..sed etiam=>not only..but also];

nĕquĕo, ire, quiui-quii, quitum : to be unable, cannot;

nēquīquăm, adv. : in vain; uselessly

Nērēus, i (os), m. : the son of Oceanus and Tethys, a seagod, the husband of Doris, and father of the Nereids, sea-monsters

nērvus, i, m. : string/cord; bowstring; bow; (leather) thong; fetter (for prisoner); prison;

nēscĭo, ire, iui (ii), itum : to not know (how); to be ignorant/unfamiliar/unaware/unacquainted/unable/unwilling;

nēscĭus, a, um : unaware, not knowing, ignorant;

nī, conj. sub. : if ... not; unless;

nĭhĭl, pron. : nothing

nĭhĭlō, adv. : with compp., by nothing, no

nĭhĭlum, i, n. : nothing

nīl, cf. nemo : nobody

nīmbus, i, m. : rainstorm, cloud;

nĭmĭs, adv. : very much; too much; exceedingly;

nĭmĭŭm, adv. : too, too much; very, very much, beyond measure, excessive, too great;

nĭmĭum, ii, n. : too much, superabundance, excess, too mighty, too powerful

nĭmĭus, a, um : excessive, too great;

nĭsĭ, conj. sub. : if not; except, unless;

nĭtĕo, ere : to shine, glitter, look bright; to be sleek/in good condition; to bloom, thrive;

nĭtĭdus, a, um : shining, bright;

nītŏr, eris, eris, nixus sum : to bear or rest upon something; To make one's way with an effort, to press forward, advance; to mount, climb, fly; To strain in giving birth, to bring forth;

nīx, niuis, f. : snow;

nŏ, are : to swim, float;

nōbĭlĭs, e : nobles (pl.);

nōbĭlĭtās, atis, f. : nobility/noble class; (noble) birth/descent; fame/excellence; the nobles; rank;

nōbĭlĭto, are : To make known, to render famous, renowned, to render notorious

nŏcĕo, ere, nocui, nocitum : to harm, hurt; to injure (with DAT);

nōcte, adv. : de nuit, nuitamment

nōctūrnus, a, um : nocturnal, of night, at night, by night;

nōdus, i, m. : knot; node;

nōlo, non uis, nolle, nolui : to be unwilling; to wish not to; to refuse to;

nōmĕn, inis, n. : name, family name; noun; account, entry in debt ledger; sake; title, heading;

nōmĭno, are : to name, call;

nōn, adv. neg. : not, by no means, no; [non modo ... sed etiam => not only ... but also];

nōnnĕ, adv. interr. : est-ce que … ne pas

nōs, nostrum pron. pl. : we (pl.), us;

nōsco, ere, noui, notum : to get to know; to learn, find out; to become cognizant of/acquainted/familiar with;

nōstĕr, tra, trum, adj. pron. : our;

nŏta, ae, f. : mark, sign, letter, word, writing, spot brand, tattoo-mark;

nŏtātus, a, um : marked, known, noted

nōti, orum, m. : acquaintances, friends

nŏto, are : to observe; to record; to brand; to write, inscribe;

nōtus, a, um : well known, familiar, notable, famous, esteemed; notorious, of ill repute;

nŏvĕm, num. : nine;

nŏvo, are : to make new, renovate; to renew, refresh, change;

nŏvus, a, um : new, fresh, young; unusual, extraordinary; (novae res, f. pl. = revolution);

nōx, noctis, f. : night [prima nocte => early in the night; multa nocte => late at night];

nūbo, ere, psi, ptum : to marry, be married to;

nūdo, are : to lay bare, strip; to leave unprotected;

nūdus, a, um : nude; bare, stripped;

nūllŭs, a, um : no; none, not any; (PRONominal ADJ)

nūmĕn, inis, n. : divine will, divinity; god;

nŭmĕrō, adv. : Just, precisely, at the right time, on the instant

nŭmĕrō, are : to count, reckon, number;

nŭmĕrus, i, m. : - number/sum/total/rank; (superior) numerical strength/plurality; category; - rhythm/cadence/frequency; meter/metrical foot/line; melody; exercise

nūmquăm, adv. : never;

nūnc, adv. : now, today, at present;

nūntĭo, a, are : to announce/report/bring word/give warning; to convey/deliver/relate message/

nūntĭum, ii, n. : nouvelle, message

nūntĭus, a, um : That announces, signifies, makes known; announcing, informing

nūntĭus, ii, m. : announcing, bringing word (of occurrence); giving warning; prognosticatory;

nūpĕr, adv. : recently, not long ago; in recent years/our own time; (SUPER) latest in series;

nŭrus, us, f. : daughter-in-law; prospective daughter-in-law; wife of grandson, etc. (leg.);

nūsquăm, adv. : nowhere; on no occasion;

ō, excl. : Oh!;

ōbdūro, are : to be hard, persist, endure;

ōbēx, ĭcis, m. : a bolt, bar; a barrier, wall

ōbĭcĭo, ere, ieci, iectum : to throw before/to, cast; to object, oppose; to upbraid; to throw in one's teeth; to present;

ōbjēcta, orum, n. : charges, accusations

ōbjēcto, are : to expose/throw (to); to throw/put in the way; to lay to one's charge, put before;

ōbjēctŭs, us, m. : a casting before, a putting against, in the way, opposite, an opposing;, neutr., a lying before, opposite, the opposing of the shield

ōbjĭcĭo, ere, ieci, iectum : to throw before/to, cast; to object, oppose; to upbraid; to throw in one's teeth; to present;

ōbjūrgo, are : to scold, chide, reproach;

ōbrŭo, ere, obrui, obrutum : to cover up, hide, bury; to overwhelm, ruin; to crush;

ōbscūro, are : to darken, obscure; to conceal; to make indistinct; to cause to be forgotten;

ōbscūrum, i, n. : -I. dim light, twilight, the dark, darkness, obscurity -II. darkling, unseen

ōbscūrus, a, um : - dim, dark, obscure; dusky, shadowy, only faintly/dimly seen; dingy; gloomy; inaudible; - not open; vague/uncertain/dim/faint, poorly known; unclear; incomprehensible;

ōbsĕquĭŭm, i, n. : - compliance (act /form /sex /orders); consideration /deference/solicitude; - obedience/allegiance /discipline (military); tractability/docility (animals);

ōbsērvo, are : to watch, observe; to heed;

ōbsēs, idis, m. : hostage; pledge, security;

ōbsĭdĕo, ere, edi, essum : to blockade, besiege, invest, beset; to take possession of;

ōbsĭdĭŏ, onis, f. : siege; blockade;

ōbsĭdĭum, ii, n. : -I. a siege, investment, blockade -II. the condition of a hostage, hostageship

ōbsīdo, ĕre : to beset, invest, besiege, blockade

ōbsīsto, ere, stiti, - : to oppose, resist; to stand in the way; to make a stand against, withstand;

Ōbsĭus, ii, m. : a Roman surname

ōbstĭnātus, a, um : firm, resolved, resolute; obstinate;

ōbstĭno, are : to set about, with firmness, resolution, to set one's mind firmly on, to persist in, be resolved on

ōbsto, are, stiti, staturus : to oppose, hinder; (w/DAT);

ōbstŭpĕfăcĭo, ere, fēci, factum : to astonish, amaze, astound, stupefy; to render senseless, deprive of feeling, benumb, Pass.

ōbstŭpēsco, ōbstĭpēsco, ere, stupui (stipui), - : to be stupefied; to be struck dumb; to be astounded;

ōbsŭm, esse, fui : to hurt; to be a nuisance to, tell against;

ōbtēstŏr, aris, ari : to call to witness; to implore

ōbtĭnĕo, ere, tinui, tentum : to get hold of; to maintain; to obtain; to hold fast, occupy; to prevail;

ōbtrūnco, ōptrūnco, are : to cut off, lop away; to trim, prune.

ōbvērsus, a, um : turned towards, against, directed towards.

ōbvērto, ōbvŏrto, ere, uerti, uersum : to turn or direct towards; to direct against;

ōccāsĭŏ, onis, f. : opportunity; chance; pretext, occasion;

ōccāsus, us, m. : setting; fall

ōccĭdēns, entis, m. : the quarter of the setting sun, the west, the occident

ōccĭdo, ere, occidi, occasum (ob + cado) : to fall down, fall; to perish, be ruined, lost;

ōccīdo, ere, occidi, occisum (ob + caedo) : to strike down, strike to the ground; to beat, smash, crush

ōccŭlo, ere, cului, cultum : to cover; to cover up, hide, cover over, conceal;

ōccūlto, are : to hide; to conceal;

ōccūltŭm, i, n. : secrecy; hiding;

ōccūltus, a, um : caché, secret, occulte

ŏcŭlus, i, m. : eye;

ōdio, isse : to hate; to dislike; to be disinclined/reluctant/adverse to

ŏdĭōsus, ŏdĭōssus, a, um : distasteful, disagreeable, offensive; tiresome, boring, troublesome, annoying;

ŏdĭum, i, n. : - hate/hatred/dislike/antipathy; odium, unpopularity; boredom/impatience;

Ōedĭpūs, ŏdis, m. : A king of Thebes, the son of Laius and Jocasta

ŏffēro, fers, ferre, obtuli, oblatum : to offer; to present; to cause; bestow; (medieval form of offerre);

ŏffĭcĭo, ere, fec, fectum : to block the path (of), check, impede;

ŏffĭcĭum, ii, n. : duty, obligation; kindness; service, office;

ŏlĭm, adv. : formerly; once, once upon a time; in the future;

Ōlўmpĭus, a, um : Olympic

Ōlўmpos, i, m. : The name of several mountains, the most celebrated of which is one on the borders of Macedonia and Thessaly, Lacha, of great height, and consequently regarded as the seat of the gods

ŏmĕn, inis, n. : omen, sign; token;

ŏmītto, ere, misi, missum : to lay aside; to omit; to let go; to disregard;

ŏmne, n. : every thing

ŏmnĭs, e : all men (pl.), all persons;

ŏnŭs, eris, n. : load, burden; cargo;

ŏpĕra, ae, f. : work, care; aid; service, effort/trouble; [dare operam => pay attention to];

ŏpĕrĭo, ire, perui, pertum : to cover (over); to bury; to overspread; to shut/close; to conceal; to clothe, cover/hide

ŏpīmus, a, um : rich, fertile; abundant; fat, plump; [opima spolia => spoils from a general];

ŏpīnĭŏ, onis, f : belief, idea, opinion; rumor (Plater);

ŏpōrtĕo, v. :it is right/proper/necessary; it is becoming; it behooves; ought

ŏppōno, ere, posui, positum : to oppose; to place opposite;

ŏppōrtūnus, a, um : suitable; advantageous; useful, fit, favorable/opportune, ready; liable/

ŏppŏsĭtus, a, um : Part. from oppono

ŏppūgno, are : to attack, assault, storm, besiege;

ŏps, opis, f. : power, might; help; influence; resources/wealth (pl.);

ŏptĭmum, i, n. : a good, goods, a moral good, a blessing

ŏpto, are : to choose, select; to wish, wish for, desire;

ŏpŭlēnto, are : to make rich, to enrich

ŏpŭlēntus, a, um : wealthy; rich in wealth/resources; well supplied; sumptuous, opulent, rich;

ŏpus, indecl. n. : usually with esse, necessary

ŏpŭs, operis, n. : need; work; fortifications (pl.), works; [opus est => is useful, beneficial];

ōra, ae, f. : shore, coast;

ōrātĭō, onis, f. : speech, oration; eloquence; prayer;

ōrātŏr, oris, m. : speaker, orator;

ōrbĭs, m. : circle; territory/region; sphere; [orbis terrarum => world/(circle of lands)];

ōrbo, are : to bereave (of parents, children, etc), deprive (of);

ōrbus, a, um : bereft, deprived,childless;

Ōrcus, i, m. : god of the underworld, Dis; death; the underworld;

ōrdĭno, are : to order/arrange, set in order; to adjust, regulate; to compose; to ordain/appoint (Bee);

ōrdō, inis, m. : row, order/rank; succession; series; class; bank (oars); order (of monks)

ŏrĭēns, entis : rising (sun/star); eastern; beginning, in its early stage (period/activity);

ŏrīgō, ginis, f. : origin, source; birth, family; race; ancestry;

ŏrĭŏr, iris, iri, ortus sum : to rise, arise; to spring from, appear; to be descended; to begin, proceed, originate

ŏrĭūndus, a, um : descended; originating from;

ōrnātus, us, m. : a furnishing, providing, preparing; a preparation;

ōrno, are : to equip; to dress; to decorate, honor; to furnish, adorn, garnish, trim;

ōro, are : beg, ask for, pray; beseech, plead, entreat; worship, adore;

ōrtus, us, m. : descended/born/sprung (from w/ex/ab/ABL); [a se ~ => w/out famous ancestors];

ōs, oris, n. : the mouth; the face, countenance; A mouth, opening, entrance, aperture, orifice;

ŏs, ossis, n. : bone; (implement, gnawed, dead); kernel (nut); heartwood (tree); stone (fruit)

ōscŭlo, are : to kiss; to exchange kisses;

ōscŭlŭm, i, n. : kiss; mouth; lips; orifice; mouthpiece (of a pipe);

ōstēndo, ere, tendi, tentum : to show; to reveal; to make clear, point out, display, exhibit;

ōtĭŭm, ii, n. : leisure; spare time; holiday; ease/rest/peace/quiet; tranquility/calm; lull;

Ŏvĭdĭus, ii, m. : Ovid, the name of a Roman gens, A contemporary of Martial

ŏvĭs, f. : sheep;

ŏvo, are : to rejoice;

ōvŭm, i, n. : egg; oval;

pācātus, a, um : peaceful, calm;

pāco, are : to bring into a state of peace and quietness, to make peaceful, to quiet, pacify, subdue, soothe

pāenĕ, adv. : nearly, almost; mostly;

pāenĭtĕo, ere, ui : it displeases, makes angry, offends, dissatisfies, makes sorry;

pāgĭna, ae, f. : a written page, leaf

Pălātīnus, a, um : of or belonging to the Palatium, Palatine, the tenth region, also called simply, one of the four city tribes, Subst. m. an officer of the palace, a chamberlain, Domitian's chamberlain

pălātĭum, ii, n. : a palace, the palace of the sky

Pălātĭŭm, ii, n. : Palatine Hill;

pălātum, i, n. : the palate

pāllĭŭm, i, n. : cover, coverlet; Greek cloak;

pālma, ae, f. : palm/width of the hand; hand; palm tree/branch; date; palm award/first place;

pālŏr, aris, ari : to wander abroad stray; to scatter; to wander aimlessly

pāndo, ere, pandi, passum : to spread out [passis manibus => with hands outstretched];

pār, paris : - equal (to); a match for; of equal size/rank/age; fit/suitable/right/proper; - corresponding in degree, proportionate, commensurate (unlike qualities); - balanced/level;

părātus, a, um : ready, an, easy victory, prepared

pārcē, adv. : Sparingly, frugally, thriftily; penuriously, parsimoniously.

pārco, ere, peperci, parsum : forbear, refrain from; spare; show consideration; be economical/thrifty with;

pārcus, a, um : sparing, frugal; scanty, slight;

pārēns, entis, comm. : -parent

părēnto, are : to perform rites at tombs; to make appeasement offering (to the dead);

pārĕo, pārrĕo, ere, ui, itum : - to obey, be subject/obedient to; to submit/yield/comply; to pay attention; to attend to;

părĭēs, etis, m. : wall, house wall;

părĭo, ere, peperi, partum : to acquire (accounts); to settle a debt; to settle up;

părĭtĕr, adv. : equally; together;

Pārnāssŏs, i, m. : a high mountain in Phocis with two peaks, sacred to Apollo and the Muses, at whose foot was the city of Delphi and the Castalian spring, range of Liakhoura

păro, are : to prepare; to furnish/supply/provide; to produce; to obtain/get; to buy; to raise; to put up; to plan;

pārs, partis, f. : - part, region; share; direction; portion, piece; party, faction, side; monthly];

pārtĭcēps, ĭpis, m. : a partner, comrade, fellow-soldier

pārtĭcēps, ipitis : sharing in, taking part in;

pārtĭcĭpo, are : to make partaker, for a community of interests.mdash; To share, impart, To share in, partake of, participate in

pārtus, us, m. : birth; offspring;

părūmpĕr, adv. : for a short/little while; for a moment; in a short time; quickly, hurriedly;

pārvum, i, n. : a small amount of

pārvus, a, um : small, little, cheap; unimportant; (SUPER) smallest, least;

pāsco, ere, paui, pastum : to feed, feed on; to graze;

pāssĭm, adv. : here and there; everywhere;

pāssum, i, n. : prose

pāssus, a, um : outspread, outstretched, extended, open.

pāstŏr, oris, m. : shepherd, herdsman;

pāstus, us, m. : pasture, feeding ground; pasturage;

pătĕo, ere, patui : to stand open, be open; to extend; to be well known; to lie open, be accessible;

pătĕr, tris, m. : father; [pater familias, patris familias => head of family/household];

pătērnus, a, um : father's, paternal; ancestral;

pătēsco, ere : to be opened/open/revealed; to become clear/known; to open; to extend, spread;

pătĭēns, entis : - patient/long-suffering; tolerant/easy-going; submissive/liable/susceptible - hardy; able/willing to endure; capable of bearing/standing up to hard use;

pătĭēntĭa, ae, f. : - endurance/hardiness; patience/persistence; apathy; sufferance; hardship;

pătĭŏr, eris, i, passus sum : to suffer; to allow; to undergo, endure; to permit

pătrĭa, ae, f. sing. : native land; home, native city; one's country;

pătrĭus, a, um : father's, paternal; ancestral;

pătro, are : to accomplish, bring to completion;

pătrōnus, i, m. : patron; advocate; defender, protector;

pătrŭus, a, um : of or belonging to a father's brother, of an uncle, an uncle's, sup.

pătrŭus, i, m. : "- father's brother; paternal uncle; [~ magnus/major/maximus => gr/gr-gr/gr-gr- - severe reprover; type of harshness/censoriousness/finding fault; ""Dutch"

pāuci, orum, m. : few, a few, the few, the select few, the more distinguished

pāucus, a, um : little, small in quantity/extent; few (usu. pl.); just a few; small number of;

pāulŭlŭm, adv. : little; to small extent, somewhat; only a small amount/short while/distance;

pāulŭlum, i, n. : a little bit, a trifle., a little, somewhat

pāupĕr, (pauperus) eris, adj. et subst. : poor/meager/unproductive; scantily endowed; cheap, of little worth; of poor

pāupĕro, are : to make poor, to impoverish

păvĕo, ere, pavi : to be frightened or terrified at;

păvĭdus, a, um : fearful, terrified, panicstruck;

păvŏr, oris, m. : fear, panic;

pāx, pacis, f. : peace; harmony;

pēccātum, i, n. : a fault, error, mistake, transgression, sin

pēcco, are : to do wrong, commit moral offense; to blunder, stumble; to be wrong;

pēctŭs, oris, n. : breast, heart; feeling, soul, mind;

pĕcūnĭa, ae, f. : money; property;

pĕcūnĭōsus, a, um : rich, wealthy; profitable;

pĕcŭs, oris, n. : sheep; animal;

pĕcŭs, udis, f. : cattle, herd, flock

pĕcus, us, m. : cattle, a herd

pĕdĕs, itis, m. : on foot;

pēdo, ere, pepedi, peditum : to break wind;

pĕdum, i, n. : a shepherd's crook, a sheep-hook

pējŭs, adv. : worse

pĕlăgus, i, n. : sea; the open sea, the main; (-us neuter, only sing.);

Pēlĭa, ae, m. : a king of Thessaly, son of Neptune and the nymph Tyro

Pēlīdēs, ae, m. : The son of Peleus, i. e. Achilles

Pēlĭus, a, um : of or belonging to Pelion, Pelian

pēllĭs, f. : skin, hide; pelt;

pēllo, ere, pepuli, pulsum : to beat; to drive out; to push; to banish, strike, defeat, drive away, rout;

Pĕnātēs, ium, m. pl. : gods of home/larder/family; home/dwelling; family/line

pēndĕo, ere, pependi, - : to hang, hang down; to depend; [~ ab ore => hang upon the lips, listen attentively];

pēndo, ere, pependi, pensum : to weigh out; to pay, pay out;

Pēnēlēus, ĕi (ĕōs), m. : son of Hippalmus and Asterope, one of Helen's suitors

pĕnĕtrāle, n. : innermost parts/chambers/self (pl.); spirit, life of soul; gimlet (Latham);

pĕnĕtrālĭs, e : inner, innermost;

pĕnetro, are : to enter, penetrate;

pĕnĭtŭs, (penite) adv. : inside; deep within; thoroughly;

pĕr, prép. + acc. : through (space); during (time); by, by means of;

pĕrăgo, ere, egi, actum : to disturb; to finish; to kill; to carry through to the end, complete;

pĕrăro, are : to plough through; to traverse

pĕrcēllo, ere, culi, culsum : to strike down; to strike; to overpower; to dismay, demoralize, upset;

pĕrdo, ere, didi, ditum : to ruin, destroy; to lose; to waste;

pĕrēnnĭs, e : continual; everlasting, perpetual, perennial; eternal;

pĕrĕo, ire, ii, itum : to die, pass away; to be ruined, be destroyed; to go to waste;

pĕrēxĭgŭus, a, um : very small, very little.

pĕrfēctus, a, um : perfect, complete; excellent;

pĕrfĕro, fers, ferre, tuli, latum : to carry through; bear, endure to the end, suffer; to announce;

pĕrfĭcĭo, ere, feci, fectum : to complete, finish; execute; to bring about, accomplish; to do thoroughly;

pĕrfŭga, ae, m. : deserter;

pĕrfŭgĭo, ere, fugi, - : to flee, desert; to take refuge;

pĕrfŭgĭŭm, i, n. : refuge; asylum; excuse;

pĕrfūndo, ere, fudi, fusum : to pour over/through, wet, flood, bathe; to overspread, coat, overlay; to imbue;

Pērgăma, orum, n. pl. : the citadel of Troy, Troy

Pērgămum, i, n. : -I. the citadel of Troy, Troy -II. a city in Creta, founded by Agamemnon -III. a city in Mysia, on the Caystrus, the residence of the Attalian kings, with a celebrated library, Bergamo

pĕrīcŭlōsus, a, um : dangerous, hazardous, perilous; threatening;

pĕrīcŭlŭm, pĕrīclŭm, i, n. : danger, peril; trial, attempt; risk; responsibility for damage, liability;

Pĕrĭphās, antis, m. : A king of Attica

pērjūrĭum, ii, n. : a false oath, perjury.

pērjūrus, a, um : perjured, who lies under oath, false, lying

pērlĕgo, ere, legi, lectum : to read over/through (silent/aloud); to scan, survey, run one's eyes over; to recount;

pērlĭcĭo, ere, lexi, lectum : to attract/draw away; to allure/seduce/entice/captivate; to coax/induce/wheedle/win

pērmītto, ere, misi, missum : to let through; to let go through; to relinquish; to permit, allow; to entrust; to hurl;

pērmŏvĕo, ere, moui, motum : to stir up; to move deeply; to influence; to agitate;

pērmūltus, a, um : very much; very many (pl.);

pērpĕtŭē, adv. : constantly

pērpĕtŭus, a, um : continuous, uninterpreted; whole; perpetual, lasting; everlasting;

pērrūmpo, ere, rupi, ruptum : to break through;

pērsōlvo, ere, solui, solutum : to pay;

pērsōna, ae, f. : mask; character; personality;

pērtērrĕo, ere, terrui, terrĭtum : to frighten, terrify thoroughly

pērtērrĭtus, a, um : very frightened, thoroughly frightened; completely terrified;

pērvĭgĭlo, are : to remain awake all night; to keep watch all night; to keep a religious vigil;

pērvĭus, a, um : passable, traversable; penetrable;

pēs, pedis, m. : foot; [pedem referre => to retreat];

pēssĭmus, a, um : worst, most incapable; wickedest; most disloyal/unkind; lowest in quality/rank;

pĕto, ere, iui, itum : to attack; to aim at; to desire; to beg, entreat, ask (for); to reach towards, make for;

pĕtŭlāns, antis : insolent, unruly, smart-alecky; forward, aggressive; impudent; reprobate/

pĕtŭlāntĕr, adv. : pertly, wantonly, impudently, petulantly

pĕtŭlāntĭa, ae, f. : impudent or boisterous aggressiveness; wantonness, immodesty;

phărĕtra, ae, f. : a quiver

phărĕtrātus, a, um : furnished with, wearing a quiver, quivered

phĭlŏsŏphĭcus, a, um : of or belonging to philosophy, philosophic, Adv.

Phŏebus, i, m. : a poetical appellation of Apollo as the god of light, the sun

Phŏenīx, īcis, m. : -I. -I. the Carthaginians, a Carthaginian, a Phoenician -II. The son of Amyntor, who was given by Peleus to Achilles as a companion in the Trojan war -II. Phoenician;

phŏenīx, īcis, m. : the phoenix, a fabulous bird in Arabia. It was said to live, years, and from its ashes a young phoenix arose

Pīĕrĭa, ae, f. : A country of Macedonia, south of the Haliacmon

Pīĕrĭdes, um, f. : Pierides daughters of Pierus

Pīĕris, ĭdis, f. : a Muse (first worshipped in Pieria),

Pīĕrĭus, a, um : Pierian, Thessalian; sacred to the Muses, poetic

pĭĕtās, atis, f. : responsibility, sense of duty; loyalty; tenderness, goodness; pity; piety

pĭgĕr, gra, grum : lazy, slow, dull;

pīgnŭs, oris, n. : pledge (security for debt), hostage, mortgage; bet, stake; symbol; relict;

pīnna, ae, f. : lobe (of the liver/lung);

pĭo, are : to appease, propitiate; to cleanse, expiate;

plăcĕo, ere, cui, citum : it is pleasing/satisfying, gives pleasure; is believed/settled/agreed/decided;

plăcĕt, v. impers. : it is pleasing/satisfying, gives pleasure; is believed/settled/agreed/decided

plăco, are : to appease; to placate; to reconcile;

plănēta, ae, m. : a wandering star, planet

plāngŏr, oris, m. : outcry, shriek;

plānta, ae, f. : cutting, heel, young shoot detached for propagation; seedling, young plant;

plānum, i, n. : level ground, a plain

plānus, a, um : level, flat;

plāudo, ere, si, sum : to clap, strike (w/flat hand), pat; to beat (wings); to applaud; to express (dis)approval;

plēbēĭus, a, um : plebeian;

plēbēĭus, i, m. : a plebeian

plēbēs, ei, f. : common people, general citizens, commons/plebeians; lower class/ranks; mob/

plēbs, plebis, f. : common people, general citizens, commons/plebeians; lower class/ranks; mob/

plēnus, a, um : full, plump; satisfied;

plōro, are : to cry over, cry aloud; to lament, weep; to deplore;

plūrĭmŭm, adv. : most/great number of things; greatest amount; very much; the most possible;

plūrĭmus, a, um : most, greatest number/amount; very many; most frequent; highest price/value;

plūrĭs, plura : (pl.) plus de, plus nombreux

plūs, adv. : more, too much, more than enough; more than

plūs, plurĭs : more; several. many; (COMP of multus)

pōcŭlŭm, pōclum, i, n. : cup, bowl, drinking vessel; drink/draught; social drinking (pl.); drink;

pōena, ae, f. : penalty, punishment; revenge/retribution; [poena dare => to pay the penalty];

pŏēta, ae, m. : poet;

Pŏlītēs, ae, m. : a son of Priam, killed by Pyrrhus

pŏlītĭcus, a, um : of or belonging to civil polity, to the State, political, civil

pōllūtus, a, um : polluted, unchaste

pōmpa, ae, f. : procession; retinue; pomp, ostentation;

pōnĕ, prép. + acc. : behind (in local relations) (rare);

pōno, ere, posui, situm : - to put/place/set; to station/post (troops); to pitch (camp); to situate; to set up; to erect; to bury; - to put/lay down (load/arms), take off (clothes); to shed (leaves); to cut (nails);

Pōns, ntis, m. : a geographical proper name.

pōns, pontis, m. : bridge;

pōntus, i, m. : sea;

pŏpŭlārēs, ium, m. : Acceptable to the people, agreeable to the multitude, popular

pŏpŭlārĭs, e : "- compatriot, fellow citizen/from same community; partner/associate; - member of ""Popular"" party, promoter of ""Popular"" policies;"

pŏpŭlātĭŏ, onis, f. : plundering, ravaging, spoiling; laying waste, devastation; plunder, booty;

pōpŭlus, i, f. : poplar tree; (long o)

pŏpŭlus, pŏplus, i, m. : people, nation, State; public/populace/multitude/crowd; a following

pōrrīgo, pōrgo, ere, rexi, rectum : to stretch out, extend;

Pōrsĕna, Pōrsēnna, Pōrsīna, ae, m. : a king of Etruria, who made war on Rome on account of the banished Tarquins, to sell Porsena's goods, to sell goods at auction

pōrta, ae, f. : gate, entrance; city gates; door; avenue; goal (soccer);

pōrtĭcus, us, f. : colonnade, covered walk; portico; covered gallery atop amphitheater/siege

pōrto, are : to carry, bring;

pōrtōrĭŭm, i, n. : port duty; customs duty; tax;

pŏsĭtŭs, us, m. : a position, situation; disposition, order, arrangement, ways of arranging

pōssĭdĕo, ere, sedi, sessum : to seize, hold, be master of; to possess, take/hold possession of, occupy; to inherit;

pōssŭm, potes, posse, potui : to be able, can; [multum posse => have much/more/most influence/power];

pōst, adv, prép. + acc. : behind (space), after (time); subordinate to (rank);

pōstĕā, adv. : afterwards;

pōstĕri, orum, m. : inferior

pōstĕrĭŭs, adv. : later, at a later day; by and by;

pōstĕrus, a, um : coming after, following, next; COMP next in order, latter; SUPER last/hindmost

pōstĭs, m. : doorpost;

pōstmŏdŭm, adv. : after a while, later, a little later; afterwards; presently;

pōstquăm, conj. sub. : after;

pōstrēmō, adv. : at last, finally;

pōstrēmus, a, um : last/final/latest/most recent; nearest end/farthest back/hindmost; worst/

pōstŭlo, are : to demand, claim; to require; to ask/pray for;

pŏtēns, entis : powerful, strong; capable; mighty;

pŏtēntĭa, ae, f. : force, power, political power;

pŏtēstās, atis, f. : power, rule, force; strength, ability; chance, opportunity;

pŏtĭŏ, ionis, f. : drinking, drink;

pŏtĭŏr, oris : better/preferable/superior; more useful/effective; more important; - having better claim, more entitled/qualified, carrying greater weight;

pŏtĭs, pote : able, capable; possible; (early Latin potis sum becomes possum);

pŏtĭssĭmŭm, pŏtīssŭmŭm, adv. : chiefly, principally, especially, in preference to all others, above all, most of all

pŏtīssĭmus, a, um : chief, principal, most prominent/powerful; strongest; foremost;

pŏtĭŭs, adv. : rather, more, preferably;

pŏto, are : to drink; to drink heavily/convivially, tipple; to swallow; to absorb, soak up;

prăctĭcē, f. : la pratique [par oppos. à la théorie]

prăctĭcus, a, um : active

prăe, adv., prép. : before, in front; in view of, because of;

prăebĕo, ere, bui, bitum : - to present/show/put forward; to offer; to expose physically oneself; to expose/submit; - to make available, supply, provide; to be the cause, occasion, produce; to render;

prăecēps, (praecip-) cĭpĭtis, n. : -I. a steep place, a precipice -II. Great danger, extremity, extreme danger, critical circumstances

prăecēps, cipitis : head first, headlong; steep, precipitous

prăecĭpĭtĭŭm, i, n. : a steep place, an abrupt descent, a precipice

prăecĭpĭto, are (svt pronominal) : to throw headlong, cast down;

prăeda, ae, f. : booty, loot, spoils, plunder, prey;

prăedātŏr, ōris, m. : a plunderer, pillager.

prăedico, are : proclaim/declare/make known/publish/announce formally; praise/recommend

prăedīco, ere, dixi, dictum : say beforehand, mention in advance; warn/predict/foretell; recommend/prescribe;

prăedō, onis, m. : robber, thief; pirate (if at sea);

prăedŏr, aris, ari : to acquire loot (by robbery/war/depredation); to obtain food by hunting/preying

prăefĕro, fers, ferre, tuli, latum : to carry in front; to prefer; to display; to offer; to give preference to;

prăemĭŭm, ii, n. : prize, reward; gift; recompense;

prăerĭpĭo, ere, ripui, reptum : to snatch away (before the proper time); to seize first; to forestall;

prăesērtĭm, adv. : especially; particularly;

prăesĭdĭŭm, ii, n. : protection; help; guard; garrison, detachment;

prăestāns, antis : excellent, remarquable, souverain, supérieur

prăesto, are : to excel, surpass, be outstanding/superior/best/greater/preferable (to); - to furnish/supply, make available, hand over; to tender/offer/present; to play part

prăetĕr, conj. coord., prép. + acc. : besides, except, contrary to; beyond (rank), in front of, before; more than;

prăetĕrĕo, ire, ii, itum : to pass/go by; to disregard/neglect/omit/miss; to surpass/excel; to go overdue; to pass over;

prăetŏr, oris, m. : praetor (official elected by the Romans who served as a judge);

prātŭm, i, n. : meadow, meadowland; meadow grass/crop; broad expanse/field/plain (land/sea);

prĕcŏr, aris, atus sum : to beg/implore/entreat; to wish/pray for/to; to pray, supplicate, beseech

prĕmo, ere, pressi, pressum : to press, press hard, pursue; to oppress; to overwhelm;

prēndo, ere, prendi, prensum : to catch, take hold of; to arrest, capture; to reach; to understand; to seize, grasp; to occupy;

prēnso, a, are : to grasp/clutch at/constantly; to lay hold of; to accost/buttonhole; to canvass, solicit;

prĕtĭōsus, a, um : expensive, costly, of great value, precious; rich in;

prĕtĭŭm, ii, n. : price/value/worth; reward/pay; money; prayer/request; [~ natalis => weregeld];

prēx, precis, f. (nom. sg. inusité) : prayer, request

Prĭămēïus, a, um : of or belonging to Priam

Prĭămus, i, m. : Priam

prīma, orum, n. : the first part, the beginning, the first principles, elements, from the beginning, at first, in front, before, in the beginning, first

prīmō, adv. : at first; in the first place; at the beginning;

prīmŭm, adv. : at first; in the first place;

prīmus, a, um : first, foremost/best, chief, principal; nearest/next

prīncēps, cĭpis, m. : The first man, first person; the first, chief, principal, most distinguished person; A chief, head, author, originator, leader, contriver; A chief, superior, director; A prince, i. e. a ruler, sovereign, emperor

prīncēps, ipis, adj. : first, foremost, leading, chief, front; earliest, original; most necessary;

prīncĭpĭŭm, ii, n. : beginning;

prīscē, adv. : in ancient style, summarily

prīscus, a, um : ancient, early, former;

prĭŭs, adv. : earlier times/events/actions; a logically prior proposition

prĭŭsquăm, + subj. : before; until; sooner than;

prīvātus, a, um : private; personal; ordinary;

prīvo, are : to deprive, rob, free;

prō, prép. + abl. : on behalf of; before; in front/instead of; for; about; according to; as, like;

prŏăvus, i, m. : great-grandfather; remote ancestor;

prŏbābĭlĭs, e : that may be assumed, believed, proved; likely, credible, probable

prŏbo, are : - to approve (of), esteem/commend/recommend/certify; to give assent/approval/ - to let; to show to be real/true; to examine/test/try/prove/demonstrate; to get accepted;

prŏcēdo, ere, cessi, cessum : to proceed; to advance; to appear;

prŏcēlla, ae, f. : storm, gale; tumult, commotion;

prŏcĕr, ĕris, m. cf. proceres : chiefs, princes; leading men of the country/society/profession

prŏcērēs, um, m. pl. : chiefs, princes; leading men of the country/society/profession

prŏcērĭtās, atis, f. : height/tallness; altitude, distance up; great length (some up); metrical feet;

prŏcŭbo, āre, intr. : to lie stretched out, to lie along

prŏcŭl, adv. : away; at distance, far off;

prŏcūmbo, ere, cubui, cubitum : sink down, lie down, lean forward;

prŏdūco, ere, duxi, ductum : to lead forward, bring out; to reveal; to induce; to promote; to stretch out; to prolong; to bury;

prŏdūcta, orum, n. : preferable things

prŏelĭŭm, ii, n. : battle/fight/bout/conflict/dispute; armed/hostile encounter; bout of strength;

prŏfēctĭŏ, ionis, f. : departure;

prŏfēctō, adv. : surely, certainly;

prŏfĭcĭo, ere, feci, fectum : to make, accomplish, effect;

prŏfĭcīscŏr, eris, i, fectus sum : to depart, set out; to proceed

prŏgēnĭes, ei, f. : race, family, progeny;

prŏgrĕdĭŏr, eris, i, gressus sum : to go, come forth, go forward, march forward; to advance, proceed, make progress

prŏīcĭo, prōjĭcĭo, ere, ieci, iectum : to throw down, throw; to abandon; to throw away;

prŏīndē, prŏin, adv. : hence, so then; according to/in the same manner/degree/proportion;

prōjēctus, a, um : stretched out, extended, jutting out, projecting.

prōlābŏr, eris, i, lapsus sum : to glide or slip forwards, fall into decay, go to ruin; to collapse

prōmītto, ere, misi, missum : to promise;

prŏpĕ, adv., prép. + acc. : near, nearly; close by; almost;

prŏpēllo, ere, puli, pulsum : to drive forward/forth; to drive away/out/off; to defeat;

prŏpĕrē, adv. : hastily, in haste, quickly, speedily

prŏpĕrus, a, um : quick, speedy;

prŏpīnquo, are : to bring near; to draw near;

prŏpīnquum, i, n. : neighborhood, vicinity

prŏpīnquus, a, um : near, neighboring;

prŏpīnquus, i, m. : a relation, relative, kinsman

prŏpĭtĭo, are : to propitiate, render favorable, win over; to sooth (feelings);

prŏpĭtĭus, a, um : favorably inclined, well-disposed, propitious;

prŏprĭē, adv. : Specially, peculiarly, properly, strictly for one's self

prŏprĭus, a, um : own, very own; individual; special, particular, characteristic; adv. ,ore closely

prŏptĕr, prép. + acc. : near; on account of; by means of; because of;

prōsĕcūtŏr, ōris, m. : an accompanier, companion, an attendant

prōsĭlĭo, ire, ui : to jump/leap up/forward; to rush/leap/spring forth/to; to gush/break/jut out;

prōspĭcĭo, ere, spexi, spectum : to foresee; to see far off; to watch for, provide for, look out for;

prōstĭtūta, ae, f. : unchaste, prostitute

prōstĭtūtus, a, um : prostituted

prōsŭm, prodes, prodesse, profui : to be useful, be advantageous, benefit, profit (with DAT);

prōtĕgo, ere, texi, tectum : to cover, protect;

prōtĭnŭs, prŏtĭnăm, adv. : straight on, forward; immediately; without pause; at once;

prōvĕnĭo, ire, ueni, uentum : to come forth; to come into being; to prosper;

prōvĭdĕo, ere, uidi, visum : to foresee; to provide for, make provision; with DAT;

prōvŏco, are : to call forth; to challenge; to provoke;

prōxĭmŭm, i, n. : the neighborhood, vicinity

prōxĭmus, prōxŭmus, a, um : neighbor; nearest one;

prūdēns, entis : aware, skilled; sensible, prudent; farseeing; experienced;

prūdēntĭa, ae, f. : discretion; good sense, wisdom; prudence; foresight;

pūbēs, eris, adj. : adult, grown-up; full of sap;

pūbēs, f. : the signs of manhood, the hair which appears on the body at the age of puberty

pŭblica, ae, f. : courtisane, prostituée.

pŭblīco, are : public, publicly (in publico);

pŭblĭcŭm, i, n. : Possessions of the State, public territory, communal property

pŭblĭcūs, a, um : public; common, of the people/state; official; [res publica => the state];

pŭblĭcūs, i, m. : A public officer, public functionary, magistrate, the police

Pŭblĭus, i, m. : Publius (Roman praenomen); (abb. P.);

pŭdīcĭtĭa, ae, f. : chastity; modesty; purity;

pŭdŏr, oris, m. : decency, shame; sense of honor; modesty; bashfulness;

pŭella, ae, f. : girl, (female) child/daughter; maiden; young woman/wife; sweetheart; slavegirl;

pŭer, eri, m. : boy, lad, young man; servant; (male) child; [a puere => from boyhood];

pūgna, ae, f. : battle, fight;

pūgno, are : to fight; to dispute; [pugnatum est => the battle raged];

pūgnum, i, n. cf. pugnus : fist;

pūlchĕr, pūlcĕr, chra, chrum : pretty; beautiful; handsome; noble, illustrious;

pūlso, are : to beat; to pulsate;

pūlvĕrŭlēntus, a, um : full of dust, dusty, covered with dust

pūnĭo, ire, iui, itum : to punish (person/offense), inflict punishment; to avenge, extract retribution;

pūnĭŏr, iris, nīri, nītus sum, cf. punio : to punish (person/offense), inflict punishment; to avenge, extract retribution;

pūrĭtās, ātis, f. : -I. cleanness, purity -II. purulency

pūrpŭrĕus, a, um : purple, dark red;

pūrus, a, um : - pure, clean, unsoiled; free from defilement/taboo/stain; blameless, innocent; - clear, limpid, free of mist/cloud; ringing (voice); open (land); net; simple;

pūs, pūris, n. : white, viscous matter, pus

pūsĭo, ōnis, m. : A little boy

pŭto, are : to think, believe, suppose, hold; to reckon, estimate, value; to clear up, settle;

pŭtrĭs, e : rotten, decaying; stinking, putrid, crumbling;

Pўrrhus, Pўrrus, i, m. : on of Achilles and Deïdamia (otherwise called Neoptolemus), founder of a kingdom in Epirus, slain at Delphi by Orestes

Q, : Quintus (Roman praenomen); (abb. Q.);

quā, conj. et adv. : where; by which route;

quācūmquē, adv. conj. : by whatever way, wherever, wheresoever

quaero, ere, siui, situm : to search for, seek, strive for; to obtain; to ask, inquire, demand;

quaesītum, i, n. : A question

quaesītus, a, um : select, special, extraordinary

quaestĭō, ionis, f. : questioning, inquiry; investigation;

quālĭs, e : what kind/sort/condition (of); what is (he/it) like; what/how excellent a ...;

quālus, i, m. : a wicker basket, hamper, a fruit-hamper, wool-basket, winestrainer

quām, quāmdĕ, quāndĕ, adv. : how, than;

quāmdĭū, adv. interr. : - for how long?; how long (ago)?; how long!, what a long time!; until; as long - for the preceding period until; up to the time that; inasmuch as; (quam diu);

quāmquăm, quānquăm, conj. sub. + ind. : though, although; yet; nevertheless;

quāmvīs, conj. sub. : however much; although;

quāndŏ, conj. sub. : when, since, because; [si quando => if ever];

quāntŭm, adv. : so much as

quāntŭm, quantum ... tantum : how much; how far;

quāntus, a, um, adj., pron. excl et interr : how great; how much/many; of what size/amount/degree/number/worth/price;

quāsĭ, conj. : as if, just as if, as though; as it were; about;

quĕmādmŏdŭm, conj. et adv. interr. : in what way, how; as, just as; to the extent that;

quĕo, ire, ii or iui, itum : to be able;

quĕrŏr, eris, i, questus sum : to complain; to protest, grumble, gripe; to make formal complaint in court of law

quĕstus, us, m. : complaint;

quī, adv. : how?; how so; in what way; by what/which means; whereby; at whatever price;

quī, quae, quod, pron. rel. : who; that; which, what; of which kind/degree; person/thing/time/point that

quĭă, conj. sub. : because;

quīcūmquĕ, quae-, quod- (-cun-) : Whoever, whatever, whosoever, whatsoever, every one who, every thing that, all that

quĭd, adv. interr. : how? why? wherefore?

quĭdăm, quaedam, quoddam/quiddam : a certain, a certain one, somebody, something

quĭdĕm, adv. : indeed (postpositive), certainly, even, at least; ne...quidem -- not...even;

quĭēsco, ere, quieui, quietum : to rest, keep quiet/calm, be at peace/rest; to be inactive/neutral; to permit; to sleep;

quīn, conj. : so that not, without; that not; but that; that; quin etiam = moreover

quīnquāgīntă, num. : fifty

quīnquĕ, num. : five;

quĭs, quae, quid, pron. interr. : who? which? what? what man?

quīsquăm, quaequam, quidquam or quic- : any, any one, any body, any thing, something

quīsquĕ, quaeque, quidque, pron. : whoever, whatever it be, each, every, every body, every one, every thing

quīsquĭs, quidquid or quicquid : whoever, whosoever, whatever, whatsoever, every one who, each, every, all

quīvīs, quaeuis, quoduis/quiduis : who, what you please, any whatever, any one, any thing

quō, adv., conj. sub. : où ? (avec chgt de lieu), pour que; adv. quelque part

quŏăd, conj. sub. + subj. : as long as, until;

quŏd, conj. sub. : That, in that, because; Wherefore, why, that

quōmŏdŏ, conj. sub. : how, in what way; just as;

quōndăm, adv. : un jour, à un certain moment, autrefois

quŏnĭăm, conj. sub. : because, since, seeing that;

quŏquĕ, adv. : likewise/besides/also/too; not only; even/actually; (after word emphasized);

quōquō, adv. : wherever, in whatever place/direction; whatever; anywhere; in each direction;

quŏt, pron. : tant de (tot... quot, autant de... que ; totidem... quot, aussi souvent... que)

rādīx, icis, f. : root; base; square-root (math);

rādo, ere, rasi, rasum : to shave; scratch, scrape; to coast by;

rāmus, i, m. : branch, bough;

răpācĭtās, ātis, f. : greediness, rapacity

răpĭdē, adv. : hurriedly, rapidly

răpĭdus, a, um : rapid, swift;

răpĭo, ere, rapui, raptum : to drag off; to snatch; to destroy; to seize, carry off; to pillage; to hurry;

rătĭō, ōnis, f. : account, reckoning, invoice; plan; prudence; method; reasoning; rule; regard;

rătĭs, f. : raft; ship, boat;

rătus, a, um : established, authoritative; fixed, certain;

rāucus, a, um : hoarse; husky; raucous;

rĕcēdo, ere, cessi, cessum : to recede, go back, withdraw, ebb; to retreat; to retire; to move/keep/pass/slip away;

rĕcēns, adv. : lately, freshly, newly, just, recently

rĕcēns, entis : fresh, recent; rested;

rĕcēntĕr, adv. : nouvellement, récemment

rĕcēntŏr, āri : to renew itself

rĕcēpto, are : to recover; to receive, admit (frequently);

rĕcēptum, i, n. : subst., an engagement, obligation, guaranty

rĕcīpĭo, ere, cepi, ceptum : to keep back; recover; to undertake; to guarantee; to accept, take in; to take back;

rĕcōgnōsco, ere, oui, itum : reconnaître, retrouver; passer en revue

rĕcōndo, ere, condidi, conditum : to hide, conceal; to put away;

rēctā, adv. : directly, straight;

rēctum, i, n. : that which is right, good, virtuous; uprightness, rectitude, virtue, subjective-clause

rēctus, a, um : right, proper; straight; honest;

rĕcūso, are : to reject, refuse, refuse to; to object; to decline;

rēddo, ere, ddidi, dditum : to return; to restore; to deliver; to hand over, pay back, render, give back; to translate;

rēdĕo, ire, ii, itum : to return, go back, give back; to fall back on, revert to; to respond, pay back;

rĕdīmĭo, ire, ii, itum : to encircle with a garland, wreathe around; to surround, encircle;

rĕdīntĕgro, are : to renew; revive;

rĕdītus, us, m. : return, returning; revenue, income, proceeds; produce (Plater);

rĕfērcĭo, ire, fersi, fertum : to fill up, stuff, cram

rĕfĕro, fers, ferre, tuli, latum : it matters/makes a difference/is of importance; to matter/be of importance (PERS);

rĕfērtus, a, um : stuffed, crammed, filled full to bursting with, replete; crowded; loaded;

rēflēcto, ere, reflexi, reflexum : to bend back; to turn back; to turn round;

rĕfōrmīdo, are : to fear greatly, to dread, to stand in awe of, to shun, avoid through fear

rĕfŭgĭo, ere, fugi : to flee back; to run away, escape;

rĕgĕro, ere, gessi, gestum : to bear, carry, bring back

rēgĭa, ae, f. : palace, court; residence;

rēgĭŏ, onis, f. : area, region; neighborhood; district, country; direction;

rēgĭus, a, um : royal, of a king, regal;

rēgnātŏr, ōris, m. : a ruler, sovereign.

rēgno, are : reign, rule; be king; play the lord, be master;

rēgnŭm, i, n. : royal power; power; control; kingdom;

rĕgo, ere, rexi, rectum : to rule, guide; to manage, direct;

rēĭcĭo, ere, ieci, iectum : to throw back; to drive back; to repulse, repel; to refuse, reject, scorn;

rĕlīnquo, ere, reliqui, relictum : to leave behind, abandon; (pass.) to be left, remain; to bequeath;

rĕmănĕo, ere, mansi, mansum : to stay behind; to continue, remain;

rĕmāno, are : to flow back

rĕmīssē, adv. : - loosely; without vehemence/passion; placidly; unconstrainedly; light- - half-heartedly/feebly; inattentively; w/laxity of discipline; mildly/

rĕmīssus, a, um : - relaxed/slack/sagging; loosely spaced; remiss; mild/gentle/free-and-easy/ - lenient, forbearing; moderate, not intense/potent; low (valuation); fever-

rĕmītto, ere, misi, missum : to send back, remit; to throw back, relax, diminish;

rĕmōtus, a, um : remote; distant, far off; removed, withdrawn; removed/freed from;

rĕmŏvĕo, ere, moui, motum : to move back; to put away; to withdraw; to remove;

rĕmūnĕrŏr, aris, ari : to reward, repay, recompense, remunerate; to requite; to pay back, retaliate

rĕnŏvo, are : to renew, restore; to revive;

rĕnŭmĕro, are : to count over, count up., to pay back, repay

rĕŏr, reris, reri, ratus sum : to think, regard; to deem; to suppose, believe, reckon

rĕpēllo, ere, rep(p)uli, repulsum : to drive/push/thrust back/away; to repel/rebuff/spurn; to fend off; to exclude/bar; to refute;

rĕpēns, tis : subit, imprévu ; récent

rĕpēntĕ, adv. : suddenly, unexpectedly;

rĕpēntīnō, adv. : suddenly, unexpectedly

rĕpēntīnus, a, um : sudden, hasty; unexpected;

rĕpĕrĭo, ire, rep(p)eri, repertum : to discover, learn; to light on; to find/obtain/get; to find out/to be, get to know;

rĕpērtŏr, oris, m. : discoverer, inventor, author;

rĕpĕto, ere, iui/ii, titum : to return to; to get back; to demand back/again; to repeat; to recall; to claim;

rĕpĕtūndāe, arum, f. : réclamées (sommes d'argent)

rĕpo, ere, repsi, reptum : to creep, crawl;

rĕpōno, ere, posui, positum : to put back; to restore; to store; to repeat;

rĕprĕhēnso, āre : to hold back continually, detain from time to time

rĕprĭmo, ere, pressi, pressum : to press back, repress; to check, prevent, restrain;

rĕpūlsŭs, us, m. : a driving back, repulsion, rebounding, reflection, reverberation, abl. sing., reechoing

rĕquĭēsco, ere, quieui, quietum : to quiet down; to rest; to end;

rĕquīro, ere, i, quisitum : to require, seek, ask for; to need; to miss, pine for;

rēs, rei, f. : a thing, object, being; a matter, affair, event, fact, circumstance, occurrence, deed, condition, case

rēscīndo, ere; scidi, scissum : to cut out; to cut down, destroy; to annul; to rescind;

rēscrībo, ere, scripsi, scriptum : to write back in reply;

rĕsĕco, are, secui, sectum : to cut back, trim; to reap, cut short;

rĕsĭdĕo, ere, sedi, sessum : to sit down/on/in; to settle; to be perched; to remain seated/idle/fixed/in place; to squat;

rĕsīdo, ere, sēdi, sessum, intr. : to sit down, to settle

rĕsīsto, ere, stiti : to pause; to continue; to resist, oppose; to reply; to withstand, stand (DAT); to make a stand;

rĕspĭcĭo, ere, spexi, spectum : to look back at; to gaze at; to consider; to respect; to care for, provide for;

rēspōndĕo, ere, di, sum : to answer;

rēspōnso, are : to return an answer, to answer, reply, respond

rēspōnsŭm, i, n. : answer, response;

rēspōnsŭs, us, m. : An answer, reply

rēspŭo, ere, ui, - : to reject, spit, spew out; to turn away, repel; to reject, destain, spurn, refuse;

rēstĭtŭo, ere, tui, tutum : to restore; to revive; to bring back; to make good;

rĕsūrgo, ere, rexi, rectum : to rise/appear again; to rare up again, lift oneself, be restored/rebuilt, revive;

rĕtĭnĕo, ere, ui, tentum : to hold back, restrain; to uphold; to delay; to hold fast; to retain, preserve;

rĕtōrquĕo, ere, torsi, tortum : to twist back; to cast back; to fling back; to turn aside;

rĕtrăho, ere, traxi, tractum : to draw back, withdraw; to make known again, divert; to bring back;

rĕtrō, adv. : backwards, back, to the rear; behind, on the back side; back (time), formerly;

rĕus, i, m. : liable to (penalty of); guilty; [mens rea => guilty mind (modern legal term)];

rĕvĕnĭo, ire, ueni, uentum : to come back, return;

rĕvērto, ere, i, sum : to turn back, go back, return; recur;

rĕvērtŏr, rĕvŏrtŏr, eris, i, reuersus sum : to turn back, go back, return; to recur

rĕvīso, ere, uisi, uisum : to revisit, go back and see;

rĕvŏco, are : to call back, recall; to revive; regain;

rĕvōlvo, ere, uolui, uolutum : to throw back, roll back;

rēx, regis, m. : king;

Rhēsus, i, m. : the son of a Muse, a king in Thrace, who was robbed of his horses and killed by Diomede and Ulysses before Troy

Rhīpēus, ĕi (ĕos), m. : Rhipée (nom d'un Centaure, d'un guerrier)

rīdĕo, ere, risi, risum : to laugh at (with dat.), laugh; to ridicule;

rīpa, ae, f. : bank;

rīvālĭs, m. : rival; (esp. in love); one who shares use of a stream/mistress; neighbor ;

rōbŏro, are : to give physical/moral strength to; to reinforce; to strengthen, make more effective;

rōbŭr, rōbus, oris, n. : - oak (tree/ timber/ trunk /club /post/cell); tough core; - strength /firmness /solidity; vigor, robustness; potency, force, effectiveness;

rōdo, ere, rosi, rosum : to gnaw

rŏgo, are : to ask, ask for; to invite; to introduce;

Rōma, ae, f. : Rome;

Rōmānus, a, um : Roman, a Roman

rŏsa, ae, f. : rose; (also as term of endearment); rose bush; rose oil;

rŏta, ae, f. : wheel (rotate);

rŭbĕo, ere, rubui : to be red, become red;

rŭbĕr, bra, brum : red, ruddy, painted red;

rŭīna, ae, f. : fall; catastrophe; collapse, destruction;

rŭmpo, ere, rupi, ruptum : to break; to destroy;

rŭo, ere, rui, rutum : to destroy, ruin, overthrow; to rush on, run; to fall; to charge (in + ACC); to be ruined;

rūrsŭs, adv. : turned back, backward; on the contrary/other hand, in return, in turn, again;

rūstĭcus, a, um : country, rural; plain, homely, rustic

rūstĭcus, i, m. : peasant, farmer

săcĕr, cra, crum : sacred, holy, consecrated; accursed, horrible, detestable;

săcērdōs, dotis, m. : priest, priestess;

săcrātus, a, um : hallowed, consecrated, holy, sacred, deified, Augustus

săcrĭfĭcĭŭm, ii, n. : sacrifice, offering to a deity;

săcrĭfĭco, săcrŭfĭco, are : to sacrifice; to celebrate the Mass (Erasmus);

săcrĭfĭcus, a, um : of or belonging to a sacrificing, sacrificial, mindful of sacrifices, of religion

săcro, are : to consecrate, make sacred, dedicate;

săcrŭm, i, n. : sacrifice; sacred vessel; religious rites (pl.);

sāepĕ, adv. : often, oft, oftimes, many times, frequently;

sāepēs, f. : hedge; fence; anything planted/erected to form surrounding barrier;

sāepĭo, ire, psi, ptum : to surround with a hedge, to hedge in, fence in, enclose

sāepta, orum, n. : a fence, enclosure, wall, stakes.mdash;An enclosed place, enclosure, fold, An enclosure for voting, the polls, booths

sāeptŭm, i, n. : fold, paddock; enclosure; voting enclosure in the Campus Martius

sāevē, adv. : savagely

sāevĭo, ire, ii, itum : to rage; to rave, bluster; to be/act angry/violent/ferocious; to vent rage on (DAT);

sāevus, a, um : savage; fierce/ferocious; violent/wild/raging; cruel, harsh, severe; vehement;

săgītta, ae, f. : arrow;

Sāïs, f. : the capital of Lower Egypt, Sa el-Hajar

sāl, salis, m. : salt; wit;

sălĕ, n. : salt

sălĭo, ire, salui, saltum : to leap, jump; to move suddenly/spasmodically (part of body under stress), twitch;

sāllĭo, sălĭo, ire, ii, itum : To salt down, to salt

sălŭm, i, n. : open sea, high sea, main, deep, ocean; sea in motion, billow, waves;

sălūs, utis, f. : health; prosperity; good wish; greeting; salvation, safety;

sălūto, are : to greet; to wish well; to visit; to hail, salute;

sāncĭo, ire, sanxi, sanctum : to confirm, ratify; to sanction; to fulfill (prophesy); to enact (law); to ordain; to dedicate;

sānctē, adv. : solemnly, conscientiously, scrupulously, religiously, with holy awe

sānctītās, atis, f. : inviolability, sanctity, moral purity, virtue, piety, purity, holiness;

sānctus, a, um : consecrated, sacred, inviolable; venerable, august, divine, holy, pious, just;

sānguĭnĕus, a, um : bloody, bloodstained; blood-red;

sānguĭno, are : to be bloody; to bleed, run with blood

sānguĭnŏlēntus, a, um : bloody; blood-red; blood-stained;

sānguĭs, inis, m. : blood; family;

sănĭes, ei, f. : ichorous/bloody matter/pus discharged from wound/ulcer; other such fluids;

sāno, are : to cure, heal; to correct; to quiet;

săpĭēns, entis : rational; sane, of sound mind; wise, judicious, understanding; discreet;

săpĭēntĕr, adv. : wisely, sensibly;

săpĭo, ere, ii : to taste of; to understand; to have sense;

săta, orum, n. : standing corn, crops

sătēllĕs, tellitis, m. or f. : attendant; courtier; follower; life guard; companion; accomplice, abettor;

sătĭs, adv. : enough, adequately; sufficiently; well enough, quite; fairly, pretty;

sătŭs, us, m. : a sowing, planting

săucĭus, a, um : wounded; ill, sick;

Sāus, i, m. : a river in Pannonia, a tributary of the Danube, the Save

sāxŭm, i, n. : stone;

Scāevŏla, ae, m. : Scaevola

scālāe, arum, f. pl. : ladder (pl.)

scāndo, ere, scandi, scansum : to climb; to mount, ascend, get up, clamber;

scĕlŭs, eris, n. : crime; calamity; wickedness, sin, evil deed;

scĭo, ire, sciui, scitum : to know, understand;

scīscĭtŏr, aris, ari : to ask, question, consult

scīsco, ere, scivi, scitum : to investigate, inquire; (political) to vote; to ordain;

scrība, ae, m. : a public, official writer, a clerk, secretary, scribe

scrībo, ere, scripsi, scriptum : to write; to compose;

scrīptum, i, n. : A line;, a game played with colored stones, on a draught-board marked into spaces by twelve oblique lines

scūtŭm, i, n. : shield; (heavy shield of Roman legion infantry);

scūtus, i, m. : An oblong shield, a buckler, of the infantry

Scȳrĭus, a, um : of or belonging to Scyros, Scyrian

sē, sui, pron. réfl. : himself, herself, itself, themselves

sēcerno, ere, creui, cretum : separate, distinguish

sĕco, are, secui, sectum : to follow; to escort/attend/accompany; to aim at/reach after/strive for/make for/seek; to attain;

sēcrētō, adv. : separately; secretly, in private;

sēcrētŭm, i, n. : secret, mystic rite, haunt;

sēcrētus, a, um : separate, apart (from); private, secret; remote; hidden;

sēcŭm, pron. contr. sēcum = cum se : suet; tallow; hard animal fat; (sebum);

sĕcŭndo, are : to make conditions favorable (winds/deities), favor; to adjust, adapt; prosper;

sĕcūndŭm, + acc : after; according to; along/next to, following/immediately after, close behind;

sĕcūndus, a, um : next, following; second; substituted; secondary/inferior; subordinate;

sĕcūrĭs, f. : ax (battle/headsman's), hatchet, chopper; (death) blow; vine-dresser's blade;

sĕcūrus, a, um : secure, safe, untroubled, free from care;

sĕcŭs, adv. : by, beside, alongside; in accordance with;

sĕd, conj. : but, but also; yet; however, but in fact/truth; not to mention; yes but;

sĕdĕo, ere, sedi, sessum : to sit, remain; to settle; to encamp;

sēdēs, f. : seat; home, residence; settlement, habitation; chair;

sēdo, are : to settle, allay; to restrain; to calm down;

sēdŭlus, a, um : attentive, painstaking, sedulous;

sĕgĕs, etis, f. : grain field; crop;

sēgnĭs, e : slow, sluggish, torpid, inactive; slothful, unenergetic; slow moving, slow;

sēgnĭtĭēs, ei, f. : slowness, tardiness, dilatoriness, sluggishness, inactivity

sĕmĕl, adv. : once, a single time

sēmpĕr, adv. : always;

sĕnātŏr, oris, m. : senator;

sĕnātus, us, m. : the council of the elders, the Senate;

sĕnēctus, a, um : very old, aged

sĕnēctūs, utis, f. : old age; extreme age; senility; old men; gray hairs; shed snake skin;

sĕnēx, sĕnis : old, aged, advanced in years

sĕnēx, senis, m. : aged, old; [senior => Roman over 45];

sĕnīlĭs, e : senile, aged;

sĕnĭŏr, oris, m. : older/elderly man, senior; (in Rome a man over 45);

sēnsus, us, m. : feeling, sense;

sēntĭo, ire, sensi, sensum : to perceive, feel, experience; to think, realize, see, understand;

sēntĭs, f. : thorn, briar;

senus, a, um, cf. seni : six each

sĕpūlchrŭm, i, n. : grave, tomb;

sĕquēstĕr, tra, : inter mediate, mediating, negotiating, m., a depositary, trustee, mediator, agent of bribery, go-between, f., under the protection of a truce

sequēstĕr, tris, : inter mediate, mediating, negotiating

sĕquēstĕr, tris, m. : a depositary, trustee

sĕquŏr, eris, i, secutus sum : to follow; to escort/attend/accompany; to aim at/reach after/strive for/make for/seek

sĕră, adv. : late at night

sĕra, ae, f. : bar (for fastening doors); rail of post and rail fence; lock (Cal)

sĕro, ere, seui, satum : to sow, plant

sērpēns, entis, m. et f. : serpent, snake;

sērpo, ere, serpsi, - : to crawl; to move slowly on, glide; to creep on;

sērus, a, um : late; too late; slow, tardy; after the expected/proper time; at a late hour;

sērva, ae, f. : a slave, servant, serf, serving-man; a female slave, maid-servant.

sērvāns, antis : keeping, observant

sērvĭo, ire, ii or iui, itum : serve; be a slave to; with DAT;

sērvĭtĭŭm, i, n. : slavery, servitude; slaves; the slave class;

sērvĭtūs, utis, f. : slavery; slaves; servitude;

sērvo, are : to watch over; to protect, store, keep, guard, preserve, save;

sērvus, i, m. : slave; servant;

sēu, conj. sub. : or if; or; [sive ... sive => whether ... or, either ... or];

sĕvērē, adv. : gravely, seriously, severely

sĕvērĭtās, atis, f. : strictness, severity;

sĕvērus, a, um : stern, strict, severe; grave, austere; weighty, serious; unadorned, plain;

sēx, adj. num. : six;

sī, sĕī, conj. sub. : si

sībĭla, orum, n. : a hissing, a whistling

sībĭlo, are : to hiss; to hiss at;

sībĭlus, a, um : hissing, whistling; hiss of contempt or disfavor

sīc, sĕic, adv. : ainsi (... ut, ainsi que)

sīcŭt, adv. : as, just as; like; in same way; as if; as it certainly is; as it were;

sīcŭtī, adv. : as, just as; like; in same way; as if; as it certainly is; as it were;

sīdŭs, ĕris, n. : star; constellation; tempest (Vulgate 4 Ezra 15,39);

sīgnĭfĭco, are : to signify, indicate, show;

sīgno, are : to mark, stamp, designate, sign; to seal;

sīgnŭm, i, n. : battle standard; indication; seal; sign, proof; signal; image, statue;

sĭlēntĭŭm, ii, n. : silence;

sĭlĕo, ere , ui, - : to be silent, not to speak (about); to be quiet; not to function;

sĭlēx, icis, m. : pebble/stone, flint; boulder, stone;

sīlva, ae, f. : wood, forest (sylvan);

sĭmĭlĭs, e : like, similar, resembling;

sĭmĭlĭtĕr, adv. : similarly;

Sīmŏīs, entis, m. : a small river in Troas that falls into the Scamander, Mendere Tchai

sīmplĭcĭtās, atis, f. : simplicity, candor;

sĭmŭl, sĕmŭl, adv. : en même temps, [conj.] dès que

sĭmŭlācrŭm, i, n. : likeness, image, statue;

sĭmŭlo, are : to imitate, copy; to pretend (to have/be); to look like; to simulate; to counterfeit; to feint;

sīn, conj. sub. : but if; if on the contrary;

sĭnĕ, prép. + abl. : without; (sometimes after object); lack; [Johannis sine Terra => John

sīngŭla, ae, f. : singula, sembella (monnaie d'argent)

sīngŭli, ae, a : One to each, separate, single

sīngŭlus, cf. singuli : One to each, separate, single

sĭnīstĕr, tra, trum : left, improper,adverse; inauspicious;

sĭnīstra, ae, f. : left hand;

sĭnīstrum, i, n. : lucky, favorable, auspicious, unlucky, unfavorable, inauspicious

sīno, ere, siui, situm : to allow, permit;

Sīnōn, ōnis, m. : son of Æsimus, through whose perfidy the Trojans were induced to take the wooden horse within their city

sīnŭo, are : to bend into a curve; to bend; to billow out;

sīnŭōsus, a, um : full of bendings, windings, curves; full of folds, bent, winding, sinuous

sīquĭs, conj. + pron. : = si quis

sīsto, ere, stiti, statum : to stop, check; to cause to stand; to set up;

sĭtus, us, m. : situation, position, site; structure; neglect, disuse, stagnation; mould

sōbrĭus, a, um : sober;

sŏcĕr, eri, m. : father in law;

sŏcĭa, ae, f. : relative and wife

sŏcĭo, are : to unite, join, ally; to share in;

sŏcĭus, a, um : sharing, joining in, partaking, united, associated, kindred, allied, fellow

sŏcĭus, ii, m. : associate, companion; ally

sŏdālis, e : of companions, friendly, companionable, sociable

sŏdālĭs, m. : companion, associate, mate, intimate, comrade, crony; accomplice, conspirator;

sōl, solis, m. : sun;

sōlēmnĭs, sōllēmnĭs, sōllēmpnĭs, e : solemn, ceremonial, sacred, in accordance w/religion/law; traditional/

sōlĕo, ere, solitus sum : to be in the habit of; to become accustomed to;

sŏlĭdo, are : to make solid/whole/dense/firm/crack free; to strengthen, consolidate; to solder; to knit;

sŏlĭdŭm, i, n. : solid figure; firm/hard material; firm/solid/unyielding ground; a whole;

sŏlĭdus, sōldus, a, um : solide, massif, compact; entier

sŏlĭtus, a, um : wonted, accustomed, usual, habitual, ordinary, common

sōllēmne, n. : - solemn observance, religious ceremony; customary practice/usage;

sōllĭcĭto, are : to disturb, worry; to stir up, arouse, agitate, incite;

sōllĭcĭtus, a, um : concerned, worried; upset, troubled, disturbed, anxious, apprehensive;

sōlo, are : to make lonely, desolate; to lay waste, desolate

sōlŭm, i, n. : only/just/merely/barely/alone;

sōlus, a, um : only, single; lonely; alone, having no companion/friend/protector; unique;

sōlūtum, i, n. : a state of looseness

sōlūtus, a, um : unbound, released; free, at large; unrestrained, profligate; lax, careless;

sōlvo, ere, ui, utum : to loosen, release, unbind, untie, free; to open; to set sail; to scatter; to pay off/back;

sōmnĭŭm, ii, n. : dream, vision; fantasy, day-dream;

sōmnus, i, m. : sleep;

sŏnĭtus, us, m. : noise, loud sound;

sŏno, are, sonui, sonitum : - to make a noise/ sound; speak/utter, emit sound; to be spoken of (as); to express - to echo/resound; to be heard, sound; to be spoken of (as); to celebrate in speech;

sōns, sontis : guilty, criminal;

sŏnus, i, m. : noise, sound;

Sŏphŏclēs, m. : Sophocles (Greek poet);

Sŏphŏclēus, a, um : of or in the manner of Sophocles

sōpĭo, ire, iui, itum : to deprive of feeling or sense; esp. by sleep, to put or lull to sleep.

sŏpōrātus, a, um : laid to sleep, unconscious, buried in sleep, stupefied, allayed, Medicated, soporific

sŏpōro, are : to put, lay asleep, cast into sleep; to deprive of sense, feeling, to stupefy, part. perf.

sŏrŏr, oris, f. : sister; (applied also to half sister, sister-in-law, and mistress!);

sōrs, sortis, f. : lot, fate; oracular response;

sōspĕs, itis : safe and sound; auspicious;

sōspīto, are : to preserve, defend;

Sp, npr. : Spurius (Roman praenomen); (abb. Sp.);

spārgo, ere, sparsi, sum : to scatter, strew, sprinkle; to spot;

spărus, i, m. : -I. neutr., a small missile weapon with a curved blade, a huntingspear -II. a kind of fish, the gilt-head, gilt-bream.

spĕcĭes, ei, f : sight, appearance, show; splendor, beauty; kind, type;

spĕcĭo, ere, spexi, spectum : to look, look at, behold

spĕctācŭlŭm, i, n. : show, spectacle; spectators' seats (pl.);

spĕcto, are : to observe, watch, look at, see; to test; to consider;

spĕcŭlātŏr, oris, m. : spy, scout;

spĕcŭlŏr, aris, ari : to watch, observe; to spy out; to examine, explore

spērno, ere, spreui, spretum : to scorn, despise, spurn;

spes, ei, f. : - hope/anticipation/expectation; prospect/hope/promise; (inheriting/ - object/embodiment of hope; [optio ad ~ => junior hoping to make centurion];

spīcŭlum, i, n. : a little sharp point, sting

spīra, ae, f. : coil;

splēndĭdus, a, um : splendid, glittering;

spŏlĭŭm, i, n. : spoils, booty; skin, hide;

spōntĕ, adv. : of one's own will; voluntarily; for one's own sake;

spūmĕus, a, um : foaming, frothy, foamlike, dappled

spūmo, are : to foam, froth; to be covered in foam; to cover with foam;

spŭrĭus, a, um : of illegitimate birth; subst., an illegitimate, spurious child, a bastard

spŭrĭus, i, m. : an illegitimate, spurious child, a bastard

Spŭrĭus, ii, m. : a Roman proenomen;

squāmĕus, a, um : scaly;

stăbŭlŭm, i, n. : - stall/stable/enclosure/fold; lair/den; herd; garage (Cal);

stătĭm, adv. : at once, immediately;

stătĭŏ, onis, f. : outpost, picket; station; watch;

stătŭa, ae, f. : statue; image;

stătŭo, ere, statui, statutum : to set up, establish, set, place, build; to decide, think;

stătus, a, um : a day of trial

stătus, us, m. : appointed;

stēlla, ae, f. : star; planet, heavenly body; point of light in jewel; constellation; star

stēllo, no perf., ātum, 1 : semer d'étoiles

stērno, ere, straui, stratum : to spread, strew, scatter; to lay out;

stĭmŭlus, i, m. : spur/goad; trap/spike in earth; prick/sting/cause of torment/torture

stīpēndĭŭm, ii, n. : tribute, stipend; pay, wages; military service;

stō, are, steti, statum : to stand, stand still, stand firm; to remain, rest;

strātŭm, i, n (strata, orum) : coverlet; bed, couch; horse-blanket;

strēnŭus, a, um : active, vigorous, strenuous;

strīctīm, adv. : -I. straitly, closely. -II. accurately

strīctus, a, um : drawn together, close, strait, tight

strīdo, ere, stridi, intr. : to make, utter any harsh, shrill, hissing, whistling, grating, creaking sound; to creak, hiss, whizz, whistle, rattle, buzz.

strīngo, ere, strinxi, strictum : to draw tight; to draw; to graze; to strip off;

strīx, strĭgis, f. : I. a screech-owl II. a furrow, channel, groove, flute.

stŭdĕo, ere, ui : to desire, be eager for; to busy oneself with; to strive;

stŭdĭōsus, a, um : eager, keen, full of zeal; studious; devoted to, fond of;

stŭdĭŭm, ii, n. : eagerness, enthusiasm, zeal, spirit; devotion, pursuit, study;

stŭpĕfĭo, fis, fĭĕri, factus sum : to strike dumb

sŭb, prép. + acc. / abl. : under; up to, up under, close to (of motion); until, before, up to, about;

sŭbĕo, ire, ii, itum : - to go/move/pass/sink/extend underneath/into; to climb/come/go up, ascend; to steal in - to place/be placed under/in support; to come up w/aid; to assume a form; to undergo;

sŭbĕūndus, a, um : qu'il faut fléchir, qu'il faut gagner

sŭbĭtō, adv. : suddenly, unexpectedly; at once, at short notice, quickly; in no time at all;

sŭbĭtum, i, n. : a sudden, unexpected thing, a sudden occurrence, whether he spoke after deliberation, off-hand

sŭbĭtus, a, um : sudden; rash, unexpected;

sŭblātus, a, um : elated;

sŭblīcĭus, a, um : consisting of, resting upon piles, the pile-bridge

sŭblīmĭs, e : high, lofty; eminent, exalted, elevated; raised on high; in high position;

sŭblīmus, a, um : uplifted, high, lofty, exalted, elevated

sŭbrĭgo, ere, surrexi (subr-), surrectum (subr-) : I. Act., to lift or raise up, to raise, erect, elevate II. Neutr., to rise, arise, to get up, stand up

sūbscrībo, ere, scripsi, scriptum : to write below, subscribe;

sūbsĭsto, ere, stiti, - : to halt, stand; to cause to stop;

sūbvĕho, ere, uexi, uectum : to convey upwards; to convey up; to sail upstream (PASS);

sūccēdo, ere, cessi, cessum : to climb; to advance; to follow; to succeed in;

sūccēssus, us, m. : approach, advance uphill, outcome, success;

sūccŭrro, ere, succurri, cursum : to run to the aid of, help;

sūffĕro, fers, ferre, sustuli, - : to bear, endure, suffer;

sūffĭcĭo, ere, feci, fectum : to be sufficient, suffice; to stand up to; to be capable/qualified; to provide, appoint;

sŭm, esse, fui : to be; to exist; (also used to form verb perfect passive tenses) with NOM PERF PPL

sūmma, ae, f. : sum; summary; chief point, essence, principal matter, substance; total;

sūmmās, atis : high-born; eminent (Collins);

sūmmŭm, adv. : -I. at the utmost, farthest -II. for the last time

sūmmum, i, n. : the top, surface; the highest place, the head of the table, the extremities

sūmmus, a, um : highest, the top of; greatest; last; the end of;

sūmo, ere, sumpsi, sumptum : to accept; to begin; to suppose; to select; to purchase; to obtain;

sūmptus, us, m. : cost, charge, expense;

sŭo, ere, sŭi, sūtum : to sew, stitch, to sew, join, tack together

sŭpĕr, era, erum cf. superus : above, high; higher, upper, of this world; greatest, last, highest;

sŭpĕr, prép. + acc. / abl. : upon/on; over, above, about; besides (space); during (time); beyond (degree);

sŭpērbĭo, ire : to show pride or disdain on account (of); to be proud/haughty; to be splendid;

sŭpērbus, a, um : arrogant, overbearing, haughty, proud;

sŭpĕrīncĭdo, ere : to cut into above

sŭpĕrĭŏr, oris : that is above, upper, higher

sŭpĕro, are : to overcome, conquer; to survive; to outdo; to surpass, be above, have the upper hand;

sŭpērstĕs, itis : outliving, surviving; standing over/near; present, witnessing;

sŭpērsto, are : to stand upon, over

sŭpērsŭm, esse, fui : to be left over; to survive; be in excess/superfluous (to); to remain to be performed;

sŭpĕrus, a, um : above, high; higher, upper, of this world; greatest, last, highest;

sūpplēx, ĭcis, m. : a suppliant, humble petitioner

sūpplēx, plicis : suppliant, kneeling, begging;

sūpplĭcĭŭm, i, n. : punishment, suffering; supplication; torture;

sŭprā, adv. : above, beyond; over; more than; in charge of, in authority over;

sŭprēmus, a, um : le plus haut, le dernier

sūrgo, ere, surrexi, surrectum : to rise, lift; to grow;

sūrrĭgo, surrexi (subr-), surrectum (subr-) : I. Act., to lift or raise up, to raise, erect, elevate II. Neutr., to rise, arise, to get up, stand up

sūrrĭpĭo, ere, ripui, reptum : to take away secretly; to steal, filch;

sūs, suis, m. f. : swine; hog, pig, sow;

sūscēnsĕo, ere, sŭi, sum : to be inflamed with anger, to be angry, irritated, enraged

sūspēctō, are : in suspicious circumstances; suspiciously;

sūspēndĭŭm, i, n. : act of hanging oneself;

sūspīcĭŏ, ionis, f. : suspicion; mistrust;

sūstĭnĕo, ere, tinui, tentum : to support; to check; to put off; to put up with; to sustain; to hold back;

sŭus, a, um, adj. et pron. : his/one's (own), her (own), hers, its (own); (pl.) their (own), theirs;

sȳmphōnĭa, ae, f. : harmony of sounds; singers/musicians; symphony ; instrument; war signal;

T, npr. : Titus, Roman praenomen; (abb. T.);

tăbēlla, ae, f. : small board; writing tablet; picture; ballot; deed (pl.), document, letter;

tăbŭla, ae, f. : - writing tablet (wax covered board); records (pl.); document, deed, will; - plank/board, flat piece of wood; door panel; counting/playing/notice board;

tăbŭlātum, i, n. : a layer, row

tăcĕo, ere, cui, citum : to be silent; to pass over in silence; to leave unmentioned, be silent about something;

tăcĭtum, i, n. : -I. a secret -II. silence

tăcĭtus, a, um : silent, secret;

tāetĕr, tētĕr, tra, trum : foul, offensive;, ugly; disgraceful; black, blackish (Souter);

Tăgus, i, f. : a river in Lusitania, celebrated for its golden sands, Tajo

tālĭs, e : such; so great; so excellent; of such kind;

tālus, i, m. : ankle; ankle/pastern bone; sheep knucklebone (marked for dice); dice game

tăm, adv. : so, so much (as); to such an extent/degree; nevertheless, all the same;

tămĕn, āttămĕn, adv. : yet, nevertheless, still;

tămquăm, adv. : as, just as, just as if; as it were, so to speak; as much as; so as;

tāndĕm, adv. : finally; at last, in the end; after some time, eventually; at length;

tāngo, ere, tetigi, tactum : to touch, strike; to border on, influence; to mention;

tāntŭm, adv. : so much, so far; hardly, only;

tāntus, a, um : of such size; so great, so much; [tantus ... quantus => as much ... as];

tārdus, a, um : slow, limping; deliberate; late;

Tārquĭnĭa, ae, f. : Tarquinia

Tārquĭnĭus, ii, m. : Etruscan name; (T~ Priscus, 5th Roman king; T~ Superbus, last king 534-510 BC);

tāurus, i, m. : bull;

tēctŏr, ōris, m. : one that overlays walls with plaster, stucco, a plasterer, pargeter

tēctŭm, i, n. : roof; ceiling; house;

tēctus, a, um : covered, roofed, decked, secret, concealed, hidden, in reserved language. mdash;Secret, close, reserved, cautious

tēcŭm, pron. contr. tēcum = cum te : avec toi

tĕgo, ere, texi, tectum : to cover, protect; to defend; to hide;

tēla, ae, f. : web; warp (threads that run lengthwise in the loom);

tēlŭm, i, n. : dart, spear; weapon, javelin; bullet (gun);

tĕmĕrē, adv. : rashly, blindly;

tĕmĕrĭtās, atis, f. : rashness; temerity;

Tēmpē, indecl. n. : I. a charming valley in Thessaly, through which ran the river Peneus, between Olympus and Ossa, now valley of Lykostomo or Dereli II. Transf., of other beautiful valleys

tēmpĕro, are : to combine, blend, temper; to make mild; to refrain from; to control oneself;

tēmpēstās, atis, f. : season, time, weather; storm;

tēmplŭm, i, n. : temple, church; shrine; holy place;

tēmpto, tēnto, are : to test, try; to urge; to worry; to bribe;

tēmpŭs, oris, n. : time, condition, right time; season, occasion; necessity;

tĕnāx, tenacis : holding fast, clinging; tenacious; retentive; close-fisted/tight/niggardly;

tēndo, ere, tetendi, tensum : - to stretch/spread/extend; to distend; to aim/direct weapon/glance/steps/course; - to pitch tent, encamp; to pull tight; to draw (bow); to press on, insist; to exert oneself;

Tĕnĕdŏs, i, f. : a celebrated island in the Ægean Sea, off the coast of Troas

tĕnĕo, ere, ui, tentum : to represent; to support;

tĕnĕr, era, erum : tender (age/food); soft /delicate /gentle; young /immature; weak/fragile/frail;

tĕnŭe, n. : weak, trifling, insignificant, mean, low

tĕnŭĭs, e : thin, fine; delicate; slight, slender; little, unimportant; weak, feeble;

tĕnŭo, are : to make thin; reduce, lessen; wear down;

tĕnŭs, prép. + gén. or abl. : as far as, to the extent of, up to, down to;

tĕr, adv. : three times; on three occasions;

tērgo, ere : to rub, wipe; to wipe off, wipe dry; to clean, cleanse (sometimes tergeo);

tērgŭm, i, n. : back, rear; reverse/far side; outer covering/surface; [terga vertere => flee];

tērra, ae, f. : earth, land, ground; country, region;

tērrĕo, ere, ui, itum : to frighten, scare, terrify, deter;

tērrĭbĭlĭs, e : frightful, terrible;

tērrĭto, are : to intimidate; to keep on frightening;

tērrŏr, oris, m. : terror, panic, alarm, fear;

tēstĭmōnĭŭm, i, n. : testimony; deposition; evidence; witness; (used of ark and tabernacle)

tēstĭs, m. : witness;

tēsto, are, cf. testor : to give as evidence; to bear witness; to make a will; to swear; to testify

tēstŏr, aris, ari : to give as evidence; to bear witness; to make a will; to swear; to testify

tēstūdō, dinis, f. : tortoise; testudo; armored movable shed; troops locking shields overhead;

Tēucĕr, cri, m. : Son of Telamon, king of Salamis, and brother of Ajax

Tēucri, orum, m. pl. : the Trojans

Tēucrĭa, ae, f. : Troy; ancient city taken by the Greeks;

Tēucrus, a, um : of or belonging to Teucer

tēxo, ere, texui, textum : to weave; to plait (together); to construct with elaborate care;

thălămus, i, m. : bedroom; marriage;

thēsāurus, thēnsāurus, i, m : treasure chamber/vault/repository; treasure; hoard; collected precious objects;

Thrēĭcĭus, a, um : Thracian

Thȳbris, ĭdis, m. : le Tibre (fleuve, dieu-fleuve)

Tĭbĕrīnus, a, um : of or belonging to the Tiber, Tiberine, Father Tiber

Tĭbĕrīnus, i, m. : Tiber-; of the river Tiber

Tĭbĕrĭs, m. : Tiber; (the river at Rome);

Tĭbĕrĭus, ii, m. : Tiberius (praenomen); abb. Ti./Tib.; (Tiberius Julius Caesar Emperor, 14-37

Tĭbūllus, i, m. : a celebrated Roman elegiac poet, born about, died about, a contemporary and friend of Ovid and Horace

tĭmēns, tis : fearful, afraid, afraid for, m, the shrinking girl

tĭmĕo, ere, timui : to fear, dread, be afraid (ne + SUB = lest; ut or ne non + SUB = that ... not);

tĭmĭdē, adv. : fearfully, timidly, bravely, hesitatingly

tĭmĭdĭtās, ātis, f. : fearfulness, cowardice, timidity

tĭmĭdus, a, um : timid; cowardly; fearful, apprehensive; without courage; afraid to;

tĭmŏr, oris, m. : fear; dread;

tīngo, ere, tinxi, tinctum : to wet/ moisten/ dip/ soak; to color/dye/tinge/tint, stain (w/blood); to imbue; to impregnate;

tĭtŭbāntĕr, adv. : loosely, totteringly.

tĭtŭlus, i, m. : - title (person/book); label; heading; placard/tablet; pretext, ostensible - distinction, claim to fame; honor; reputation; inscription; monument

Tĭtus, i, m. : Titus; Roman praenomen, abb. T.; (~ Flavius Vespasianus, Emperor, 79-81 AD);

Tītÿrus, i, m. : the name of a shepherd in Virgil's Eclogues

tŏga, ae, f. : toga; (outer garment of Roman citizen);

tōllo, tollere, sustuli, sublatum : to lift, raise; to destroy; to remove, steal; to take/lift up/away;

tōrquĕo, ere, torsi, tortum : to turn, twist; to hurl; to torture; to torment; to bend, distort; spin, whirl; to wind (round);

tōrrĕo, ere, torrui, tostum : to parch, roast, scorch, bake, burn; to dry up; to begin to burn; to harden by charring;

tŏt, adv. : as/so often, so many times, such a great number of times; that number of times;

tŏtĭēns, adv. : so often, so many times, as often, as many times

tōtum, i, n. : all, the whole

tōtus, a, um : whole, all, entire, total, complete; every part; all together/at once;

tōxĭcŭm, i, n. : poison;

trābs, trabis, f. : tree trunk; log, club, spear; beam, timber, rafter; ship, vessel; roof, house;

trādo, ere, didi, ditum : to hand over, surrender; to deliver; to bequeath; to relate;

trăgŏedĭa, ae, f. : tragedy;

trăho, ere, traxi, tractum : to draw, drag, haul; to derive, get;

trāĭcĭo, ere, ieci, iectum : to transfer; to transport; to pierce, transfix;

trāno, are : to swim across;

trānquĭllo, are : to make calm, still, to calm, still.

trānquĭllum, i, n. : a calm; a quiet sea

trānquĭllus, a, um : quiet, calm;

trāns, prép. + acc. : across, over; beyond; on the other side; (only local relations);

trānsĕo, ire, ii, itum : to go over, cross;

trānsfĕro, fers, ferre, tuli, latum : - to transport/convey/transfer/shift; to transpose; to carry/bring across/over; - to copy out (writing); to translate (language); to postpone, transfer date; to transform;

trānsfīgo, ere, fixi, fixum : to transfix, pierce through;

trānsfŭga, ae, m. : deserter;

trānsfŭgĭo, ere, fugi, fugitum : to go over to the enemy, desert;

trānsĭtus, us, m. : passage; crossing;

trĕcēnti, a, ae : three hundred; (used to denote a large number);

trĕmēndus, a, um : terrible, awe inspiring;

trĕmēns, entis : trembling

trĕmo, ere, ui, - : to tremble, shake, shudder at;

trĕpĭdo, are : to tremble, be afraid, waver;

trĕpĭdus, a, um : nervous, jumpy, agitated; perilous, alarming, frightened; boiling, foaming;

trēs, ium : three;

trĭbūnăl, alis, n. : raised platform; tribunal; judgement seat;

trĭbūnus, i, m. : tribune; [~ plebis => tribune of the people; ~ militum => soldier's tribune];

trĭbŭo, ere, bui, butum : to divide, assign; to present; to grant, allot, bestow, attribute;

trĭbus, us, m. : third part of the people; tribe, hereditary division (Ramnes, Tities, Luceres);

trĭbūtŭm, i, n. : tax, tribute;

trĭbūtus, a, um : formed, arranged into tribes

trĭbūtŭs, i, m. cf. tributum : tax, tribute;

trĭdēns, entis, m. : with three teeth;

trīste, n. : a sad thing

trīstĭs, e : sad, sorrowful; gloomy;

trĭsūlcus, a, um : with three furrows, three-cleft, three-forked, trifid, triple, forked lightning

Trītōnĭs, idis, f. : a surname of Athena

trĭūmpho, are : to triumph over; to celebrate a triumph; to conquer completely, triumph;

trĭūmphus, i, m. : triumph, victory parade;

trĭvĭŭm, i, n. : trivium, first group of seven liberal arts (grammar/rhetoric/logic);

Trōes, um, m. : Trojan

Trōĭus, a, um : of Troy, Trojan

Trōja, ae, f. : Troy, a city of Phrygia

Trōjānus, a, um : Trojan;

Trōs, ōis, m. : -I. a king of Phrygia, after whom Troy was named; he was the son of Erichthonius and grandson of Dardanus -II. a Trojan.

trŭcīdo, are : to slaughter, butcher, massacre;

trūncus, a, um : maimed, mutilated, mangled, dismembered, disfigured, deprived of some of its parts;

trūncus, i, m. : trunk (of a tree)

trūx, trucis : wild, savage, fierce;

tū, tui, sing. pron. : you (sing.); thou/thine/thee/thy (PERS); yourself/thyself (REFLEX);

tŭĕŏr, eris, eri, tuitus sum : to look at; to protect, watch; uphold

tŭlo, ere, tĕtŭli : to bring, bear, lift up

tŭm, adv. : moreover; (frequent in Cicero and before; rare after);

tŭmĕo, ere : to swell, become inflated; to be puffed up; to be bombastic; to be swollen with conceit;

tŭmĭdus, a, um : swollen, swelling, distended; puffed up with pride or self; confidence;

tŭmūltŭārĭus, a, um : raised to deal with a sudden emergency; improvised; unplanned, haphazard;

tŭmūltŭo, āre, intr. : Impers. pass., that there is a tumult, disturbance in the camp

tŭmūltŭŏr, ari : to make a commotion/disturbance/armed rising; to scrap, scrimmage; to be in confusion

tŭmūltŭōsus, a, um : full of bustle, confusion, tumult, restless, turbulent, tumultuous.

tŭmŭltus, us, m. : commotion, confusion, uproar; rebellion, uprising, disturbance;

tŭmŭlus, i, m. : mound, hillock; mound, tomb;

tūnc, adv. : then, thereupon, at that time;

tŭnĭcātus, a, um : covered with a coat, skin, peel, coated

tŭŏr, eris, i, tŭi : to see, to look, gaze upon, to watch, view;, to see, look to, to defend, protect

tūrba, ae, f. : commotion, uproar, turmoil, tumult, disturbance; crowd, mob, multitude;

tūrbo, are : to disturb, agitate, confuse, disorder; to throw into disorder or confusion

tūrbŏ, inis, f. : A whirlwind, hurricane, tornado

tūrgĭdus, a, um : swollen, inflated, distended; swollen (body of water); inflamed with passion;

tūrpĕ, adv. : repulsively, disgracefully, shamelessly; in an ugly/unsightly manner;

tūrpĭs, e : ugly; nasty; disgraceful; indecent; base, shameful, disgusting, repulsive;

tūrpĭtĕr, adv. : repulsively, disgracefully, shamelessly; in an ugly/unsightly manner;

tūrpo, are : to make ugly; to pollute, disfigure;

tūrrĭs, f. : tower; high building, palace, citadel; dove tower, dove cot;

Tūsci, orum, m. : the inhabitants of Etru, ria, the Tuscans, Etruscans, Etrurians

Tūscĭa, ae, f. : Etruria, the Etruscan territory

Tūscus, a, um : Tuscan, Etruruan, Etruscan

Tūscus, i, m. : Tuscus

tŭtŭlus, i, m. : a high head-dress, formed by plaiting the hair in a cone over the forehead

tūtum, i, n. : watchful, careful, cautious, prudent

tūtus, a, um : safe, prudent; secure; protected;

tŭus, a, um : your (sing.);

Tўdīdēs, ae, m. : Tydudes

ŭbĭ, adv. interr. or rel. : where, whereby;

ŭbīquĕ, adv. : anywhere, everywhere (ubiquitous);

Ŭlīxĕs, m. : Ulysses/Odysseus; (crafty hero of Trojan war and the Odyssey; King of Ithaca);

ūllus, a, um : any;

ūltĭmum, i, n. : the last, the end

ūltĭmus, a, um : the farthest, most distant, most remote, the uttermost, extreme, last

ūltŏr, oris : avenger, revenger;

ūltŏr, ōris, m. : a punisher, avenger, revenger.

ūltrŏ, adv. : en plus, spontanément

ŭlŭlo, are : to howl, yell, shriek; to celebrate or proclaim with howling;

Ŭlўssēs, m. : the Latin name for Odysseus, Ulysses, king of Ithaca, famed among the Grecian heroes of the Trojan war for his craft and eloquence; the son of Laertes and Anticlea, husband of Penelope, and father of Telemachus and Telegonus

ūmbo, ōnis, m. : a shield boss

ūmbra, ae, f. : shade; ghost; shadow;

ūmbro, are : to shade, shadow, overshadow, overspread, cover; to make, cast a shade

ūmĕo, ere : to be wet; to be moist;

ŭmĕrus, i, m. : upper arm, shoulder;

ūmquăm, adv. : ever, at any time;

ūnā, adv. : together, together with; at the same time; along with;

ūnda, ae, f. : wave;

ūndĕ, adv. interr. or rel. : from where, whence, from what or which place; from which; from whom;

ūndĕcĭm, num. : eleven;

ūndēni, ae, a : eleven each, eleven

ūndĭquĕ, adv. : - from every side/direction/place/part/source; on all/both sides/surfaces;

ūndo, are : to surge/flood/rise in waves; to gush/well up; to run, stream; to billow; to undulate; to waver;

ūnĭvērsus, ūnĭvŏrsus, a, um : whole, entire; all together; all; universal;

ūnquăm, adv. : at any time, ever; at some time;

ūnus, a, um, sing. : alone, a single/sole; some, some one; only (pl.); one set of (denoting entity);

ūnūsquīsque, unaquaeque, unumquodque : each, every, every body, every one, every thing

ūrbānē, adv. : Courteously, civilly, affably, politely, urbanely

ūrbānus, a, um : of the city; courteous; witty, urbane;

ūrbānus, i, m. : devoted to the city, fond of city life

ūrbs, urbis, f. : city; City of Rome;

ūrgĕo, ere, ursi, - : - to press/squeeze/bear hard/down; to tread/traverse continually; to push/shove/thrust; - to hem in; to threaten by proximity; to press verbally/argument/point; to follow up;

ūrgŭeo, ere, ursi, - : - to press/squeeze/bear hard/down; to tread/traverse continually; to push/shove/thrust; - to hem in; to threaten by proximity; to press verbally/argument/point; to follow up;

Urĭŏs, ii, m. : a title of Jupiter

ūro, ere, ussi, ustum : to burn;

ūsquĕ, prép. + acc. : up to (name of town or locality);

ūsus, us, m. : use, enjoyment; experience, skill, advantage; custom;

ŭt, ŭtŭt, conj. sub. + ind. or subj. : to (+ subjunctive), in order that/to; how, when, while; even if;

ŭtĕr, tra, trum : - which (of two), whichever, no matter which; one, either, one or other;

ŭtĕrque, utraque, utrumque : each, either, each one, one and the other, one as well as the other, both

ūtī, conj. : in order that; that, so that; as, when; [ut primum => as soon as];

ūtĭlĭs, e : useful, profitable, practical, helpful, advantageous;

ūto, ĕre : Act. form only imp. utito, use, employ, make use of

ūtŏr, eris, i, usus sum : to use, make use of, enjoy; to enjoy the friendship of

ŭtrīmquĕ, adv. : on/from both sides/parts; at both ends; on one side and on the other;

ŭtrŭm, ūtrum : whether; (introducing an indirect question); [utrum...an => whether...or];

ūva, ae, f. : grape;

ūxŏr, oris, f. : wife; [uxorem ducere => marry, bring home as wife];

ūxōrĭus, a, um : of or belonging to a wife; of marriage; excessively fond of one's wife;

văcātĭŏ, ionis, f. : freedom, exemption; privilege;

văco, are : to be empty; to be vacant; to be idle; to be free from, be unoccupied;

văcŭŭm, i, n. : an empty space, an open or vacant place, a void, vacuity

văcŭus, a, um : empty, vacant, unoccupied; devoid of, free of;

vădĭmōnĭŭm, i, n. : bail, security, surety;

vădo, ere : to go, walk; esp. to go hastily or rapidly, to rush;

vāldē, vălĭdē, adv. : greatly/very/intensely; vigorously/strongly/powerfully/energetically; loudly;

vălē, adv. : "farewell, adieu (the Roman equivalent of ""Live long and prosper"");"

vălĕo, ere, ui, itum : to be strong;

Vălērĭus, a, um : of or belonging to a Valerius

Vălērĭus, ii, m. : of Valerius, Roman gens; P. V. Publicola, one of the first consuls (509 BC);

vălĭdus, a, um : strong, powerful; valid;

vāllēs, f. : a valley, vale.

vāllĭs, f. : valley, vale, hollow;

vāllo, are : to surround/fortify/furnish (camp, etc) with a palisaded rampart;

văpŏr, oris, m. : sound; cry;

vărĭo, are : to mark with contrasting colors, variegate; to vary, waver; to fluctuate, change;

vărĭus, a, um : different; various, diverse; changing; colored; party colored, variegated;

Vārrō, onis, m. : a surname in the gens Terentia

vārus, a, um : bent, stretched, grown inwards, awry.

vāstus, a, um : huge, vast; monstrous;

vātēs, m. : prophet/seer, mouthpiece of deity; oracle, soothsayer; poet (divinely

vātīs, m. : prophetess/ mouthpiece of deity; oracle/soothsayer; poetess (divinely

vēcto, are : to transport, carry; (of habitual agent/means); (PASS) to ride, be conveyed, travel;

vĕhĕmēns, vēmēns, entis : violent, severe, vehement; emphatic, vigorous, lively;

vĕhĕmēntĕr, vēmēntĕr, adv. : vehemently, vigorously; exceedingly, very much;

vĕhes, f. : a carriage loaded, a cart-load, wagon-load

vĕho, ere, uexi, uectum : to bear, carry, convey; to pass, ride, sail;

Vējēns, entis : of or belonging to Veii, Veientian

vĕl, adv. : or; [vel ... vel => either ... or];

vēllo, ere, uelli/uulsi, uulsum : to pluck/pull/tear out; to extract; to pull hair/plants; to uproot; to depilate; to demolish;

vēlŭm, i, n. : sail, covering; curtain; [vela vento dare => sail away];

vēlŭt, adv. : just as, as if;

vēlŭtī, adv. : just as, as if;

vēna, ae, f. : blood-vessel, vein; artery; pulse; fissure, pore, cavity; vein of ore/talent;

vēndo, ere, didi, ditum : to sell;

vĕnēno, are : to imbue or infect with poison; to injure by slander;

vĕnēnŭm, i, n. : poison; drug;

vēnĕo, ire, īvi (ii), ītum, intr. : to go to sale, to be sold

Vĕnĕrĭus, a, um : of or belonging to Venus; lascivious

vĕnĭa, ae, f. : favor, kindness; pardon; permission; indulgence;

vĕnĭo, ire, ueni, uentum : to come;

vēnŏr, aris, ari : to hunt, chase

vēntĕr, tris, m. : stomach, womb; belly;

vēntĭlo, are : to expose to a draught; to fan; to brandish;

vēntus, i, m. : wind;

vēnŭm, i, n. : sale, purchase; (only sg. ACC/DAT w/dare); [venum dare => put up for sale];

vĕnŭs, ĕris, f. : Venus, qualities that excite love, loveliness, attractiveness, beauty, grace, elegance, charms; - love, sexual activity/appetite/intercourse; [~ tali => best dice throw];

Vĕnŭs, neris, f. : - Venus, Roman goddess of sexual love and generation; planet Venus;

vēr, ēris, n. : spring; spring-time of life, youth; [ver sacrum => sacrifice of spring-born];

vērbĕr, ĕris, n. : a lash, whip, scourge, rod

vērbĕră, um, n. pl. : lashes, whips, scourges, rods

vērbĕro, are : to scoundrel;

vērbōsus, a, um : full of words, wordy, prolix, verbose.

vērbŭm, i, n. : word; proverb; [verba dare alicui => cheat/deceive someone];

vērē, adv. : really, truly, actually, indeed; rightly, correctly, exactly; truthfully;

vĕrĕŏr, eris, eri, ueritus sum : to feel awe of, to reverence, revere, respect; to fear, be afraid of any thing

Vērgīlĭus, Vīrgīlĭus, i, m. : Vergil

vērō, adv. : yes; in truth; certainly; truly, to be sure; however;

vērro, ere, -, uersum : to sweep clean; to sweep together; to sweep (to the ground); to skim, sweep; to sweep along;

vērsātus, a, um : experienced, skilled, versed

vērso, are : to move about; to live, dwell; to be;

vērsŏr, aris, ari, atus sum : to dwell, live, remain, stay, abide, be in a place or among certain persons

vērsŭs, adv. : turned in the direction of, towards

vērsus, us, m. : toward, in the direction of; (placed after ACC); -ward (after name of town);

vērto, vŏrto, ere, uerti, uersum : to turn, turn around; to change, alter; to overthrow, destroy;

vērŭm, conj. : yes; in truth; certainly; truly, to be sure; however; (rare form, usu. vero);

vērus, a, um : true, real, genuine, actual; properly named; well founded; right, fair, proper;

Vēstālĭs, e : a priestess of Vesta, a Vestal

Vēstālĭs, f. : a priestess of Vesta, a Vestal

vēstĕr, tra, trum : your (pl.), of/belonging to/associated with you;

vēstībŭlŭm, i, n. : entrance, court;

vēstīgĭŭm, ii, n. : step, track; trace; footstep;

vēstīmēntŭm, i, n. : garment, robe; clothes;

vēstĭo, ire, iui, itum : to clothe;

vēstĭs, f. : garment, clothing, blanket; clothes; robe;

vĕtĕra, um, n. : the old, old things, antiquity

vĕtŭs, eris : old, aged, ancient; former; veteran, experienced; long standing, chronic;

vĭa, ae, f. : way, road, street; journey;

vĭbro, are : to brandish, wave, crimp, corrugate; to rock; to propel suddenly; to flash; to dart; to glitter;

vīcīnum, i, n. : a neighboring place, the neighborhood, vicinity

vīcīnus, a, um : nearly resembling in quality, nature, like, similar

vīcīnus, i, m. : near, neighboring, in the neighborhood or vicinity

vĭcĭs, gén. acc. uicem. : turn, change, succession; exchange, interchange, repayment; plight, lot;

vīctŏr, oris, m. : triumphant;

vīctōrĭōsus, a, um : victorious, Sup.

vīctrīx, icis, f. : conquering;

vīctus, us, m. : living, way of life; that which sustains life; nourishment; provisions; diet;

vīcus, i, m. : village; hamlet; street, row of houses;

vĭdĕo, ere, uidi, uisum : to see, look at; to consider; (PASS) to seem, seem good, appear, be seen;

vĭgĕo, ere, ui, - : to be strong/vigorous; to thrive, flourish, bloom/blossom; to be active, be effective;

vĭgĭl, ilis : awake, wakeful; watchful; alert, vigilant, paying attention;

vĭgĭl, ĭlis, m. : a watchman, sentinel

vīlĭs, e : cheap, common, mean, worthless;

vīncĭo, ire, uinxi, uinctum : to bind, fetter; to restrain;

vīnco, ere, uici, uictum : to conquer, defeat, excel; to outlast; to succeed;

vīncŭlŭm, i, n. : chain, bond, fetter; imprisonment (pl.);

vīndēx, icis, m. : defender, protector;

vīndĭco, are : to claim, vindicate; to punish, avenge;

vĭŏlēns, entis : violent;

vĭŏlēntĭa, ae, f. : violence, vehemence, impetuosity, ferocity

vĭŏlēntus, a, um : violent, vehement, impetuous, boisterous;

vĭr, uiri, m. : man; husband; hero; person of courage, honor, and nobility;

vīrgĭnĕus, a, um : - virgin; of/appropriate for/haunted by marriageable age girls; unworked - married (couple) when wife still girl; of constellation Virgo; of aqua Virgo;

vīrgĭnĭtās, atis, f. : maidenhood; virginity; being girl of marriageable age; being sworn to celibacy;

vīrgō, ginis, f. : maiden, young woman, girl of marriageable age; virgin, woman sexually intact;

vĭrīlĭs, e : manly, virile; mature;

vīrtūs, utis, f. : manliness, manhood, i. e. the sum of all the corporeal or mental excellences of man, strength, vigor; bravery, courage; aptness, capacity; worth, excellence, virtue; Military talents, courage, valor, bravery, gallantry, fortitude; class of Angels; [Dominus ~ => Lord of hosts];

vīrus, i, n. : a slimy liquid, slime.

vīs, -, f. : strength (bodily) (pl.), force, power, might, violence; resources; large body;

vīso, ere, uisi, uisum : to visit, go to see; to look at;

vīsum, i, n. : something seen, sight, appearance, vision.

vīsus, us, m. : look, sight, appearance; vision;

vīta, ae, f. : life, career, livelihood; mode of life;

vĭtĭo, are : to make faulty, to injure, spoil, mar, taint, corrupt, infect, vitiate

vītĭs, f. : vine; grape vine;

vītĭŭm, ii, n. : fault, vice, crime, sin; defect;

vīto, are : to avoid, shun; to evade;

vĭtrĭcus, i, m. . : a step-father

vītta, ae, f. : band, ribbon; fillet;

vīvo, ere, uixi, uictum : to be alive, live; to survive; to reside;

vīvum, i, n. : that which is alive

vīvus, a, um : alive, fresh; living;

vīvus, i, m. : a living man

vīx, adv. : hardly, scarcely, barely, only just; with difficulty, not easily; reluctantly;

vŏco, are : to call, summon; to name; to call upon;

vŏlo, are : to fly

vŏlo, uis, uelle, uolui : to wish, want, prefer; to be willing, will

Vōlsci, orum, m. : the most considerable people in Latium, the Volsci, Volscians

Vōlscus, a, um, nom et adj. : the most considerable people in Latium, the Volsci

vŏlŭcrĭs, f. : bird, flying insect/creature; constellation Cycnus/Cygnus;

vŏlūmĕn, inis, n. : book, chapter, fold;

vŏlūptās, atis, f. : pleasure, delight, enjoyment;

vōlvo, ere, uolui, uolutum : - to roll, cause to roll; to travel in circle/circuit; to bring around/about; to revolve; - to roll along/forward; (PASS) to move sinuously (snake); to grovel, roll on ground;

vōs, uestrum, pl. pron. : you (pl.), ye;

vōx, uocis, f. : voice, tone, expression;

Vūlcānus, i, m. : Vulcan, god of fire; fire;

vūlgō, vōlgō, adv. : generally, usually; universally; publicly, in/to the crowd/multitude/world;

vūlgo, vōlgo, are : to spread around/among the multitude; to publish, divulge, circulate; to prostitute

vūlgus, vōlgus, i, n. : common people/general public/multitude/common herd/rabble/crowd/mob; flock;

vūlnĕro, vōlnĕro, are : to wound/injure/harm, pain/distress; to inflict wound on; to damage (things/interest)

vūlnŭs, vōlnŭs, ĕris, n. : wound; mental/emotional hurt; injury to one's interests; wound of love;

vūltŭr, vōltŭr, uris, m : vulture;

vūltŭrĭus, ii, m. : a vulture, bird of prey.

vūltus, vōltus, us, m. : face, expression; looks;

Zĕphўrus, i, m. : Zephyr, the west wind;

The following sources helped inform my understanding of these texts, and I highly recommend them for those that want more in depth coverage for themselves.

Perseus.tufts for Latin texts

Printed in Great Britain
by Amazon